The Buddha

The Social-Revolutionary Potential of Buddhism

नमो तस्स भगवतो
अरहतो सम्मासम्बुद्धस्स

Trevor Ling

THE BUDDHA

The Social-Revolutionary Potential of Buddhism

Pariyatti Press

Onalaska, WA, USA

The transliteration of the Devanāgari (Indian) script on the title-page is as follows:

namo tassa bhagavato
arahato sammasambuddhassa

These words, which are in Pāli, the language of Theravada Buddhism, may be translated as follows:

Honour to Him, the Blessed One,
the Worthy One, the fully Enlightened.

Gotama, the Buddha, is frequently referred to in the Buddhist texts as 'Bhagavā', or the Blessed One. This sentence is customarily said three times before any Buddhist devotions, as a mark of respect, and in praise of the Buddha.

Pariyatti Press
an imprint of
Pariyatti Publishing
867 Larmon Road, Onalaska, WA, USA
www.pariyatti.org

 Pariyatti enriches the world by disseminating the words of the Buddha, providing sustenance for the seeker's journey and illuminating the meditator's path.

From the first edition (1973)

Dedicated with her permission to
SHRIMATI INDIRA GANDHI
Prime Minister of India
in the 25th Anniversary Year
of the Republic of India

Contents

Editor's Note

by Professor S. C. F. Brandon

No founder of a great religion ever lived before his time. To win disciples, his message had to be relevant to current needs and presented in a contemporary idiom. Hence such a message drew upon a tradition of culture, and it cannot be truly understood apart from it. But it contained also something new, some fresh and dynamic insight into the nature and destiny of man that derived from a unique religious sensitivity, and was embodied in the personal being of the genius concerned. It is because of such factors that the emergence of a new religion marks the beginning of a process of change destined to affect the lives of untold generations of individuals and have incalculable cultural, and often political and economic, consequences. To that process of transformation many others in time contribute, possibly altering in varying degrees the founder's message or deflecting the development of his intention. Thus from the alchemy of the founder's own genius, which transmutes the cultural tradition in which he was nurtured, there gradually evolves a new culture and civilization. And so, to take a random example, a causal nexus of infinite complexity connects Jesus of Nazareth, a Galilean Jew of the first century, with the building of the Cathedral of Chartres, that supreme epitome of Western medieval culture.

It is the aim of this series of books to show something of the fascinating transformation of cultural traditions that the founders of the great religions have wrought in the course of history. Starting with the world into which such a founder was born, each volume will attempt to explain how, from the stimulus of his personality and teaching, a new cultural world eventually emerged.

Introduction

by Paul R. Fleischman, MD

The Buddha, by Trevor Ling, has become more important today, in the 21st Century, than it was in 1973 when it originally appeared. This growth in value over time is the hallmark of an excellent book, but it is also due to the rebirth of the Buddha's teaching. When Professor Ling wrote *The Buddha* there were few English language readers who were trying to walk the Buddha's path, but today tens of millions of English readers in both Western and Eastern countries are deep students and practitioners of it and Dr. Ling's book now provides a potentially large readership with a relatively short, lively, non-pedantic but scholarly study of the environmental, social and historical context of the Buddha's teaching.

Professor Ling addressed the Buddha's legacy from a particular standpoint, asking us to consider whether it provides a model with which we can build a better world today. Dr. Ling thrust the Buddha into our contemporary situation in a manner that demanded active consideration. Because of this particular angle, I have read, reread, underlined and treasured my out-of-print copy of the 1973 hardcover edition. For people who are casting about in the tides of history to find elevating and directive models for society, Trevor Ling's understated passion for the Buddha's example will be riveting. But he didn't merely elevate the Buddha's message. He compelled us to examine its context, goals, problems, and potentials.

This book was written with the intention that its readers be shaken into awareness of, "...the social-revolutionary potential of Buddhism..."

II

Trevor Oswald Ling was born in 1920 into a religious English family. The Second World War drew him to India, where despite his plans to become a Baptist clergyman, he became a student of Sanskrit, Pāli and classical Indian literature. After the war, he completed a degree at Oxford, taught college and was a parish minister, and, in 1960, obtained a doctorate from the School of

Oriental and African studies. His dissertation compared the concept of evil in Buddhism and Christianity, and led to his first book. His distinguished academic career evolved into a uniquely free-spirited pursuit of authenticity, that led him to leave Baptism for Anglicanism, and then to resign his Anglican priesthood, while he published numerous books, held academic posts in both England and Asia, and eventually declared himself to be (according to his wife, Dr. Jeanne Openshaw) "...a Buddhistic sort of person..." and finally, "...a human being." Among other positions, he held a Personal Chair in Comparative Religion at the University of Leeds and was Chair of Comparative Religion at Manchester University. He was also a visiting professor at Shantiniketan, the university founded by India's Nobel Prize winning poet, Rabindranath Tagore, and later a Senior Research Fellow in Singapore.

Ling's numerous books were wide ranging, but at the center was usually original Buddhism. *A History of Religion East and West* was a text that made him a prominent figure in the field of comparative religion. Although Professor Ling's capacity to absorb languages, history, sociology, and to write voluminously, made him a prominent academic, he was never purely dispassionate, and his writing always seems to bear upon his deepest concern. In an obituary after his death from Alzheimer's in 1995, Cynthia Chou wrote that she and others remembered him most by his advice, "You should always leave the world a better place than you found it." In another obituary, Haddon Wilmer wrote, "Ling never gave up seeking good religion and advocating what he found."

It is in the light of Trevor Ling's commitment to improve the world that we can best understand the strengths, holes, and power of *The Buddha*.

III

The Buddha is ironically not exactly about the Buddha. This book might have been more accurately if clumsily titled, "The Historical, Cultural, and Ecological Context of the Buddha's Message and its Ongoing Challenges and Relevance." For actual biographical details of the Buddha's life, as well as they can be known from the texts left in his name, a reader would be better served by *The Life of the Buddha*, by another Oxford graduate and

World War II veteran, Bhikkhu Ñāṇamoli. Trevor Ling sets out not only to tell us about the Buddha, but also to correct what he felt were widespread misperceptions, and to offer reasons for renewed interest.

The book has two major themes. First, it argues that the Buddha's message is intrinsically social, political, and progressive. Second, it implies that despite the decay of its seminal context, and despite its relative eclipse on the world stage, the way of life portrayed in the Pāli Canon offers us implicit, workable guidance towards the future.

In addition, Trevor Ling wanted to pound in a corrective correlate to his first theme: the Buddha's teaching has been inaccurately stereotyped as otherworldly escapism, when, in reality, its sweeping program is to improve humankind. Dr. Ling was emphatic in his position that the Buddha's teaching is not merely, "...a message of private consolation...for the suburban West..." but is a "...vision for a new civilization." To anchor this most important message of his text, Trevor Ling added, "Buddhism could never be a private salvation...its concerns were with the public world."

Trevor Ling wrote with brilliant phrases. He described Buddhism as "...not a religion, but a non-religious philosophy...a way of attempting to restructure human consciousness and the common life of men in accordance with the nature of what it conceives to be the sacred reality." He understood Buddhism as something bigger than religion, as prescriptions for civilization, "...so comprehensive and diffuse that they are virtually coextensive with human life itself." He seemed to be implicitly referring to his contemporary historian of religions, Mircea Eliade, who wrote in, *Myths, Dreams, and Mysteries* that "religion is the exemplary solution of every existential crisis." Trevor Ling believed that religions were the residue of civilizations with their embracing way of life, and that Buddhism, understood as a religion, was only a reduced form of the larger platform of Buddhist civilization. This generous perception also leads us to the book's major tilt.

IV

The Buddha is not exactly about the Dhamma, the practical path out of suffering that is in fact the essence of what the Buddha taught. Instead, Trevor Ling was so determined to correct the misperception of Buddha as an otherworldly mystic, that he devoted the majority of his book almost entirely to the Buddha's wish to reform human society. For a description of the Buddha's path and technique, the reader would be better served by reading a text from the contemporary Vipassana tradition, such as William Hart's, *The Art of Living.* To Trevor Ling, meditation was an essential yet poorly understood aspect of the Buddha's dispensation. His description of the Dhamma was a clear but brief digest: "...a noble quest that seeks the unborn, the unaging, the undecaying...*nibbāna*...release...the state of coolness..." His relatively terse condensation of what to many people is the heart of Dhamma skewed Trevor Ling's writing and placed it to one side of books that facilitate walking the path. He approvingly quoted Rabindranath Tagore's poetic, facile and somewhat misleading description of the Buddha's teaching as "elimination of all limits on love." Of what value then is *The Buddha?*

Trevor Ling gave us a reality check against which the new world of emerging practices, paths, and ways of life can be calibrated for insight and authenticity.

As the Buddha's teaching has reemerged in the 20th and 21st centuries, finding itself located in the West where it has no cultural roots, or in Asia, where its cultural roots may be fixated and automatic rather than inspired, it needs to be adjusted to avoid two errors.

On the one hand, there is the danger of literalism, Buddhist fundamentalism. Are we imitating a dead past? Are we mimicking an ancient culture? Are we sentimental and archaic? We want to know what is essential and trans-cultural in the teaching, rather than what is merely situational. Are we walking a path, or trying on costumes?

On the other hand, as soon as traditions are modified, their practitioners face the danger of "anything goes." If we can modify one aspect, why not another, and another? In this scenario, token adherence to a tradition, which in fact has been radically altered, leads to the sanctification of new and inauthentic accretions that are slipped in beneath the marquee of the old name. Have we made practical compromises, or have we drained away the essence?

What a gift it is to have Trevor Ling's voice, with its historical and textual knowledge, its analytic skills, and its breadth of information across scholarly disciplines. The Buddha's teaching occurred in one place and at one time, and we are faced with the question of what is to be modified and what is to be kept; this book is a valuable resource: "...some aspects of the teaching have permanent validity because they are relevant to some enduring feature of the human situation, whereas others will be understood as having only limited validity since they refer in a very particular way to special situations which existed in the teacher's own day and which now no longer exist..."

V

Trevor Ling described the world within which the Buddha emerged, his embeddedness within that world, his transformation of it, the new institutions he founded, preeminently the Sangha, his relationship with other institutions, such as kings and republics; and then, the evolution of all of these components within the new contexts of Buddhist India under Emperor Ashoka, and Buddhist Sri Lanka. Dr. Ling's narrative of historical sociology helps us to understand the teaching as a unique social institution. He put his finger on the anatomy of a breakthrough moment in consciousness and civilization.

The Buddha was born into a rich, fertile landscape that was still heavily forested, with attendant moderation of climate, and groves for solitude in "the all encircling forest." There was relative political and social stability. But at the same time the forests were being actively cleared for productive rice-based agriculture, that enabled rapid population growth, and a food surplus, both of which in turn facilitated urbanization. Within the rural, agrarian Gangetic Valley, the Buddha was a part of an urban, affluent, commercial, artistic and intellectual society. Urbanized classes, predominantly merchants, intellectuals, and royalty, sought new answers to the new questions triggered by their new way of life. "It was precisely there, in the cities, that most of the Buddha's public activity took place..." Almost all of the Buddha's discourses were delivered in major cities, and one city alone, Shravasti, accounts for the majority of them.

Travel and trade abounded. Caste divisions were fluid. Food surplus supported royalty, armies, scholars, merchants, and guilds, as well as India's signature cultural contribution, wandering truth seekers who had food security without labor. Organized religion did not yet exist, and people sought existential security by participating in a plethora of competing rites and beliefs in a marketplace of religious activity where no one product had outsized market share.

In Trevor Ling's view, the Buddha was not a religious reformer, but an "opponent or critic of religion." "The notion that Gotama was a "religious" man needs careful scrutiny...the modern understanding of "religion" is being projected back into the time of the Buddha...it is an anachronism to ascribe a Hindu religious tradition to this early period..." The Buddha's teaching was particularly relevant to urban individuals who were only recently emancipated from the group cohesion of traditional agrarianism, and who were newly differentiated, individuated, and lonely. The Buddha provided these emancipated and progressive people "a new community," "a rational outlook which treats reality as causally and functionally determined..." Unlike the magical and superstitious ritualism, which the Buddha condescendingly tolerated but derided, he offered instead, "the real possibility of human choice and freedom of action..." Professor Ling emphasized that Western audiences have failed to understand the Buddha because they have mistakenly focused on "a private cult of escape" rather than on the social dimension. An "unmistakable portrait" of the Buddha emerges as the "discoverer, initiator, and exponent of a social, psychological and political philosophy..."

VI

Trevor Ling ascribed great importance to the Bhikkhu Sangha, which "provides the environment in which a new dimension of consciousness becomes possible." We are taught that "Bhikkhu" means literally "a sharesman who receives a share of the common wealth," of public resources. The begging meditative life is not for "outsiders" but for someone "integrally involved in society."

In one of his finest phrases, Trevor Ling described the teaching of Buddha as "a narrowing down of consciousness, followed by expansion." But in his vigorous corrective emphasis, Dr. Ling overstated his case, when he wrote, "Buddha was not concerned with the private destiny of the individual, but with something

18

much wider, the whole realm of sentient being, the whole of consciousness…a concern with social and political matters…" It might be more correct to say that the Buddha hoped to build continuity from individual to social liberation, and to eliminate any gap or dichotomy between the two. As if to correct his own over emphasis, Trevor Ling also wrote that the Buddha's teaching, "…is essentially a therapy for individualism." Dr. Ling forcefully reminded us, however, that implicit in the Buddha's message is a collective elevation of the totality of consciousness.

Dr. Ling challenged us with other provocative perspectives. He believed that the emphasis on face-to-face ideological consensus within the Sangha necessitated and augmented schism as a practical and non-violent resolution to any unsolvable dissent. He also reminded us of the ambivalent relationship between Sangha and laity, who, on the one hand provided the life-sustaining "share" to the Sangha, but who were often pejoratively devalued in the Pāli Canon as "common…addicted to pleasure…greedy and lustful…" We are reminded that it is the Sangha that provided "the growth point for…the social restructuring of human life."

VII

Regarding laity, we are reminded that the Buddha's teaching to them follows "the noble spirit of justice" but was also "naïve and simple." Once again, Trevor Ling mingled reverence and daring by reminding us that "the crux of the matter is…a practicability gap." He asked us whether the teaching can really establish and maintain itself in historical and social contexts that differ so much from the Buddha's era.

Along with the Bhikkhu Sangha, who represent and model the path, there was the concurrent problem of political power and authority: "how to deal with potentially violent or antisocial elements." The Buddha is once again described as "a social and political theorist…in constant touch with current problems of government…one who had something to say on matters of policy." The low regard for common people and the need for social stability placed the teaching in the context of oligarchic, patriarchal republics, which eventually self-destructed, or in absolutist, authoritarian kingdoms. The Buddha was the friend and confidant of kings who fomented war, used capital punishment, and practiced slavery. "The King's duty is to defend his territory and people by force of arms...and to inflict punishment on wrongdoers...the king should be neither too severe or too mild...the violence of many individuals was to be met and overcome by the violence of one supreme individual...a strong and benevolent monarch against the unwisdom of the multitude..."

The historical seating of original Buddhism within rule-bound and schismatic monasticism on the one hand, and authoritarian government on the other hand, gives the modern reader challenging issues to rethink.

Within the context of situations that seem alien to us today, there arose, in Trevor Ling's acute phrases, "...a theory of existence...an awareness of a transcendental dimension...necessary loyalty to that which transcends immediate personal gain...to recognize that the structure of being was different from what was commonly supposed...the individual was not the key concept to the understanding of the human situation...a reorganization of human affairs directed towards a new, non-individualistic society."

No one has more eloquently pointed to the elevated social dimension of the teaching, although Professor Ling's insights shortchange the role of meditation as the catalyst to activate social ideals within the renewed individuals whose participation is essential to the newly formatted society.

VIII

Trevor Ling led us beyond the Buddha's world to its subsequent expressions in India and Sri Lanka. He wanted to gather information that would influence our view about two very important questions. How did the teaching impact society when it was freshest and strongest? Why did it decay and regress from civilization to mere religion?

Professor Ling was a tough realist in his evaluation of the Ashokan Empire, which covered most of India about three hundred years after the Buddha, and which is sometimes praised as an example of the ideal Buddhist state. Dr. Ling pointed to several flaws in this retrospective idealization. The famous inscriptions left by Ashoka throughout his empire praised and promoted the Buddha's moral principles, such as "...good behavior towards slaves and servants...abstention from killing...non-injury to living beings..." Dr. Ling commented: "This is an ethical system whose primary characteristic principles are non-violence and generosity...there appears to be very little in the way of specifically Buddhist doctrine..." In this analysis, Trevor Ling followed exactly what T.W. Rhys Davids wrote in *Buddhist India* seventy years earlier; "It was Dhamma for laymen...not a word about Buddha or Buddhism." Ashoka's government was remarkably progressive, devoting resources of the state to various public works, and promoting concord among sects and groups. But Dr. Ling challenged the idea that the Buddha's practices were actually widely followed: "...the stupa served as a focus for reverential feeling...In India the tendency to pay elaborate respect and reverence to great men to the point of deifying them, is well attested...the desire to surrender oneself in self-abnegating adoration." Professor Ling concluded: "...popularly-based religious cult...was one of the chief causes of its (Buddhism's) eventual decline and virtual disappearance from India." He further reminded us, "Without doubt, Ashoka's rule was autocratic," and even the tolerance for various sects had clear economic and political motives: the Sangha needed the protection provided by kings, and food and shelter, donated by a widely dispersed laity.

In Sri Lanka there was a long and noble effort to create a state that would implement what Trevor Ling saw as the essence of the Buddha's mission: "a restructured humanity." But Professor Ling cautioned us about historical texts written eight or nine centuries after the events, or about stories of lay people who attain *nibbāna*'s entry stage after hearing a single sermon. Furthermore, "It is evident from the style of the Pāli chronicles that already popular ideas of miracles and marvels had made themselves at home in the Buddhist tradition." He clarified that "...the political dimension was an accepted feature of Buddhism." The King of Sri Lanka had to be Buddhist, protect territory, and wage war against Tamils "...with the intention of establishing firmly the *sāsana* of the Buddha." Trevor Ling's main point was not scepticism about the ethics of Sri Lankan Buddhist Kingdoms, but emphasis on the notion that the Buddha's teaching was understood to be a pervasive and embracing program, and not merely an interior, individual salvation. He reserved particular praise for governmental attention given to healthcare, both for people and animals! His view was that Sri Lankan Buddhism understood the great transformative agenda of the Buddha, but never could exemplify it.

IX

Finally, Dr. Ling arrived at his analysis of the fate of Buddhist Civilization, which was "short-lived in India." He believed that the Buddha's humanism was undermined by widespread theistic devotionalism, and that entrenched priesthoods and orthodoxies censored its political and ethical concerns. From within supposed Buddhism itself, theistic worship cults eroded the original teaching. "Theravada form, committed to the concept of Buddhist national and international structure...ran into the shifting sands of Indian polytheism and was lost." Finally, Muslim invasions eliminated the supportive laity that had funded the Sangha. Indian Buddhism disappeared under "a violent and determined invasion by bearers of an alien culture."

In Sri Lanka, Buddhism as a religion has endured for over two thousand years, but what Dr. Ling called "Buddhist civilization" on the island met a similar fate of foreign aggression, crop failure, famine, disease, decay, and political disunity. Eventually, serial European invasions led to subjugation. Christian missions considered the Buddha's teaching to be idolatry, and aspired to mass conversion. In unaffected villages, "non-Buddhist supernaturalism" became the dominant religion. Sri Lankan Buddhism, according to Dr. Ling, placed *nibbāna* beyond the reach of ordinary people, and eventually came to emphasize only otherworldly escape.

Although Dr. Ling did not seem to find enduring examples in history, he seemed animated by his own faith in the *"Buddha sāsana* as a system of mind training, for the restructuring of human consciousness and thus, ultimately of human society...a humanistic ethic seeking full embodiment in a political and social community, an ideology seeking to become a civilization." With such beautiful phrasemaking, Dr. Ling seems to be writing his own *Sutta* for coming generations. He added that the Buddha's teaching "...adumubrates a reconstituted humanity...which lead men towards *nibbāna*...the affirmation of transcendent sacred reality..."

X

I would like to point to four problems with *The Buddha*. First, as I have mentioned, the centrality of meditation is vastly understated. Second, the relative diminution of Theravada on the world stage is often considered by other historians to be a result of its over emphasis on monasticism, and its alienation from the family life around which almost all people in almost all historical conditions center themselves. A frequent historical interpretation of the disappearance of the Buddha's teaching from India, for example, emphasizes that it provided inadequate format for familial participation. Dr. Ling's analysis focused on the negative side of Indian "polytheism" and "devotionalism," but did not consider the need for any enduring social system to vigorously embrace the family.

Third, Dr. Ling confused *Anattā* and *Mettā*. He was the preeminent champion of Buddhism's potentially revolutionary social impact, penning echoing phrases, like: "The Buddha addresses himself not to man's need for religion, but man's need to overcome his condition of self-centeredness, and to identify with a greater, completely comprehensive reality." Still, this is *Mettā*, not the selflessness of *Anattā*, which is not merely social, but the bedrock biophysical-existential recognition of the impermanence of everything in the human "self."

Finally, Dr. Ling himself provided us with this problem. The historical record in India and Sri Lanka is sketchy and rarely definitive. It gives us a historical sociology that is porously bounded and intermittent. History cannot eliminate guess, hunch, and myth from its narrative reconstructions. The best history can only make us self-aware of how little we know as fact. Expert historians, like Trevor Ling, remind us to be careful of intoxication from our own spurious historical inventions.

XI

The Buddha is intended to stir up the reader to ponder many unresolved questions. Can a worldwide reconstitution of human ethics and consciousness ever really occur? Can such an effort be simultaneously pragmatic and non-violent? Can "Buddhistic" societies ever defend themselves against foreign aggression? Must they center around a celibate Sangha? Can the interiority of the meditative pursuit of *nibbāna* ever escape from the self-centered narcissism that some Western critics claim are intrinsic to the pursuit of *nibbāna*? Is that why Dr. Ling shortchanged meditation in his text? Where is Myanmar in this text, and why is it ignored? Is it possible that the Buddha's teaching is inescapably rooted in authoritarian monasticism, monarchy, or oligarchy? In 1973, when Dr. Ling completed *The Buddha*, it was not yet mandatory to ask, as readers today will, what about women and slaves? Is there a "practice gap" that will permanently sideline the Buddha's teaching away from common human life? Is the Pāli Canon of Theravada Buddhism actually built on rejection of "common" people, or on simplistic and patronizing condescension towards them?

Thoughtful friends of *The Buddha* will find this book a learned and challenging teacher that can be repeatedly pulled off the bookshelf for one more provocative class. The text pushes its reader beyond stereotypes and clichés into realpolitic.

Trevor Ling's unblinking historical realism was by no means intended to discourage us. He wanted us to raise our efforts out from under nostalgic fantasy and sentimental, chauvinistic pseudo-history. His goal was to encourage pragmatism and efficacy in wielding the Buddha's teaching as a hopeful tool for personal, communal, and widespread humanism, rationality and political regeneration. He believed that the Buddha had put forth a big salutary program for our planet that remained worthy of very serious attention.

For those people who wish to pursue the teaching of the Buddha beyond the stage of wishes and promises, into a stage of mature implementation, Trevor Ling, with his learning, his unabashedly positive bias, and his seasoned historical lessons and lenses, spoke with a clarifying voice. His vivid history lets us feel we are walking around inside ancient India and Sri Lanka. Forty years after he wrote *The Buddha*, his book emits tempered hope.

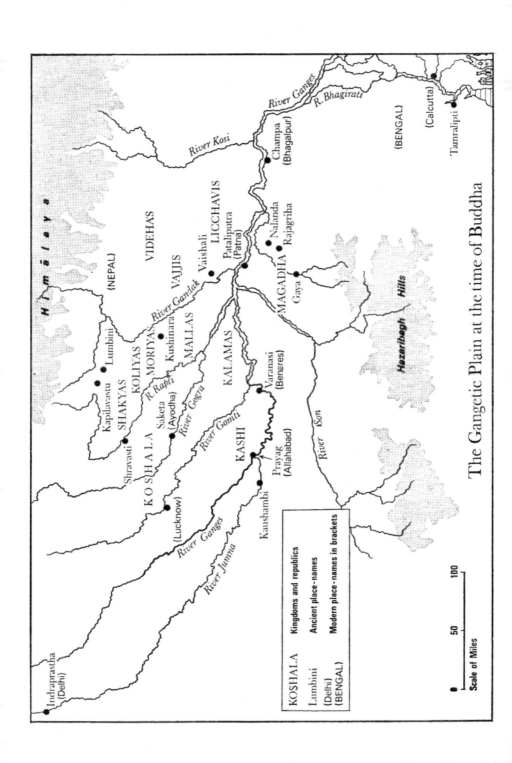

The Gangetic Plain at the time of Buddha

Himālaya

Indraprastha
(Delhi)

River Jumna

River Ganges

(Lucknow)

KOSHALA

Shravasti

Kapilavastu

SHAKYAS

Lumbini

KOLIYAS

(NEPAL)

MORIYAS

R. Rapti

Saketa
(Ayodha)

River Gogra

Kushinara

River Gandak

MALLAS

VIDEHAS

VAJJIS

Vaishali

LICCHAVIS

Pataliputra
(Patna)

River Gomti

KALAMAS

KASHI

Varanasi
(Beneres)

Prayag
(Allahabad)

Kaushambi

River Son

MAGADHA

Gaya

Nalanda
Rajagriha

River Kosi

River Ganges

Champa
(Bhagalpur)

R. Bhagirati

(BENGAL)

(Calcutta)

Tamralipti

Hazaribagh
Hills

KOSHALA   Kingdoms and republics

Lumbini   Ancient place-names

(Delhi)
(BENGAL)   Modern place-names in brackets

Scale of Miles

0   50   100

Part 1

Perspectives

1   Buddhism and Religion

To say that Gotama the Buddha founded a religion is to prejudice our understanding of his far-reaching influence. For in modern usage the word religion denotes merely one department of human activity, now regarded as of less and less public importance, and belonging almost entirely to the realm of men's private affairs. But whatever else Buddhism is or is not, in Asia it is a great social and cultural tradition. Born of a revolution in Indian thought it has found sponsors in many of the countries of Asia outside the land of its origin. What is a particularly interesting fact about these sponsors is that very often they were men concerned with *public* affairs, kings, emperors and governors. Yet it was not only to rulers that Buddhism appealed. Through its own special bearers, representatives and guardians, the orange-robed *bhikkhus*,[1] it has found its way into the common life of the towns and villages of much of Asia. Especially in Sri Lanka and South-East Asia it has continued to the present day to impart to the ordinary people its own characteristic values and attitudes, and has had a profound influence on the life of the home, as well as of the nation.

Buddhism has its own long and noble tradition of scholarship, and of education of the young, with the result that some of the traditionally Buddhist countries of South-East Asia have an unusually high rate of literacy for Asia. It has encouraged equality of social opportunity but without frantic economic competition. Buddhist values have inculcated a respect for the environment and a realistic attitude towards the importance of material things, an attitude which sees the folly of plundering and extravagantly wasting what cannot be replaced. For Buddhism has not encouraged ideas of dominance, in the sense that man should, by some divine sanction, dominate either his environment, or his fellow men. Neither exploitation nor colonialism have any place in Buddhist civilization; the key word is cooperation, at every level of being. The values and attitudes implicit wherever Buddhist culture survives have proved resistant to the campaigns and the blandishments directed from the West towards Buddhist Asia. From the time of the first contacts with European culture represented by the sixteenth-century Portuguese, hungry for spices and Christian converts, to the more recent work of American, British and French missionaries, the people of Buddhist Asia have not seen in either the doctrines or the fruits of Christianity anything sufficiently compelling to cause them to abandon their own tradition and culture in any large numbers. In Burma in 1931, the year in which the last decennial census under British rule was taken, Christians were 2.3 per cent of the total population, and Buddhists were 84 per cent.[2] Christian missionary activity in Burma had begun in the early eighteenth century. In Thailand, to take another example, according to the official report for 1965 issued by the Department of Religious Affairs in the Ministry of Education, 0.53 per cent of the total population were Christians and 93 per cent were Buddhists.[3]

IS BUDDHISM A RELIGION?

It is clear that in entering the world of the Buddha we are confronted by something more than a religion, if by religion is meant a system of *personal* salvation. The question could also be raised, and in fact often has been raised, as to whether Buddhism is a religion at all. It is possible from the historical perspective to answer both 'yes' and 'no' to this question.

Some attempts to deal with it appear to end inconclusively, in a circular argument. If one asks, 'Is Buddhism a religion?' it is obvious that one needs to know what a religion is, in order to say whether Buddhism is one or not. And when one asks, 'What is religion?' the definition will frequently be found to include reference to belief in a god or gods. If this is to be regarded as an essential constituent of religion, and if the absence of such belief denotes something other than religion, then the objection is likely to be raised, 'But what about Buddhism?' By this is usually meant early Buddhism, which does not appear to *require* belief in a god or gods as an essential part of the belief system. Emile Durkheim ran into this difficulty in his attempts to define religion. He pointed out that early Buddhism was not covered by such a definition of religion as E. B. Tylor's: that religion consists of 'belief in Spiritual Beings'.[4] In his support he quoted Burnouf's description of Buddhism as 'a moral system without a god', H.

Oldenberg's, that it is 'a faith without a god', and others of a similar kind.[5] Durkheim's argument is that Buddhism is in essence a non-theistic religion, and that in defining religion in general one should have this case in mind, and formulate a definition which will cover both theistic and non-theistic systems. The assumption which Durkheim appeared to be making was that Buddhism must be regarded as a religion, that is, a particular example of a general category, 'religion', a word about whose meaning there is some common agreement. Or he may simply be saying, 'I have a feeling that Buddhism should be included in, rather than excluded from, any survey of religions, for if it is not a religion, then what is it?' It might in fact be more useful, as Melford Spiro has pointed out, to pursue the latter question 'If not a religion, then what is it?'[6] For it may be that no conclusive answer will be found, in terms of any of the other possible conventional categories. If early Buddhism was not a religion, this does not necessarily mean that it was therefore a philosophy, or a personal code of ethics, or anything else for which a category exists. Inability to find any satisfactory answer may have the effect of stimulating further research, not only into the nature of what is generally regarded as 'Buddhism', but into the nature of what is regarded as 'Christianity', or as 'Islam', and so on. It might be found that these titles merely serve to indicate large, complex structures whose constituent factors have to be studied by the psychologist, philosopher, sociologist, the political scientist, the historian, and the economist. If this were found to be the case, then, since the entities concerned ('Buddhism', etc.) are so comprehensive and at the same time so diffuse that they are virtually coextensive with human life itself they should be known respectively as the Buddhist way of life, the Islamic way of life, and so on. Another way of dealing with the matter would be to speak, for example, of 'Buddhist civilization' or 'Islamic civilization'. In the next chapter it will be suggested that this is what they once very largely were, and that 'religions' as we know them are reduced civilizations.

BUDDHISM AND THE SACRED

First, there is the question of Durkheim's hunch, referred to a little earlier, the conviction which he seems to have had that Buddhism belonged in the category of community belief-systems of a certain kind. What distinguished such belief systems, said Durkheim, was *a sense of the sacred* which each of them manifested, and which differentiated them from secular belief systems. Furthermore, Durkheim suggested where the source of this sense of the sacred was to be found: it was in the human individual's awareness of his own dependence on the values and the collective life of the society to which he belonged, something which greatly transcended him, with his own short span of life, something to which he was indebted, which upheld him, and which provided the sanctions for his conduct. One might say that that which totally *sanctions* the life of the individual is the *sanctus*, the sacred. This need of the human individual for a collective with which he can identify, and which 'sanctions' his existence can be seen as underlying a good deal of what goes by the name of religion, and may be seen, also, as providing a powerful source of motivation for much of the activity which is called 'political'.

It was this, rather than belief in a spiritual, superhuman being or beings, according to Durkheim, which was the dominant strand in 'religion'. This very useful distinction provided by the concept of the sacred will be taken up later, in connection with the Buddhism of Sri Lanka, where the classical Theravada form exists in association with local beliefs in gods and spirits.

The answer to the question whether Buddhism is a religion is thus both Yes and No. It is not necessary to regard it as a religion if by that is meant a system of beliefs focusing in the supposed existence of a supernatural spirit being or beings, a god or gods. For in at least one of its major forms, the Theravada school, prominent in India in the early centuries, and still the dominant form in Sri Lanka and South-East Asia, Buddhism has no essential need of such beliefs. Later on in India a form of Buddhism emerged, alongside the Theravada, which was characterized by beliefs in, and practices associated with, heavenly beings who possessed superhuman spiritual power, and who were known as Bodhisattvas. This form of belief seems to be

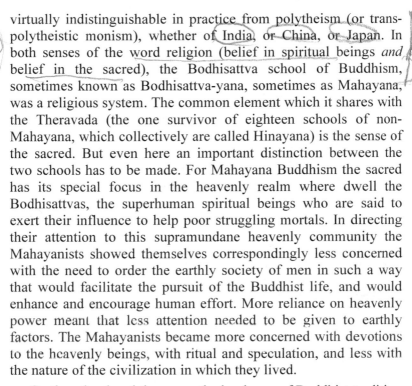

virtually indistinguishable in practice from polytheism (or trans-polytheistic monism), whether of India, or China, or Japan. In both senses of the word religion (belief in spiritual beings *and* belief in the sacred), the Bodhisattva school of Buddhism, sometimes known as Bodhisattva-yana, sometimes as Mahayana, was a religious system. The common element which it shares with the Theravada (the one survivor of eighteen schools of non-Mahayana, which collectively are called Hinayana) is the sense of the sacred. But even here an important distinction between the two schools has to be made. For Mahayana Buddhism the sacred has its special focus in the heavenly realm where dwell the Bodhisattvas, the superhuman spiritual beings who are said to exert their influence to help poor struggling mortals. In directing their attention to this supramundane heavenly community the Mahayanists showed themselves correspondingly less concerned with the need to order the earthly society of men in such a way that would facilitate the pursuit of the Buddhist life, and would enhance and encourage human effort. More reliance on heavenly power meant that less attention needed to be given to earthly factors. The Mahayanists became more concerned with devotions to the heavenly beings, with ritual and speculation, and less with the nature of the civilization in which they lived.

On the other hand there was the hard core of Buddhist tradition which never totally disappeared from Buddhist India even in the period when Mahayana flourished in such great citadels as Nalanda (in Bihar). This tradition was that reliance on the saving power of heavenly beings is contrary to the teaching of Gotama, the Buddha, who emphasized that men's supreme need was for sustained moral effort and mental discipline.[7] Where this point of view prevailed there was also a general tendency to realize Buddhist values as far as it could be done in the life of the society concerned; wherever possible this would be at the national level. In the areas where Theravada has been influential there has been a strongly developed sense of the need for a Buddhist state. It has been in the Theravada countries that Buddhism has most clearly expressed its character in this way, and that Buddhist civilization has been most strongly developed and has endured.

This should not, of course, be taken to mean that Mahayana Buddhism is of less significance for the sociological study of religion. In a sense a much greater refinement of approach is needed in dealing with the sociological interrelation of, say, economic factors with certain kinds of belief. That is an important task for the cross-cultural sociology of religion, but it is one which is not undertaken in the present work. The focus of the present study is in the idea of a Buddhist civilization, and the particular form this takes in the Buddhist state.

THE HISTORICAL PERSPECTIVE

There are various ways in which one can study the teaching of some outstanding figure such as Gotama the Buddha (or Jesus, or Muhammad). Ultimately, however, the various ways will be seen to resolve themselves into two main ones. The first of these may be called the literalist approach. The sayings of the Buddha are regarded as propositions to be understood literally without any necessary reference to the context in which they were spoken; as they stand they can be examined (if one is an historian of ideas), or thought about (if one is an interested enquirer), and acted upon (if one is a devotee). Usually it has been the devotee (of a certain type) who has been responsible for encouraging the literalist approach. For he who, in the first instance, has come to regard the total teaching of the founder of his religion, contained in the canon of scripture, as the truth will also very easily apply such an evaluation to this or that particular saying which he finds in the canon; such sayings become invested with the quality of 'eternal truths', propositions which are universally valid in all circumstances and under all conditions. The historian of ideas and the interested enquirer note this claim and proceed to work within these terms of reference: to be a Christian, or a Muslim, or a Buddhist, is to accept the canonical words of Jesus or Muhammad, or Gotama as inspired eternal truths. From such absolutist claims there follows all too easily the clash of rival 'absolutes', as well as the alienation of the more thoughtful.

The second approach may be called the historical-critical. In this case the teaching of the Buddha is related to the historical situation in which it was delivered, so far as it is possible to reconstruct and understand that situation. Attention is paid not only to the substance and meaning of the words spoken, but also

34

to the fact that they were spoken to certain hearers in a given, concrete situation.

In order to know what weight is to be given to a particular saying it is necessary to remember that the words were not uttered into the empty air, but to a specific audience. The nature of the audience, their level of understanding, their preconceptions or prejudices, and so on, all need to be taken into account in assessing how profound or how ephemeral the words are. In following such a method, difficult though it may be to apply in all cases, one is enabled to see that some aspects of the teaching have permanent validity because they are relevant to some enduring feature of the human situation, whereas others will be understood as having only limited validity since they refer in a very particular way to special situations which existed in the teacher's own day and which now no longer exist, or to beliefs which were current then but which are not held now. This second approach, like the first, may be adopted with equal appropriateness whether one is an historian of ideas, an enquirer, or a devotee.

Severe limitations attend the literalist approach. These show themselves specially clearly when one is attempting to evaluate the message of a teacher such as the Buddha in relation to the teachings of other prominent figures in the history of ideas. An extreme example will serve to highlight the difficulty. Karl Marx wrote a good deal concerning the alienation or estrangement (*Entfremdung*) which he saw as a feature of the human situation, but to search for a saying of the Buddha on this subject is to draw a blank, since Marx was dealing with industrial, capitalistic society in nineteenth-century Europe, and nothing of this sort existed in the India of the sixth century BC. To attempt to relate the teaching of the Buddha to that of Karl Marx purely in terms of propositions is likely to be an unprofitable exercise; it is like trying to get a telephone conversation going between two men who speak different languages, and one of whom cannot hear the other.

However, those who have by common convention been regarded as in some sense or other 'religious' teachers have this much in common, that they have all ultimately been concerned with a dimension to human existence other than the material and the temporal, a dimension which, in the interests of brevity, may

35

be called the transcendental dimension. This applies to the Buddha as to other so-called 'religious' teachers, even although, in his case, unlike most of the others, belief in the existence of a supreme divine being is not integral to his teaching. It is this transcendental dimension which invests the life of the human individual with a significance it would not otherwise have, and which it does not have in purely materialistic schemes of thought. 'There is, O monks' the Buddha is reported to have said, 'that which is not-born, not-become, not-made, not-compounded. If that not-born, not-become, not-made, not-compounded were not, there would be no release from this life of the born, the become, the made, the compounded.'[8] Another feature of the teaching of the Buddha which, in general terms, is shared with the other great systems which have come to be called religions is the importance given to proper moral conduct and moral attitudes on the part of the individual. This may be seen as the counterpart, at the level of human response, of the importance accorded to the transcendental dimension.

After recognizing these two common features, however, one begins to be more aware of differences than of similarities. It is at this point that the historical-critical approach is particularly relevant. It has already been pointed out that the form and even the content of a particular saying may be due to the local historical factors which have to be known and understood if the saying is to be realistically evaluated. This principle, by which we recognize this or that saying to have been conditioned by the circumstances in which it was spoken and the audience to whom it was addressed, can be extended beyond the form and content of particular sayings. The possibility which has to be considered is this: that the form and content of the teaching as a whole may be the result of conditioning by local, historical and geographical factors. It is to the exploring of this possibility, in so far as it relates to the religious teaching of the Buddha, that the first part of this book is devoted (chapters 2–4).

It should perhaps be made clear at the outset that this is not a full-scale cultural history of Buddhism. It has a more limited, simple, two-fold aim: first, to show what were the historical conditions in India—environmental, economic, political, and social—out of which the Buddha emerged, and in terms of which

36

his significance must be assessed; and second, to provide an account of the distinctively new phenomenon which resulted in due course from the Buddha's life and work, namely, Buddhist civilization. This will be examined first in principle (chapters 6–8) and then in practice (chapters 9–12).

Thus, in one sense of the word 'religion', denoting beliefs and practices connected with spirit-beings, Buddhism was in origin not a religion, but a non-religious philosophy. In the other, more sophisticated meaning of the word 'religion', which indicates awareness of that which is sacred, that which sanctions every individual existence, Buddhism in its Asian setting remains in certain respects what it was in origin, a way of attempting to restructure human consciousness and the common life of men in accordance with the nature of what it conceives to be the sacred reality. There are signs that in the modern period this important dimension of Buddhist civilization—the societal and political dimension—has been lost sight of, and that Buddhism is being reduced from a civilization to what the modern world understands by religion: that is, a system of 'spiritual' beliefs to be taken up by the minority in whatever country it happens to be who care for that sort of thing, a source of comfort to some, but in the last resort a private irrelevance, having little bearing on the real issues that shape human affairs. When Westerners have looked at Buddhism, too often they have seen only this, because this was all they were looking for. We shall examine this issue in general terms before we embark on our main purpose.

2   Religions and Civilizations

MODERN RELIGIOUS PLURALISM

In a brief but highly significant article on the role of Buddhism as a religion in modern, traditionally non-Buddhist societies, Elizabeth Nottingham indicates a number of important points for any comparative, sociological study of Buddhism.[1] One of these is the assimilation of Buddhism to the common pattern of 'religions' in urbanized societies. She observes that in contemporary situations in the United States and elsewhere 'Buddhism has had to accommodate itself to an existence as one religion among a number of other religions in a given country.' Introduced in the first place by Chinese and Japanese immigrants, Buddhism is now making itself at home in the United States and 'is already taking its place as one of the many organized "religions" of America. ... While still remaining Buddhism it is beginning to take on forms of organization and congregational services modeled on the American pattern.'[2] The same kind of process appears to be going on in parts of Europe and non-Buddhist Asia, especially in urban situations. In Malaysia, to take a random example, an organization for Buddhists, mainly residents of the capital, Kuala Lumpur, was founded in 1962, known as the Buddhist Missionary Society. The local achievements of the Society include the development of a uniform system of worship in connection with regular religious services, a Sunday School attended by hundreds of adolescent boys and girls and school children, religious classes for youths and adults, sessions for the singing of Buddhist hymns and songs, services of blessing by monks for newly-wedded couples, after the civil ceremony, and the performance of last religious rites.[3] Growth in the numbers taking part in these activities since 1962 is said to have been remarkable. Equally remarkable to the Western observer is the degree of assimilation to the pattern of activities of urban religious groups, of all kinds, in the West. One important factor in the Malaysian case may be the number of Sri Lankan Buddhist expatriates living there. Many of these are middle-class people in professional occupations who have imported urban assumptions about the proper pattern for Buddhist activities from

Sri Lanka. These assumptions appear to be largely due to accommodation to Christian concepts, encountered in Sri Lanka.[4]

To take another example, Buddhism is represented in England by a number of local associations in cities, towns and universities in various parts of the country.[5] While these groups vary to some extent in the kind of activities they engage in, and to a minor extent also in the social stratum from which their members are drawn, they share a tendency to see themselves as part of the spectrum of local religious sects and churches. Anyone who is familiar with institutionalized English Christianity will find much that is similar here, only with Buddhist terminology substituted. One characteristic which this kind of Buddhism shares with conventional middle-class suburban Christian organizations is an extreme reluctance to become involved in, or even to allow discussion of, matters of a political nature.

Thus, the temptation grows to answer the question 'What is Buddhism' by conceding that, after all, it is merely one of the *religions*, that is, one of the many organizations in the modern world which cater for men's private 'spiritual' needs, and which, competing for recruits, regard the number of those gained as the measure of the organization's success. To accept this as an adequate answer to the question 'What is Buddhism?' would, however, be to take a short-sighted and simplistic view; short sighted because it would force Buddhism permanently into the perspective of the suburban religious situation of the West; and simplistic because it would ignore the implications which Buddhist values carry in the realms of politics, economics and social structure. It would be to underestimate the social-revolutionary potential of Buddhism if it were assumed that it is merely a message of private consolation, or spiritual uplift, and that its presuppositions, and the life-style which it implies, are ultimately indistinguishable from those of the suburban residents of London or Petaling-Jaya.[6]

This phenomenon of the recent growth of Buddhist groups in the urban middle-class sector of traditionally non-Buddhist societies may, however, represent a significant new cultural development. For it may be serving to channel what in the first instance are largely negative feelings of dissatisfaction with Western society, its norms and values. Aspirations towards an alternative type of society, dimly perceived and perhaps not consciously formulated, may be nourishing this growth of Buddhist groups in non-Buddhist countries, a growth which has been particularly noticeable, not only since the end of the Second World War, but in the last decade.[7] This is a possible explanation which will be considered again at the end of this book, when the nature of Buddhist civilization has been explored.

'GREAT RELIGIONS' AS RESIDUAL CIVILIZATIONS

For Buddhism is, and has been for more than two thousand years, something very much more significant, socially, economically and politically, than is allowed by the statement 'Buddhism is one of the religions.' So also were Judaism, Christianity (for at least 1200 years) and Islam (for 1300 years), although these also today find themselves being relegated to the league of those organizations which cater mainly for the private, 'spiritual' aspirations of individual citizens, whose lives are, at the same time, being moulded and determined in the public dimension by forces quite independent of the organized 'religions'. It was not always so. There was a time when at least the major representatives of what are today identified by the reductionist term 'religions' or even 'great religions' were considerably more than institutionalized systems of private comfort and salvation which have no business to concern themselves with 'politics'; but this is what they have become today in the eyes of the majority of their adherents, especially their lay adherents.

What all these 'great' systems have in common is that each in origin was a total view of the world and man's place in it, and a total prescription for the ordering of human affairs in all the various dimensions which in the modern world are separated and distinguished from one another as philosophy, politics, economics, ethics, law and so on. Such an undifferentiated view of things is characteristic of 'unsophisticated' tribal life. But when, for one reason or another, the structure of tribal life is upset, there eventually follows, perhaps after an interval of time and after the enforced mingling of originally separate tribal cultures, some attempt at reintegration, now in a wider context than before, and with considerably extended horizons. The old tribal integration would eventually be broken by the trauma which historical events were to bring about. The new integration is on the other side of the trauma; it recognizes the traumatic events, and goes beyond them. It is an integration which would not have been possible, or would have had no relevance, in the earlier situation.

HINDU CIVILIZATION

What is popularly known as Hinduism provides a good example of this. 'Hinduism' covers, in fact, a large family of cultural systems and theistic sects. The most important of these, historically and structurally, is the system properly known as brahmanism. Metaphysics, cult, ceremonial, social structure, ethical principles, political and economic prescriptions, all are to be found in brahmanism. In this case the 'crisis' which brought it into being appears to have been the encounter of the incoming Aryan civilization with the culture which already existed in India when the Aryan immigrants arrived.[8] It was probably a fairly protracted crisis, extending over several centuries, but the result was an integrated civilization in which everything had been considered and provided for by the brahmans, the socially predominant priestly class, who were the architects of the system.[9] One of the most comprehensive treatises on the nature and structure of brahman civilization is the *Treatise on Government* (*Arthaśāstra*) of Kautilya. Another is the *Law Code of Manu* (*Manava Śāstra*) a work composed by brahmans but ascribed to Manu, the mythical father and lawgiver of the human race.

The word *artha* in the title of the first of these treatises represents an important concept in the brahmanical view of the world. The three principle concerns of man are, in this view, in order of importance: *dharma* (righteousness or duty), *artha* (the public economy) and *kāma* (aesthetic pleasure). When these are properly regulated and wisely pursued it becomes possible for man to achieve *moksha*, the spiritual goal of life. Thus, rules governing the public economy are an essential feature of brahman civilization, and so are rules governing the whole realm of aesthetic pleasures. Both of these, however, are subordinate to *dharma*, a word for which there is no single English equivalent. It indicates the eternal principle of being, that which is, and upholds all things. It also means the mode of life which is in harmony with this eternal principle. And it can mean, too, the specific code of conduct proper to each group, or to each individual according to the stage of life he has reached. It is in this context that one has to place such a treatise as the *Arthaśāstra*, the treatise on public wealth, welfare or economy.

The *Arthaśāstra* of Kautilya deals first with the life of the king: how he should discipline himself by restraining the organs of sense, the principles which should govern the appointment of his counselors, and the conduct of the meetings of king and counselors. It then goes on to describe in detail the rural economy, the development of villages and the regulation of their life with a view to the quiet and uninterrupted pursuit by the villagers of their proper occupations. It deals also with legal contracts, disputes, sexual offences, marriage and heritance laws, property purchase and sale, personal assault, betting and gambling, and so on. Other sections of the treatise deal with public finance, the civil service, defense, foreign policy and diplomacy. The emphasis, it will be seen, lies fairly heavily on legal, economic and political matters. The other treatise, the Law Code of Manu, is wider in its scope. It is more than a Legal treatise; as Keith says, 'It is unquestionably rather to be compared with the great poem of Lucretius, beside which it ranks as the expression of a philosophy of life.'[10] After a description of the creation of the universe, the text sets before us the brahmanical view of the hierarchy of living beings, of whom 'the most excellent are men, and of men [the most excellent] are brahmans'. The life of men is then covered in great detail, and regulations are laid down for every aspect of human affairs: sacramental initiation, student life, the life of the householder, marriage, types of occupation, duties of woman, rules for hermits and ascetics and rules concerning the king: how he should be honored, how he should spend his time, when he should offer worship, and how he should conduct the public affairs of the kingdom. A considerable body of civil and criminal law is also included, covering such matters as recovery of debts, agreements in respect of sale and purchase, boundaries, defamation, assault, theft, violence, adultery, inheritance, and various other matters.[11]

These two are not the only brahman treatises governing religious, political, economic and social life, but they are the best known, most important, and have been influential in the shaping of Hindu civilization. It is clear that what is described in these texts, and what was envisaged by the brahmans as their legitimate field of concern, is not adequately described as religion, as that word is now commonly used, but civilization.

ISLAMIC CIVILIZATION

Islam provides an even better example. As D. S. Margolionth wrote, 'We are apt to think of Islam as a religion, whereas the prophet probably thought of it rather as a nation.'[12] Early Islam was a complete prescription for human life as it then existed in the Arabian peninsula. A document known as *The Constitution of Medina*, together with the Quran, provided for every aspect of human needs in the early period—a view of the world and man's place in it, an account of man's destiny, the rules by which social relations and personal conduct were to be governed, how economic resources were to be used, what customs, ceremonies, festivals and so on, were to be followed. It was, in other words, the vision of a new civilization. At first it was believed that this vision was for the people of Arabia; then it came to be considered as one which had universal relevance, and which therefore could be applied to other situations outside Arabia. As Islam spread into the other lands of the Middle East it was as a civilization that it spread and developed in the initial stages. Leadership in prayer and leadership in political control were alike the responsibility of the Prophet and, after him, of each *khalifa*, or successor of the Prophet. The community of Islam was, as *The Constitution of Medina* said, one community over against the rest of mankind; it was one in theology, in government, in economic life and in social mores. But when, in the course of time, political power and economic practice became independent issues, then 'Islam' was the residue: namely the theology, the ethic and the social customs. What was originally a civilization had now, by a process of reduction, become a 'religion'. In the case of Islam, however, the original vision has never been entirely lost, and even in the modern world there have been attempts to reconstitute Islam after the earlier fashion, as a nation-state based on a theology and an ethic. An example is the Republic of Pakistan—at least, this was the hope claimed by some of the Muslims of undivided India in 1947.

Judaism has had a similar history. Its earliest identifiable form is found in the tribal confederation, united by the common vision of the prophets, a vision of what human society should be, what were its sustaining values, what its norms of social and individual behaviour, what its proper political form. But when the confederation was politically disrupted, north from south, each half thereafter maintained a theologically diminished and politically distorted version of the original theocratic civilization. The two halves each adopted instead of theocracy, the ancient Near Eastern pattern of government, which was that of a militarily maintained, city-based monarchy. Thus, Yahwistic civilization was in essence abandoned. The theological, social and ethical residue was preserved, however, in an uneasy coexistence and compromise with the urban monarchical system of government until at last, in the course of the political history of Palestine, the head of the Judean state was overthrown by the empire of Babylon; and Judaism developed in its residual form as a civilization without political or economic dimensions, that is, as a 'religion'.

JUDEO-CHRISTIAN CIVILIZATION

As in the case of Islam, so, too, in the history of Judaism there were attempts to reconstitute it as a totally integrated civilization, attempts to 'restore the kingdom to Israel'. This is not the place to examine them in detail. It may be noted, however, that yet another of the great 'religions' of the world—Christianity—may possibly have resulted from one of them. In this case, however, the early nature of the movement is now almost entirely unknown to us. Those early developments which took place in Palestine in a community of Aramean-speaking Jews are known to us only through a set of documents in Hellenistic Greek. In these not only the original words of Joshua (Hellenized as 'Jesus') of Nazareth have been translated into a foreign language, but the interpretation of the significance of the events themselves is given to us in terms

44

of Hellenistic Jewish thought, much of it that of Saul (Paul) of Tarsus, a Jew of Roman citizenship, indebted to the Hellenes for a great part of his culture. It is evident from the evidence of these documents (known by Christians as The New Testament) that there were a number of partisan interpretations of the events which had taken place in Judea in connection with Jesus, and that Paul's was one among others. Evidence from non-Christian sources concerning the movement is very scanty and tells us nothing more than that Jesus was put to death by the Romans for sedition. S. G. F. Brandon, in his examination of the available evidence, comments 'on the irony of the fact that the execution of Jesus as a rebel against Rome is the most certain thing we know about him'.[13] Professor Brandon goes on to examine the connection between Jesus and the Zealots. He points out that because the latter were rebels against an imperial power, they tended to have a poor press in the West, where they could too easily be assimilated with Russian, Irish or Indian revolutionaries, all groups who threatened the stability of Western capitalist, imperialist rule. Since the Second World War, however, with its change of sentiment towards 'resistance groups' there has, he notes, been some slight change of attitude to the Zealots among Western scholars. What is still hard for Christians, thinking of Jesus as the incarnate God is 'even to consider the possibility that Jesus might have had political views'.[14] He points out that 'if theological considerations make it necessary to prejudge the historical situation and to decide that Jesus could not have involved himself in a contemporary political issue, the judgment must accordingly be seen for what it is.... Such an evaluation of Jesus may be deemed theologically necessary and sound, but it will surely concern another Jesus than he who lived in Judea when Pontius Pilate was procurator, under whom he suffered crucifixion as a rebel against Rome.'[15]

The historical evidence concerning the period in which Jesus lived clearly points to the existence of widespread political discontent among the Jews of what had, by then, become a Roman province, and of various movements aimed at the overthrow of Roman power and the restoration of the Jewish theocratic ideal. Whether or not the movement associated with the name of Jesus of Nazareth was one such movement, aimed at the recovery of an integrated Jewish civilization, it is clear that by the time it had begun to win adherents in the Hellenistic world outside Palestine, it had lost any such total vision; in leaving Judea it very soon became non-political. Its apologists were eager to make this very clear to the Roman authorities, and later Christian theologians neither understood, nor had any interest in understanding, Jewish politics of the time of Jesus.[16] Like later Islam, and Judaism after AD 70, the early Hellenistic Christian movement had the restricted range of interests of a religion rather than of a civilization. It is noteworthy in this case, however, that when Christianity had become combined with the state religion of Rome, in the time of the Emperor Constantine, it did take on the kind of characteristics which justify its being called from this time, and throughout the medieval period, a civilization. The old gods of Rome had lost their ability to legitimate the imperial power; but once the Roman political system had found for itself a new source of legitimation, in the Jewish–Christian idea of God, it was assured of continuity, in the form of the Roman Church and the Roman Christian civilization to which it gave rise. The system lasted until, in the modern period, the theistic belief which had provided it with its sanctions began to be eroded by the rationalism of the emerging modern cities. After passing through the transitional stage which characterized it in its modern urban-rationalistic milieu, the stage of Protestantism, Christian civilization may now be said to have disappeared almost finally into the sands of modern Western secularism.

MODERN SOCIETIES AND THEISTIC BELIEF

Each of the 'major religions' which we have considered, as they now exist, may be seen as theological, ethical and ritual deposits left behind when the civilizations of which they were part lost their distinctive political and economic features. In each case the original vision on which the civilization was based had some form of theistic belief as its legitimation. Islam was realized as a civilization because there were men who were persuaded that the God of whom Muhammad spoke was a living reality, the supreme being, whose commands could not be set aside. It was the work of persuading men of this which was in the first instance the prophet's great achievement, carried out as it was in the face of the opposition and scepticism of the Meccan merchants and their followers. Initially, the prophet's success must be attributed to the power of his personality, together, perhaps, with a predisposition on the part of some of his hearers to belief in a supreme, powerful and righteous being. Given such belief there could follow, detail by detail, the realization of the prophet's vision of a new structure for human society which would transcend tribal limits and individual self-interest. When the civilization thus created eventually lost its political cohesion and its economic integrity, the theistic belief which had been its sanction remained as its central feature. As modernization advances, and Islamic life becomes by degrees more and more secularized, it is the element of belief in Allah which remains as the final distinctive feature. When a Muslim living in Britain is encouraged or forced by circumstances to conform more and more closely to the pattern of life of his workmates, and can perhaps no longer even observe properly the fast of Ramadan, then what finally marks him out as a Muslim is the distinctive nature of his belief in God, differing as it does from that of both Jew and Christian. This then, this surviving shred of the whole civilization which once encompassed the life of his forefathers, is what in the end Islam may come to mean for him: one variety among others of belief in God. What was once a civilization has now become a man's 'religion'—as that word is frequently used and understood in the West today. Perhaps some ritual practices and ethical attitudes will be preserved, but their maintenance will be precarious, depending very largely on the continuance of belief in the God of Islam. In the case of the children of such a man, brought up in modern industrial Britain, when belief in Islam's God is no longer tenable, there would seem to be little justification for practices and attitudes which mark them off from their schoolfellows; such justification as there is will then consist almost entirely in the strength of the family's own tradition.

This situation is one which all the major religions of the West share now that they have been reduced to their present state of being little more than precariously held theistic beliefs with attendant ethical attitudes and a possible modicum of ritual practice. Their viability is thus limited; they will last as long as theistic belief can be maintained in a modern industrial society. This may, of course, be longer than the unbeliever expects, especially among politically, socially or culturally deprived or depressed classes of society for whom traditional theistic belief can be a major source of satisfaction and comfort.

ALTERNATIVES TO THEISM

It is often assumed in the West that theistic belief is the only possible way in which a man or a civilization can be spiritually orientated. A major refutation of this assumption is provided by Buddhism. It is possible that Marxism may provide another but, as yet, it has not had as long a period as Buddhism in which to demonstrate its capacity in this direction. What they have in common is that they both begin from a vision of a new civilization which will enable man to grow and develop into a quality of life beyond what he has known hitherto. In neither case, however, does this vision need to be legitimated by reference to belief in a supreme divine being. The sanctions in both cases are philosophical rather than theological; in the case of Buddhism they are also to some extent derived from what, for brevity, may be called psychological experience.

Thus, one view of the relationship between religion and civilization is that religions make civilizations—or that they have done so in the past. Another view is that what are seen today as the 'great religions'—Hinduism, Buddhism, Christianity, Islam— are vestigial remains of civilizations. Mere hummocks of what were once, so to speak, great mountain ranges, they now have a mild charm, standing out a little, as they do, from the flat alluvial expanse of secularism in which they are slowly being silted up. Perhaps, to continue the geological metaphor, they will be superseded by some upthrust of new rock from the depths. The first rumblings of this movement can already faintly be heard. Whether that will be so or not we cannot tell. What we can discern is the present shape of the so-called 'great religions', and their drastically reduced dimensions, compared with what once they were. In the process of erosion by which civilizations were reduced to religions, one of the severest stages was that which occurred about a century ago. It has been described by Louis

Wirth: 'The atomistic point of view arising out of the biological and mechanistic tradition of the late nineteenth century led to the recognition of the individual organism as the solid reality constituting the unit of social life, and depreciation of "society" as a terminological construct or an irrelevant fiction.[17] The idea that human society is nothing more than the aggregate of the individual members of which it is composed is reflected in the nineteenth-century view of religion as the wholly private affair of the individual, a view which is given concrete expression in the American 'secular' state, where what is public and official has to be kept from all contact with religion which is essentially the affair of the individual.[18]

What the Buddha initiated, therefore, was not a religion—at least not in any sense that has meaning in the twentieth century. The same is true of the civilizations initiated by Moses, and Muhammad and perhaps Jesus, and the anonymous brahmans of ancient India who are represented by the name of Manu. What these all initiated were more than 'religions' in the reduced, individualistic sense of today. What exactly the Buddha did initiate it is the purpose of this book to explore. When its full scope has been revealed and its essential features have been examined, we may then decide how best it may be characterized. To do this will lead us to consider the characteristics of the Ashokan Kingdom of India in the third century BC, territorially and in other ways one of the greatest India has ever known; it will require us to look at the subsequent fate of Buddhist civilization in India, and to consider the long history of Buddhism in the island of Sri Lanka as it has existed now for twenty-two centuries.

Part 2

North India in the Sixth Century BC

3   The Physical, Economic, and Social Environment

Gotama the Buddha was born at a time when the main center of Indian civilization was located in the Ganges plain.[1] Whether there were at that time other important centers of development elsewhere in India is an open question. Certainly less is known of the peninsula or the south for this period.[2] The only other area of India for which historical evidence is available is the Indus valley. One of the indications that the Ganges valley had become the focal area of development is that in the literature which dates from this period, both brahmanical and Buddhist, it was termed 'the middle country' (*Madhyadesa*, Skt; *Majjhimadesa*, Pāli). The exact extent of the area to which this title was applied seems to have varied from one literary source to another but generally it designates the middle Gangetic plain. The Buddhist sources tend to regard the Majjhimadesa as extending farther to the east than do the brahmanical sources. For the Buddhists the eastern boundary was at a town called Kajangala, possibly the most easterly point reached by the Buddha in his travels. Kajangala was described by the Chinese Buddhist pilgrim, Hsuan Tsang, as being 400 *li* to the east of Champa (modern Bhagalpur). This would locate it at the point where the Ganges, at the eastern edge of Bihar, makes a major change of course towards the south, to flow through Bengal. In the other direction the boundary of the Majjhimadesa was a little to the west of the modern city of Delhi, along the western watershed of the Yamuna river, the major tributary to the Ganges, which flows parallel with it through most of the northern part of the Gangetic plain.

It was in this region, the 'middle' or 'central' country, comprising the Ganges valley from its upper reaches as far as the approaches to the delta, which was regarded as the most important area of India by all the ancient writers. Wherever brahmanical or Buddhist literature deals with geographical description, great attention is devoted to 'the central country' and much less to the other four regions—namely, northern, western, southern and eastern India. One does not have to seek very far for a reason for this, as B. C. Law pointed out: 'As with the brahmanical Aryans, so with the Buddhists, Middle Country was the cradle on which they staged the entire drama of their career, and it is to the description and information of this tract of land (by whatever name they called it) that they bestowed all their care and attention. Outside the pale of Madhyadesa there were countries that were always looked down upon by the inhabitants of the favored region.'[3]

THE HEART OF THE MIDDLE COUNTRY

By the time of Gotama's birth in the sixth century BC, however, it is possible to identify, even within the territory of the Middle Country, an inner heartland of the developing civilization.[4] This heartland consisted approximately of the area comprised by the rival Kingdoms of Koshala and Magadha, to which further reference will be made in the next chapter. Roughly, the territory concerned was the Gangetic plain from just west of the modern city of Lucknow to Bhagalpur in the east. Another way of identifying it is to say that it consists of the south-eastern third of the modern state of Uttar Pradesh, a small part of Nepal, and the northern half of the state of Bihar. Apart from a relatively small proportion of upland—the southern slopes of the Himalayan foothills of central Nepal and some outliers of the Bihar hills in the neighborhood of Gaya—the whole of this area of about 70,000 square miles consists of the broad, flat expanse of the middle Gangetic plain, which nowhere in this region rises above 350 feet.

Along the entire northern edge of this plain are the steeply rising slopes of the Himalayan mountain range, whose peaks are the highest in the world; from plains level to a height of 20,000 feet is reached in a horizontal distance of about seventy miles. Issuing southwards from this mountain range are the many tributaries which flow south to join the Ganges. The Ganges river itself emerges from the mountains in the extreme north of Uttar Pradesh to flow 1300 miles south-eastwards through this great plain before turning southwards to enter the Bay of Bengal. From Kanpur, where the river has yet 900 miles to go before reaching the sea, its height above sea-level is only 360 feet, so low and level are the plains from here.

For four months of the year, from June to September, the monsoon pours heavy rain over the whole region; this is heaviest in the eastern part of the region, and over the forested slopes of the Himalayas along the northern boundary. Most of the great rivers which flow south-eastwards across the plain, eventually to join the Ganges, have their source in the Himalayas, and between them they carry down the vast volume of water which the monsoon discharges. Some of the larger rivers on the northern half of the plain, such as the Gandak and Kosi, cause great damage by flooding the countryside, changing their courses, and depositing sand and stones across the plain. Ninety per cent of the total yearly rainfall comes in these four months, with the result that during the remaining eight months many of the smaller rivers dwindle away almost to nothing. The Gumti, for instance, is more than two miles wide in the rainy season, but a mere two hundred feet in the hot season.[5] The larger rivers, however, are fed from another source during the burning heat of the summer, from February to May; having their sources in the heights of the Himalayas they receive their water from the melting snows and glaciers. The Ganges 'never dwindles away in the hottest summer'.[6] Thus the plains which surround these larger rivers have a year-round supply of water, and agriculture can be maintained by irrigation. The soil of the Gangetic plain varies in quality, but in many places, especially where the Ganges, unlike the devastating Gandek and Kosi rivers, deposits rich alluvium it is suitable for intensive agriculture; 'the alluvial silt which it spills over its banks year by year affords to the fields a top-dressing of inexhaustible fertility'.[7] It is therefore not surprising that throughout the history of the region its people have held sacred the source of such fertility and life.

Between the four months of monsoon rain and the four months of burning sun and scorching wind comes the season of winter, from October to the end of January: a time of calm blue skies, when the days are warm, the nights cool and the mornings fresh and dewy. There may, however, be a period of light winter rain in January. This is the time when the *rabi* (spring-harvested) crops are grown, such as wheat and barley, and linseed and mustard for their oil.

A LAND OF ABUNDANT FOOD

In the Buddha's day the situation was in some respects very much more favorable for agriculture than it is today.[8] Much of the Gangetic plain was still forested, and land could be had for the clearing, where virgin soil was ready to produce abundant harvest. The Greek writers of the period describe the agriculture of the Ganges valley with great enthusiasm. Diodonis, who derived his knowledge of India from the work of Megasthenes, writes in this way: 'In addition to cereals there grows ... much pulse of different sorts, and rice also ... as well as many other plants useful for food, of which most grow spontaneously ... Since there is a double rainfall in the course of each year, one in the winter season, when the sowing of wheat takes place as in other countries, and the second at the time of the summer solstice which is the proper season for sowing rice and bosporum as well as sesamum and millet, the inhabitants of India always gather in two harvests annually.... The fruits, moreover, of spontaneous growth, and the esculent roots which grow in marshy places and are of varied sweetness, afford abundant sustenance for man. The fact is, almost all the plains in the country have a moisture which is alike genial whether it is derived from the river, or from the rains of the summer season which are wont to fall every year at a stated period with surprising regularity.'[9] A passage from Strabo tells the same story: 'From the vapours arising from such vast rivers and from the Etesian winds, as Eratosthenes states, India is watered by the summer rains and the plains are overflowed. During these rains, accordingly, flax is sown and millet; also sesamum, rice and bosmorum, and in the winter time wheat, barley pulse and other esculent fruits unknown to us.'[10]

Many of these fruits, then unknown to Europeans, were gathered by the people of India from the forests which at that time were far more extensive—fruits such as mango, jack-fruit, date, coconut and banana. Throughout the Buddhist and brahmanical literature one is constantly reminded of the thick growth of forest which still covered the greater part of the plains in the sixth century BC.[11]

The wagons that carried merchandise from one town to another had to pass through dense and sometimes dangerous forests where wild creatures, human or sub-human lay in wait for the unprotected traveler. But the forests were also lovely with flowering trees, especially in the cool season and early summer. Buddhist literature frequently refers to the sound of the birds 'there, where the forest is in flower'.[12] Banyan and bo-tree, palmyra, date palm, coconut, acacia, ebony and sal, all these and many other trees are mentioned in the contemporary literature as features of the everyday scene. When, in the pursuit of the spiritual life men wished to withdraw from the enclosed village area of houses and fields, it was into the all-encircling forest that they went. In a region so vast and with a population still relatively small there was plenty of space for all, whether they wished to cultivate the numerous crops the land would bear, or to withdraw into silence and solitude.

THE ARYANIZATION OF THE MIDDLE COUNTRY

Some of the inhabitants of the Gangetic plain may originally have come from the north and east, from the lands we now call Burma and Tibet. At its eastern end there were, at the time of the Buddha, a people called the Anga, whose capital was Champa (near modern Bhagalpur). Their name, as indeed that of the Ganges itself, has been identified as Tibeto-Burman, or Sino-Burman. The findings of linguists and archaeologists are summarized as follows: 'Heine Geldern believes that the south-eastern Asiatics (Austronesians), already having considerable Mongoloid mixture, who had come down into Assam and Burma, migrated westwards into India and introduced the tanged adze between 2500 and 1500 BC before the Aryan invasion. Percy Smith recognizes a Gangetic race in northern India before the Aryan invasion. He believes that a Himalayo-Polynesian race, allied to the Chinese and Tibetan formerly spread over the Gangetic basin from further India.'[13] What is generally regarded as certain is that there had, for some centuries before the time of the Buddha, been a considerable process of 'Aryanization' spreading south-eastwards from the

Indus valley, down the Ganges plain. This may have been the consequence of an actual physical invasion by Aryan-speaking peoples from the north-west beyond India, which swept away the ancient city-civilization of the Indus valley, or it may have been part of a general cultural movement, like other cultural 'invasions' which have taken place over the same territory in the centuries since that time. The invasion of north India by Islam provides a clear example of the latter possibility. While there were, it is true, actual movements of Muslim invaders from the north-west, these were only a minority among the people whom they invaded. The spread of Islam (mainly from the eleventh century AD onwards) consisted largely in the adherence of large numbers of the original inhabitants of the territory to Islamic culture and Persian language. This kind of process may well have occurred in the course of the Aryanization of northern India which marked the centuries immediately before the time of the Buddha. In north India this period was, as Kosambi points out, one of transition from a pastoral, herd-keeping mode of life to one of cultivation of the soil. The land was at the 'crucial stage where soon the plough would produce much more than cattle' in the way of food supply.[14] The stages by which this would have come about are fairly clearly traceable.

RICE CULTIVATION AND POPULATION INCREASE

The situation in the Buddha's time can be seen as one of increasingly extensive agriculture in the middle Gangetic plain. The cost of this increase in agriculture was extensive deforestation. Round each village settlement was an area of cultivated fields, beyond this some pasture, and then the forest. As the bounds of the cultivated fields were pushed outwards, the forested area retreated before the agriculturist's axe and fire. New fields were to be had for the clearing and some of the more enterprising were opening up new settlements. There was consequently a continually spreading area of cultivated field. Where cattle raising, associated with a nomadic or semi-nomadic way of life, is the main occupation, there is not normally a high density of population. The increase in cultivation would, therefore, have entailed a sharp increase in the human population of the region. The land which was being brought under cultivation was preeminently suited to rice-growing, especially when advantage was taken of the all-the-year-round water supply from the Ganges in the development of irrigation. It is known that, at the time of the Buddha this was, in fact, being done.[15] It was the rice of the Gangetic plain which became, and has remained, the major source of food supply in the eastern half of Uttar Pradesh, in Bihar and Bengal. The time spent in cultivating the land would have meant that less time and energy could be spent on herd-keeping. This, together with a decrease in the range of land available for herds, meant a gradual decline in the cattle population. In this way a change in the balance of the people's diet would have occurred, from one in which milk products and meat had a large place, to one in which the larger place was taken by rice and vegetables. It has been pointed out that the latter type of diet is a factor in further population increase. Rice, says Beaujeu-Garnier 'produces two to two-and-a-half times more grain to the acre than wheat, two-thirds more than barley, and one-third more than maize. Moreover, it is a food of high value, especially when consumed in the husk.'[16] In addition to this, whereas a high protein diet, such as that enjoyed by those whose diet consists in large measure of milk products and meat, appears to reduce fertility, a rice diet seems to have the opposite effect; rice provides 'woman with a diet which predisposes them to fertility; furthermore it can be consumed by very young infants either as gruel or as a pulp, enabling them to survive and thus to be weaned early so that the mother is ready to conceive again'.[17] The increase in human population, which had followed the beginning of the deforestation of the Ganges plain, would have resulted in a demand for yet more land to support the increasing numbers.

By the time of the Buddha a steady growth in the density of population of the Gangetic plain was taking place, and, together with this, there was probably a decline in the number of cattle being reared. To this fact has to be added another, as we shall see later: that cattle were a consumable commodity, so to speak, since they were required in considerable numbers for the brahmanical sacrificial system. Moreover, these sacrifices would probably have increased in number, if only slightly, with the increase in human population. This would have been the case especially in times of threatened shortage of cattle or food, since the sacrifice was supposed to ensure prosperity. The growth of monarchy and the aggressiveness of kings would have supplied another reason for an increase in the number of sacrifices, since success in battle was also held to be secured through priestly offerings. Over the whole area under cultivation the density of population would have remained reasonably uniform, without any very great unevenness anywhere, as is usually the case in rice-growing regions. There would, however, have been a natural and proportionate increase in size of the larger settlements. Towns or cities were certainly to be found throughout the Gangetic plain in the Buddha's day. The six great cities, named in Buddhist texts, were Savatthi, Saketa, Kaushambi, Kashi (Varanasi), Rajagriha and Champa. Apart from these a number of other large towns of the area are known to us by name, such as Kapilavastu, Vesali, Mithila and Gaya. With the rise in population and a general steady growth in the size of settlements, some of the small villages would have expanded into towns, wherever special factors were present to encourage such development, such as location at the junction of caravan routes, or near to river crossings, at places of religious importance, and at points of strategic military or political importance, wherever a stronghold had been established.

DEVELOPMENT OF URBAN LIFE

It is therefore possible to see that one of the features of life in this region in the sixth century BC was a steady growth in the numbers of people who were beginning to experience an urban way of life. They were then a small minority; but then, as now, they were a minority with a considerable social, cultural and political significance. The cities and towns were centers of industry and trade. Workers in the various industries were organized in guilds, and it is known from the brahmanical and Buddhist sources that these included guilds of wood-workers, iron-workers, leather-workers, painters, ivory-workers and others. These guilds appear from the sources to have been highly organized autonomous bodies, recognized by the state, and able to exercise control over their members.[18] Most of the cities and large towns which have been mentioned by name were also political and administrative centers, in that they were capitals of kingdoms (Shravasti, Saketa, Kashi and Rajagriha are examples) or centers for the ruling assemblies of republics (as, for example, Vaishali). They would have become so owing to their strategic situation or the existence of resources for an industry, or both; these reasons together would also have encouraged their growth as centers of trade. Connecting the urban trade centers were established and recognized routes. For example, from Shravasti the capital of the Kingdom of Koshala, there was a major route eastwards along the northern edge of the Gangetic plain. The route kept close to the Himalayan foothills because at that level the rivers flowing southwards and south-eastwards towards the Ganges could more easily be forded or ferried than lower down in their courses, where they increased in size. The towns which lay along the line of this eastward route received an added importance from the caravan traffic which passed through them and made use of their facilities as halts. Such a town was Kapilavastu, the home of Gotama, the Buddha-to-be, one of the five recognized halts on the route. This continued eastwards to the crossing of the river Gandak, then turned south-eastwards through Vesali, southwards across the Ganges at Pataligama, and thence to Rajagriha, the capital of the Magadhan Kingdom. From there another route led southwards to Gaya and beyond. In other directions, from Shravasti a route led southwards to the city of Ujjain and beyond, while yet another ran north-westwards to Hastinapura and the cities of the Punjab, including, most notably, the city of Taxila. There was a good deal of travel by river as well as by land routes, especially in the central part of the Gangetic plain, where the rivers were large enough to allow vessels of considerable size. They also provided a more convenient, safer, and sometimes quicker method of transporting goods, especially heavier ones, than the overland caravan routes. Kaushambi, Varanasi, and Champa would have been busy riverports and trade centers.[19]

The cities and towns of the Ganges plain thus began to develop a style of life which was in certain respects fairly distinct from that of the country villages. As centers of business and trade they drew in the wealth of the country, and they also became centers of learning and culture, attracting, too, what Atindranath Bose describes as 'parasite professions like stage-acting, dancing, singing, buffoonery, gambling, tavern-keeping and prostitution.'[20] In contrast with the sophisticated and heterogeneous life of the towns is the style which the Arthaśāstra considers proper for the villages; provision is made in that treatise of government for the work of agriculture to be protected from disruptive and diverting influences: 'No guilds of any kind other than local cooperative guilds shall find entrance into the villages of the Kingdom. Nor shall there be in villages buildings intended for sports and plays. Nor, with the intention of procuring money, free labor, commodities, grains and liquids in plenty, shall actors, dancers, singers, drummers, buffoons and bards make any disturbance to the work of the villagers.'[21] The existence of such a regulation, whether it was put into practice, or remained an ideal, is enough to indicate that there was felt to be a distinct difference between the relatively sophisticated life of the town, and that of the countryside. The villagers' awareness of this difference may have been the reason for their reluctance to visit the towns, observed by Megasthenes: 'husbandmen themselves with their wives and children live in the country and entirely avoid going into town'.[22]

THE SIX CITIES OF THE MIDDLE COUNTRY

Of the six great cities of the Gangetic plain at the time of the birth of Gotama, one had become particularly prominent: Shravasti, the capital of the Kingdom of Koshala. By the time of the Buddha's death, however, it was beginning to lose this position of superiority as Rajagriha, some 270 miles to the south-east, grew in importance. Nevertheless, throughout the sixth Century BC Shravasti was the great center of life and activity. In the *Jātaka* literature, cities such as Varanasi (Banaras), capital of a kingdom which had by now been conquered and absorbed by Koshala, appear as places which had lost some of their former importance and had yielded in prestige to the large, lively and wealthy city of Shravasti. According to a tradition mentioned by the great Buddhist writer of the fifth century AD, Buddhaghosa, there were in the Buddha's day 57,000 families living in Shravasti.

The city was both the capital of the Kingdom of Koshala and the leading center of commercial activity. It lay on the caravan route from north-west to south-east where this passed between the foothills of the Himalaya and the difficult terrain to the south, where the rivers became broad and difficult to cross and where there were still tracts of dense tropical jungle and marsh. Moreover, Shravasti was at the junction of this trade route with another which led southwards to the city of Kaushambi and beyond it to the Deccan. So, Shravasti, as an important junction of trade routes, had become famous for its rich merchants. One such was Anathapindika, who, at a very high price, purchased from Prince Jeta of Shravasti a pleasant piece of ground outside the city in order to give it to the Buddha and his monks as a residence and a retreat.

The explanation of the name Shravasti which is given in later Pāli Buddhist literature is itself evidence of the city's prosperity: the name, it is said, was derived from the common saying of those days that this was a place where everything was obtainable.[23] This is interesting as historical evidence of the standard of living in Shravasti, although it is questionable as etymology. A modern explanation of the name of the city, and of the river Ravati on whose bank it stood, connects them both with *Sharavati*, derived from the name of the sun-god, Savitri.

The city lay along the south bank of the Ravati; it was crescent shaped, with the concave side facing the river. Its 'walls and watch towers' are mentioned in one of the *Jātakas*, and even today, 2,500 years later, the ruins of these solid brick walls are forty feet high and the remains of the western watch tower, on the river bank, are fifty feet high. The site's modern name is Saheth Maheth, a corruption of the original name, and it is in Gonda district, in Uttar Pradesh, about ten miles by road from the railway station of Balrampur. The ruins were identified by General Cunningham in the course of his archaeological survey of India;[24] archeological excavations were carried out in 1907–8 and in 1910–11, and today the place has become a well-frequented pilgrim center. The original lay-out and character of the city can thus be fairly reliably reconstructed from both literary and archaeological evidence. The major routes entered the city through the principal gateways on the south-west, the south, and the south-east. The roads converged in an open square in the center of the city. The larger and more important buildings were in the western half; while in the eastern half were streets and lanes where were the bazaars and houses of the common people.[25] In this eastern half were gathered all kinds of specialized trades, each street-bazaar specializing in one commodity:[26] in one street were the cooks, in another the garland-makers, in another the perfumers, and so on. One of the *Jātakas* mentions a group of about five hundred page-boys in the city, who were particularly adept at wrestling. Containing a royal court and the residences of opulent merchants, the city would have been the center of attraction throughout the wide area served by the routes which converged here. It was undoubtedly the 'modern' city of the time, and had been so sufficiently long for this reputation to have been established by the time of the Buddha, even though it was by then nearing the end of its period of preeminence. The significance of these facts will be seen later, when we consider the special nature of the community founded by the Buddha.[27]

Most of the characteristic features of Shravasti were found in the other great cities, except Rajagriha, which in certain respects was distinct from the rest. But Saketa, Kaushambi, Varanasi, and Champa had much in common with one another, and with Shravasti, the greatest of them all. Each had as its original *raison d'être* the fact of being both a political and a commercial center. Each of the four had been the capital of a formerly independent kingdom, which, by the Buddha's time, had been absorbed by one or other of the two giants, Koshala and Magadha. These capital cities, which had by then lost their autonomy, had clearly been places of power and grandeur, and much of this would still have been apparent in the Buddha's day, in the impressive fortified walls and watch towers that each possessed, so massive that in some cases they still exist, like those of Shravasti, as substantial ruins even today.[28]

Situated in each case on a large river, at the junction of important trade routes, they were also prominent commercial cities. Since river boats carried a good deal of traffic, both in passengers and commodities, the cities were important *entrepôts* at the crossing of land and river routes. Their leading citizens were merchants and bankers, officials and princes from various places, who would travel about the city in horse-drawn chariots or by elephant. Within the wide extent of the city walls were contained, in addition to the houses of merchants and traders, a great variety of crafts and industries, 'perfumers, spice sellers, sugar-candy sellers, jewelers, tanners, garland-makers, carpenters, goldsmiths, weavers, washer-men, etc.'[29] Like other large cities, ancient and modern, they had also the distinction of 'abounding in rogues'.[30] In one respect Varanasi (Banaras) was distinguished from the others, in that it was, in the Buddha's day, not only a wealthy and prosperous place noted for its textiles and ironware, but also a great center of learning, with educational institutions which were among the oldest in India. Then, as for many centuries since, it was the most prominent intellectual and religious center, certainly of northern India. Its city hall had become a place used not so much for the transaction of public business as for public discussions of religious and philosophical questions.[31] This intellectual preeminence of Banaras in the Buddha's day is a fact we shall refer to again in connection with the outline of the Buddha's public activity.

Rather distinct in certain respects from these other cities was Rajagriha, the capital of the growing Magadhan kingdom. This was situated to the south of the Ganges, in what is now Bihar, where the river plain meets the first line of hills, outliers of the greater upland region of Chota Nagpur and central India. Rajagriha was one of the oldest cities of India, with a history reaching back long before the sixth century BC.[32] The original site was a stronghold encircled by five low hills as a natural rampart, with walls and embankments filling the gaps between them. For this reason, the older name of the city was Giribbaja (mountain stronghold). A new city, just outside the northern hill, was built by Bimbisara, the king of Magadha, who was an older contemporary of the Buddha. Bimbisara's action would appear to reflect both the expanding population of the city, which could no longer be contained in the original area, and the growing strength of the Magadhan kingdom; and it may indicate, too, a confidence that the security of the new city was assured against any possible attack. Northwards from Rajagriha the major trade route was the one that led to Shravasti and thence to the north-west of India. Southwards the route led to one of the major sources of Magadha's strength, the iron-bearing hills of what is today south Bihar. As the capital of an expanding kingdom Rajagriha attracted travelers of all kinds; provision is said to have been made for these to be accommodated in a large building in the center of the city. One such traveler was the rich merchant, Anathapindika,[33] from the Koshalan capital, Shravasti, who, according to Buddhist tradition, first met the Buddha in Rajagriha. At night the outer gates were closed against possible enemy attack under cover of darkness, for in spite of the buoyancy of mood which led to the building of the new city, there was apparently still some fear of invasion from hostile neighboring states. It is said that the sanitary conditions within the city left much to be desired because of the density of the population. The city was the venue for a famous festival[34] which attracted crowds of people of all social classes from the whole area of Magadha and Anga. Nautch dances formed a prominent part of the public entertainment, which was held in the open air, together with popular music, singing and other amusements. Special arrangements were made for the provision of food for the crowds. At other times troupes of players, acrobats and musicians used to visit the city and provide entertainment for days at a time.

This brief summary of some of the available information about the six major cities of the Buddha's day is enough to indicate certain common features which they shared. The life of each of these cities was conditioned by two major factors: first, a junction of trade routes, and second, a royal court. Each of these cities had been the capital of a kingdom, even though some of them (Saketa, Kaushambi, Varanasi and Champa) had been absorbed into more powerful kingdoms and had become vice-royalties. The crucial factor in the growth of each of them had been the development of monarchy in north India, although important subsidiary factors, such as a tradition of learning, had aided the original growth. Ultimately it was the presence of a royal court which seems to have determined their prosperity; it was essential to the security of a kingdom that the royal capital was strong and secure; as the kingdom grew and prospered so did the life of the city. When the kingdom became weak or lost its independence so, eventually, did the city and in some cases the end of a kingdom meant the end of the life of the city. The one exception is Varanasi (Banaras) where, in spite of the loss of political sovereignty, the city has survived to modern times. This must very largely, though not entirely, be attributed to the special sanctity which Varanasi possesses for Hindus. In addition, it had a strong tradition of brahmanical learning and the natural local advantages of its site. Since there is an important connection between the character of early Buddhist civilization and the life of the north-Indian city, and also between the latter and the growth of monarchy, it is necessary at this point to give attention to the political conditions in north India in the sixth century BC.

4   Monarchy, the City and Individualism

REPUBLICS IN DECLINE

At the time of Gotama's birth, two types of government were in competition with one another in northern India: republican and monarchical. Not only were the republics engaged in a struggle for survival in the face of the expansion of the monarchies; there were also minor feuds between different tribal republics, as well as major struggles between one monarchy and another. The general result of all this was a trend towards an increase in the size and power of the monarchies at the expense of the republics.

The republics occupied a belt of territory which ran across the middle of the Gangetic plain in a roughly north-west to south-east direction from the Himalayas to the Ganges. The most northerly of them was the Shakyan republic, in which Gotama himself was born. Adjoining its territory, to the south-east, was the Koliyan republic, and beyond this the Moriyan. To the east of these three was the territory of the Mallas, whose capital was Kushinara, where the Buddha's decease occurred. The republic of the Mallas, together with some other republics—the Licchavis, the Videhas, the Nayas, and the Vajjis—appear to have formed themselves into a loose confederation for joint action against common enemies; this was known by the name of the last one in the list, the Vajjis. It is unlikely that it was a federation in any permanent and formal sense.[1] Government by discussion was the keynote of the republics; that is to say, within these tribal groups the common life was regulated by discussion among the elders or noblemen of the tribe meeting in a regular assembly. These assemblies were known as *Sangha*s, and since this institution was the most characteristic feature of the republics, this is the general term by which the republics themselves were known. Earlier in Indian history, in the Vedic period, there appears to have been a somewhat different practice, namely, the assembly of all the members of the tribe to discuss matters of importance. The republican assemblies of the Buddha's day differed from these older folk-assemblies in that it was the elders only who assembled to discuss the affairs of the republic. They were not elected by the rest of the people; rather, they were leading men of the tribe, men belonging to the Kshatriya clan. The form of government was aristocratic rather than democratic. Final authority in all important matters lay with the assembly of the 'fully qualified members of this aristocracy'.[2]

The case of the Shakyan republic is particularly interesting. Here the form of government seems to have been a mixture of the kind of republicanism which has just been described, with features of monarchy. The Shakyas, probably for this reason, are not found in many of the lists of typical *Sanghas* (republics) found in the texts of this period; the Shakya republic was recognized as being of a somewhat different constitution. The case of the Shakyas is interesting because of its possible bearing on the question of what stage of political evolution the *Sanghas* may be taken to represent. It has been suggested that their aristocratic form of government was derived from monarchy, through the emergence of royal, princely groups among whom power was shared. On the other hand, the *Sanghas* might be seen as an intermediate stage between the earlier collectivism of fully popular tribal assemblies, and the later, fully developed autocracy of the monarchical state. On one view of the matter, the constitution of the Shakyas could be interpreted as a sign that they had not yet progressed as far as the other *Sanghas* from monarchy to republicanism, and that they still retained traces of monarchy; on the other view, it might be held that they were ahead of the others in their progress from some sort of collective tribal rule towards a fully established monarchy.[3] The case is all the more interesting in that it was to the Shakyas that Gotama belonged, and one of his most common titles serves as a reminder of this: Shakya-muni, 'the sage of the Shakyas'. It is significant that in the Pāli canonical texts both republican government and kingship are represented as subjects on which the Buddha had something relevant to say, as we shall see in more detail later (see chapter 8, p. 165 ff.)

The weakness of the republics is demonstrated by the fact that their collapse followed within a few years of the Buddha's decease, that is, by about the middle of the fifth century BC. While this was due partly to the aggression of the monarchies, it was also due in fairly large measure to internal disagreements among the republican nobles or elders, and to moral indolence, lack of discipline and justice, and an ill-founded pride.[4] In general, therefore, the collapse of the republics may be said to have been due to the prevalence of an *undisciplined individualism*.

Whether monarchy was a type of government superior to the republicanism of the Buddha's day is a question whose answer will depend on how other, prior questions are answered. For one must first ask, 'superior in whose view and for what purposes?' One needs to know how widely the effects of one form of government as distinct from another were actually felt throughout the societies concerned, and whether monarchy had more unpleasant and uncomfortable consequences for a greater number of people than republican rule. Was the condition of the people as a whole worse or better under a monarchy from the point of view of personal security, economic prosperity, social freedom, and spiritual satisfaction? To say that the aim of good government is the greatest good of the greatest number is simply to beg two questions: what is the greatest good, and how is agreement on this issue reached? Some forms of government are based on the claim that the governing elite knows what is best for the people; monarchical government may even be based on the claim of a totalitarian ruler that he possesses superior wisdom and insight, vouchsafed to him from some divine source.

On the other hand it may be that all such theoretical niceties are beside the real point, that power belongs to him who is successful in seizing it and keeping it. In this view of the matter people merely acquiesce in whatever form of government is thrust upon them until it becomes acutely intolerable, when they may be driven to rebel and overthrow the tyrant, hoping that out of the new situation will emerge a more agreeable alternative.

Such observations as these are, at best, only attempts to simplify what are, in actual historical situations, extremely complex mixtures of conscious evaluation and choice on the one hand, and environmental, economic and social determinants on the other.

With regard to India at the time of Gotama's birth, the kind of considerations which have just been mentioned are very appropriate. How far the growth of a great monarchy such as Koshala or Magadha was accepted as an evil necessity, or perhaps a *fait accompli*, in the face of which the common people were powerless, and how far it was accepted for its own sake as providing more satisfactory solutions to problems connected with the common life than republicanism was able to offer, are questions to which no clear answers can be given. Such issues were certainly discussed in the Buddha's day, and various views were taken of the origins and respective merits of different systems of political organization.[5]

THEORIES OF KINGSHIP

One view of the origin of monarchy is found in the Buddhist Pāli Canon. The *Aggañña Sutta*, or 'Discourse on Genesis', said to have been delivered by the Buddha at Shravasti, describes how the first king came to be instituted, in the early days of the human race. Men had become greedy, dishonest, quarrelsome and violent (for reasons which are set out at length in the early part of the Sutta). Recognizing this, they came together, and, bewailing the situation, reasoned in this way: 'What if we were to select a certain being, who should be wrathful when indignation is right, who should censure that which should rightly be censured, and should banish him who deserves to be banished?' In recognition of the role which such a being would play in the interests of the common good, they decided to 'give him in return a proportion of the rice'. Thereupon, we are told, they 'went to the being among them who was the handsomest, the best favored, the most attractive, the most capable' and put to him their proposal. He accepted it, and, chosen by the whole people, became their *rājā*, or ruler. The text emphasizes that he and his like (that is, other rulers among men) were in origin of the same blood as other men: 'their origin was from among those very beings, and no others; like unto themselves, not unlike; and it took place according to what ought to be, justly, and not unfittingly.' It was assumed that there was a 'norm' or ideal, of a ruler, and that actual rulers were selected according to their fitness in terms of this ideal.[6]

The theory of kingship which is set out here is well known in other contexts, where it occurs in roughly the same form: it is the

71

theory which sees the origin of kingship in a social contract. The way in which it is presented in this early Buddhist text suggests that it was at that time a commonly accepted view of the origin and proper function of the political ruler.

In his discourse on this occasion, the Buddha is represented as having gone on to describe the origin of the four social classes— they were in ancient India believed once to have existed in separation—namely, the landed ruling class, the priestly class, the trading class and the hunters (the lowest class of all). What is of interest at this point is a view of kingship which, as Ghoshal says, 'imposes upon the ruler the obligation of punishing wrong-doers in return for the payment of the customary dues by the people', and the conception of 'the temporal ruler's quasi-contractual obligation of protecting his subjects'.[7] The relation of the Buddhist monk to such a ruler, and to the other classes of society, is the real crux of this discourse, but with that we shall be concerned at a later stage (see chapter 8).

Monarchy was, it seems, recognized as being preferable to anarchy, and the monarch was a mortal man as other men: that much can safely be affirmed on the basis of these words of the Buddha. In the theory of kingship found in the brahmanical writings, however, the king was a noble, semi-divine, and beneficent being, promoting the welfare of his people, who were his subjects by right. This was a somewhat different, and certainly more exalted view of kingship from that set forth in the Buddhist texts. In the brahmanical writings the king is represented as being in origin closely associated with the gods; from this fact some, at least, of his authority is derived. The Vedic hymns, and the slightly later writings known as the *Brāhmaṇas*, which all belong to the pre-Buddhist period, set out a double theory of the origin of kingly authority: 'one theory is based upon his creation and endowment by the Highest Deity, and the other is founded upon his election by the gods in the interest of their external security.'[8] From this there developed the principle that it was his subjects' *duty* to honor and obey him. This idea is clearly affirmed in the *Law of Manu*, a treatise which, in its present form, is perhaps of roughly the same date as the Buddhist Pāli texts, but may have existed in an earlier form.[9] There the divine origin of kingship is quite explicitly affirmed: 'When creatures, being without a king, were through fear dispersed in all directions, the Lord [i.e., Bhagavan, or God] created a king for the protection of this whole creation.' 'Even an infant King must not be despised, from an idea that he is a mere mortal; for he is a great deity in human form. Let no man, therefore, transgress that law which the king decrees with respect to those in his favor, nor his orders which inflict pain on those in disfavour.'[10]

In its ancient Indian form the theory of kingship had another aspect: the kingly office carried with it an obligation to act in accordance with the highest moral principles, the king's connection with the gods giving him no right to act arbitrarily or despotically. The great epic, the *Mahābhārata*, contains a section called *Shantiparvan* (the Book on Peace), which sets out, among other things, the principle of the king's protectorship: 'One becomes a king for acting in the interests of righteousness and not for conducting himself capriciously. The king is, indeed, the protector of the world.'[11] The famous treatise of Indian statecraft, the *Arthaśāstra* of Kautilya[12] places the emphasis somewhat differently. Its author was a brahman priest and minister of state whose function was to instruct the secular ruler in his proper *dharma* or duty, and while in the course of doing so he makes formal acknowledgment of the idea of *righteous* rule, nevertheless, the real concern of this work is with the successful exercise of political power, the continual aggrandizement of the state, and the extension of its territorial empire. The tone of the work has been variously characterized as that of political realism, cynicism and Machiavellianism. It is perhaps significant that this treatise is more firmly connected with an historical person (Kautilya, or Chanakya, its brahman author) than either the *Law of Manu* or the *Mahābhārata*. It is significant, too, that its prescriptions are known to have been closely related to the actual policy of the Mauryan empire (which grew out of the Magadhan Kingdom shortly after the lifetime of the Buddha). In other words, we may, in the severely practical aspect of this treatise of statecraft, have a more realistic picture of the actual policies and procedures of ancient Indian monarchical rule than is to be found in the somewhat idealistic accounts given in *Manu* and the *Mahābhārata*.

These, however, may come nearer to the actualities of monarchical rule in India when they dwell on the shortcomings of kingship rather than when they describe its ideal merits. For the criticisms of kingly rule found in the ancient literature are more likely to have been prompted by real experience, than conceived in the abstract, as possibilities which might arise.

THE DISADVANTAGES AND ADVANTAGES OF MONARCHY

The malfunctioning of the monarchical system is again and again acknowledged. A Buddhist text makes the point that when a king becomes unrighteous, the fault soon spreads to the king's ministers, from them to the brahmans, and from them to the householders, townsmen and villagers. Before long even the environment is affected; the times are out of joint, the winds blow out of season, the rains fail, and the whole kingdom grows weak and sickly.'[13] Conversely, when a king acts righteously, benefits follow in the same sequence. Unrighteousness in a king shows itself chiefly in pride, asserts the *Shantiparvan*, and this led many kings to ruin. He who succeeds in conquering pride becomes a real king.[14] Frequently mentioned among the snares to be avoided by a king are over-indulgence in drink, gambling, hunting, women and music. In brahmanical theory of the seventh and sixth centuries BC, the king's *authority* was, as we have seen, vested in him by the gods and was exercised, in part at least, by virtue of his quasi-divine nature, but it is very clear, too, that he had no inalienable right to this kingly authority, should he by unrighteousness disgrace his office. Warnings against unrighteous conduct are too frequent for us to assume that real examples of kingly misrule were unknown. The fact that in the *Law of Manu* strong emphasis is placed on the need for the king to rule his own passions successfully if he is to be a successful ruler of his kingdom suggests that, by the time *Manu* was composed, the necessity had been very clearly seen from historical examples. 'Day and night he must strenuously exert himself to conquer his senses, for he alone who has conquered his own senses can keep his subjects in obedience."[15] *Manu* also lists certain vices which kings must shun: hunting, gambling, sleeping by day,

74

censoriousness, excess with women, drunkenness, inordinate love of dancing, singing and music, and useless travel.

Another disadvantage of monarchy is that it means the concentration of power in the hands of one individual, for an individual is more acutely vulnerable to violence, disease or some form of fatality than is a company of men such as a republican assembly. It was fully recognized in ancient India that this constituted a peculiar weakness of monarchy. In a hereditary system of monarchy, the king, especially as he grew older and his sons came to manhood, was always at risk from the latter's jealousy. Various safeguards against this danger were set out in the Indian manuals of kingship. One of them declared cynically that any prince for whom his father felt no affection should be secretly killed in infancy. Another recommended that the king should deliberately encourage his sons to indulge in sensual pleasures, for in that way they would be too preoccupied to plot against their father. Yet another advises the king to engage spies to instigate the princes to commit treason, and other spies to dissuade them from doing so. These and other similar prescriptions indicate a general agreement that the ambition of princes constituted a perennial danger to the security of the king, and that the protection of the king's person must be a fundamental aim of royal policy, for upon this rested the whole security of the state.[16]

However, the concentration of power in the hands of one individual was seen to have compensating advantages, too. One of the chief of these was the greater likelihood of uniform punishment for crime, since this was administered entirely by the king. The fact that punishment was meted out by one individual rather than by a number of different men was a guarantee of equity. The citizens of the state could depend on it that all would receive roughly the same treatment—assuming that the king administered justice impartially: so this, too, was a matter on which great emphasis had to be laid. Originally, the function of law enforcement was part of the king's military role. It was his duty to defend his territory and people by force of arms, and by the same kind of force to inflict punishment on wrongdoers; to restrain those who did not restrain themselves, to punish those who violated their prescribed duties. No one was exempt from the performance of his own special duty. The context of thought is of a strongly military kind. The stability and integration of the kingdom depended to a large extent on the manner in which justice was administered. Kautilya's manual of statecraft, the *Arthaśāstra*, though it may have been composed a century or so after the Buddha's death, nevertheless reflects the experiences of kings and their subjects in the earlier period when it declares that the king who is too harsh in administering punishment depresses and damages the whole realm, that the king who is too mild loses authority and may be overthrown, while the one who inflicts punishment justly gains the respect and support of all his subjects.[17] The great epic, the *Mahābhārata*, makes the same point: if the king is too gentle and forgives too frequently, the ordinary people will overpower him, like the little elephant driver who climbs up on the head of that great and noble animal and makes it subservient;[18] the king should be neither too severe nor too mild, but like the spring sunshine, in whose rays one experiences neither excessive cold nor excessive heat. In general the manner of inflicting punishment seems to have been one of the major criteria by which a king's rule was evaluated. If punishment was well-judged, then, it was said, the people became wise and happy; when it was ill-judged and prompted by anger or desire, people were afflicted by a sense of injustice; when it was neglected altogether the whole realm fell into anarchy. In India this was described as the state of affairs in which the larger fishes devour the smaller.[19]

THE KING AS THE SUPREME INDIVIDUAL

This might lead one to suppose that at the time of the Buddha monarchy was expanding at the expense of the tribal republics because it was popularly held to be a preferable form of government. But that would be to think that the known examples of it were, on the whole, just and beneficent rather than otherwise, and such a thought is both naive and historically unwarranted. It would be too ingenuous to imagine that monarchical rule had its origins in the free choice of the people; the king was where he was, in almost every case, largely because he had, so to speak, climbed up on the shoulders of others. Even in the case of a long-established dynasty, where a king had succeeded to his throne by hereditary right, he would almost certainly have had to deal with rival claimants, in the form of ambitious brother-princes, or powerful ministers who might easily become would-be usurpers. In India palace intrigue and the *coup d'etat* were far from uncommon. They are, in fact, envisaged in the manuals of statecraft as possible courses of action to be followed when a king failed to rule in accordance with the traditional *dhamma,** or law of righteousness laid down by generations of brahman priests. The king's quasi-divinity afforded him no protection if he defaulted in his role as the upholder of *dhamma.* It is clear that he ruled, in the first place, by virtue of his ability to protect himself from intrigue and attack. That he ruled by the grace of God or with the consent of the common people were, in reality, subordinate considerations. It was as the *de facto* solitary wielder of power that he inspired fear and reverence; to such a figure it would not be difficult to attribute divinity, especially in India, where the dividing line between men and gods is less sharply drawn than it is in some other cultures.

There was a special reason for the growth in power of one of these monarchies in particular, namely that of Magadha. The territory of this kingdom covered approximately the area which today forms the adjacent administrative Districts of Patna and Gaya. To the south of this is an area containing vast iron-ore deposits, described by modern geologists as 'one of the major iron ore fields of the world, in which enormous tonnages of rich ore are readily available'.[20] It is noteworthy that this iron ore, which is of high grade, 'occurs usually at or near the tops of hill ranges' and that most of it 'can be won by open-cast methods'.[21] Of the kingdoms of the Gangetic plain it was Magadha which was best placed to benefit from this good supply of readily available iron. Since it was nearby, the trouble and cost of transporting the ore would not have been so great for it as for other more distant kingdoms. Moreover, supplies of ore to the other kingdoms of the north Indian plain would have had to pass through Magadha's territory and it would consequently have been able to exercise

---

* Dhamma is the Pāli spelling of the Sanskrit Dharma.

77

some kind of control of iron supplies to these other states. The iron was used for agricultural tools (and so aided the development of agriculture), and also for weapons of war. The kingdom which controlled the iron supply and had easiest access to it would obviously be in a position to develop agriculturally and militarily more rapidly than others. The shift in the balance of power among the north Indian kingdoms in favor of Magadha seems to have been taking place during the Buddha's lifetime, in the reign of the Magadhan king, Bimbisara, and his son, Ajatashatru, who was also king while the Buddha was alive. Ajatashatru, especially, appears in the early Buddhist literature as a very powerful, determined and ruthless monarch.

The old maxim that nothing succeeds like success appears to find support in the history of kingship in India. What seems to have been abhorred more than anything was political anarchy. The social evils of this are depicted in the ancient texts, brahmanical and Buddhist, in a way that suggests that the common view of society was one which saw it as an aggregate of aggressive, violently self-assertive individuals whose mutual destructiveness could be held in check only by a single controller possessing the authority and the power to punish. The violence of the many individuals was to be met and overcome by the violence of the one supreme individual.

THE EMERGENCE OF INDIVIDUALISM

A question which it is important to try to answer at this point is one concerning the causes of this individualism during these early centuries of Indian history. It was a period, we have seen, characterized not only by increasingly marked individualism but also by the growth of monarchy; together with these factors there appears to have been an intensification of urban life in some of the larger cities. These three features of the life of the period certainly seem to be in some way inter-related. What has to be considered is whether one of them developed first, independently of the other two, and, if so, whether this was because of some other prior condition. The possibilities are (1) that individualism was the primary factor, that is, that the trend towards individualism facilitated the growth of monarchical government, and that this entailed increased urbanization; or (2) it may have been that monarchy was the novel factor which, once introduced into the lands of the Gangetic plain, gave rise to urbanization, which in turn led to increased individualism; or (3) it may have been that the growth of cities was the primary factor: that is, that there were non-political reasons why certain cities grew in size and density of population, and that these cities then became the growth-points of an individualism, which, by gradually spreading through the whole region, paved the way for the advance of strong monarchical government as the only solution to the evils entailed in its increase.[22] There is something to be said for each of these possibilities, but on balance the known facts seem to favor the third.

We have already seen that a considerable growth of population was taking place in the Gangetic plain at the time of the Buddha, due largely to the increased cultivation of what had formerly been forest (see p. 56). In the 'middle' country (*Madyadesa*) it was rice growing which predominated, but it is clear from the evidence of the Pāli Buddhist texts that a variety of other crops and fruits were also grown. The result of this increased population size would have been a slight increase also in population density over the whole area, with, however, more acute increases in density in the cities of the plain. We have seen, too, that there was in the cities a considerable diversity of occupations, with a fairly refined degree of specialization. This was due partly to the needs of a royal court, which each of the great cities either was or had been at some stage in its history. But it was due too, and possibly in even greater measure, to the diversification of the economy which would have followed as a consequence of the growth of population, the development of agriculture, the growing differentiation in methods of production (such as herd-keeping, fishing, the raising of rice and other cereal and vegetable crops, fruit-growing, forestry and mining) and a general increase in the economic wealth of the region. Moreover, the continual extension of the area of society which was under monarchical rule, as opposed to tribal republican government, would have meant a growing complexity in modes of social organization.

All this accords well with the general line of argument developed by Emile Durkheim, that the development of the division of labor has for its principal cause an increase in the density of a society.[23] An increase in the over-all density of population brings with it an increase in what Durkheim calls 'moral density'. By this he means increased facilities for transportation and communication throughout the area; and thus an increase in the extent to which, and the area over which, social contacts take place. Durkheim summarizes his argument at this point in the following proposition: 'The division of labor varies in direct ratio with the volume and density of societies, and, if it progresses in a continuous manner in the course of social development, it is because societies become regularly denser and generally more voluminous.'[24] This would appear to fit very well what was happening in the Ganges valley in the period we are concerned with. Among the consequences of such a development of diverse specialist occupations, according to Durkheim, is the growth of individualism: 'far from being trammelled by the progress of specialization, individual personality develops with the division of labour.'[25] He points out that in more primitive societies each man resembles his companions; there is little differentiation of tasks and statuses and it is the corporate life of the tribe which, so to speak, occurs in each and every man. But with the development of specialization there is increasingly for each man 'something in him which is his alone and which individualizes him, as he is something more than a simple incarnation of the generic type of his race and his group'.[26]

More recent work in the field of sociology confirms this view of the development of individualism in societies characterized by developed occupational specialization, particularly where this is found in an urban milieu. Louis Wirth points out that 'in contrast with earlier, more integrated societies, the social life of the city provides much greater potentials for differentiation between individuals'.[27] One passage in particular from Wirth's writings, may be quoted here for its relevance to our study of early Indian urban life:

The superficiality, the anonymity, and the transitory character of urban social relations make intelligible, also, the sophistication and the rationality generally ascribed to city dwellers. Our acquaintances tend to stand in a relationship of utility to us in the sense that the role which each one plays in our life is overwhelmingly regarded as a means for the achievement of our own ends. Whereas the individual gains, on the one hand, a certain degree of emancipation or freedom from the personal and emotional controls of intimate groups, he loses, on the other hand, the spontaneous self-expression, the morale, and the sense of participation that comes with living in an integrated society. This constitutes essentially the state of *anomie*, or the social void, to which Durkheim alludes in attempting to account for the various forms of social disorganization in technological society.[28]

This agrees with what is known of urban society in the early Buddhist period. In the *Jātaka* stories and in the many dialogues between the Buddha and various different individuals, it is precisely this sophistication, this rationality of the urban dweller that we recognize. Moreover, there was also at that time a considerable degree of what Durkheim called *anomie*, or moral and social dislocation. To be more specific, the transition which many people were then experiencing from the familiar, small-scale society of the old tribal republics to the strange, large-scale and consequently more impersonal, bleaker life of the new monarchical state, was accompanied by a psychological *malaise*, a heightened sense of dissatisfaction with life as it had to be lived. It was this *malaise* which the Buddha was to take as the starting-point of his analysis of the human condition, calling it *dukkha* (see chapter 7, p. 132 f.). Erich Fromm, too, has drawn attention to the association between the developing sense of individuality in the human person and a sense of *growing aloneness.*[29] He refers to the separation which the growing person experiences from the world which was familiar to him as a child. 'As long as one was an integral part of that world, unaware of the possibilities and responsibilities of individual action, one did not need to be afraid of it. When one has become an individual, one stands alone and faces the world in all its perilous and overpowering aspects.'[30]

INDIVIDUALISM AS A CONSEQUENCE OF URBANISM AND MONARCHY

There are thus good reasons for saying that the development of urban life, as a result of population increase, and the political

81

innovation of *monarchical rule* were both responsible for the development of an awareness of individuality and the sense of personal isolation and psychological *malaise* which accompanies such awareness. What is more, monarchical rule had the further effect of giving the development of urban life an extra stimulus, over and above the general incentive towards the development of cities which the extension of agriculture and the accelerating growth of population provided.

But kingship, as it had emerged in early Indian civilization, was itself a consequence of the specialization of functions which had developed in Aryan society in the Vedic period. The primary differentiation of functions was between the brahman priest and the kshatriya nobleman. In the earlier, nomadic period of the Aryans' history, as in the early stages of other societies, political, cultic and judicial functions appear to have been performed by the same person or class. It has been suggested that 'the tribal priests who antedated the brahmans and were not always distinguished from the kshatriya warriors developed some sort of secret organization as a preparation for sacrificial purity.'[31] It is possible, too, that changing conditions, from the more violent and insecure conditions of nomadic life to those of settled agricultural communities, deprived the kshatriya warrior of his superior authority just at a time when the development of ritual and sacrificial ideas was enhancing the authority of the brahmans. Perhaps, indeed, the stimulus for the development of these new sacrificial ideas was the need for a new source of authority in the changed conditions of life, and the need to legitimate that new authority—the authority of the brahman priest. This, certainly, is what appears to have happened: on the one hand an increasing specialization in the sacrificial *cultus* and the esoteric mysteries connected with its performance, and on the other an increasing specialization in the business of secular government, now no longer by the kshatriyas as a class, but by kings, as individual specialists in the technicalities of political administration diplomacy and so on.

So, by the time Aryan civilization reached the Gangetic midland plain it was already characterized by the first stage in the specialization of functions and an incipient trend towards urbanism,[32] in the sense that its political structure required an administrative capital. The nature of the terrain and its resources were such that these characteristics soon developed, in the way we have seen, into an increasingly diversified political and economic structure. From this situation there then emerged, as a consequence of the increasing complexity of life—especially in the cities—a growing awareness of personal differentiation, or individualism.

5   The Religious and Ideological Environment

It was suggested at the outset (see pp. 29 f. and 40 f.) that we merely prejudice our understanding of the Buddha's historical significance if we think of him as the founder of a religion in the customary modern sense of the term. A more useful way of approaching the matter is to examine the nature of the early Buddhist community—its principles, its purposes, and its social implications—and then to consider whether it is not more appropriate to regard the Buddha as the founder, in effect, of something more approaching a type of civilization. We shall not, therefore, begin by regarding the Buddha as one who was consciously a religious reformer or innovator. It is possible that his role is better understood as that of the opponent or critic of religion, who had no intention of founding yet another example of what he criticized. This is, of course, to assume that 'religion' could already be identified in the Buddha's day as a more or less distinct set of phenomena, and not as an aspect of a civilization. We have suggested that what are now identified as 'religions' may be seen as surviving elements of civilizations which tend to seek reembodiment in some new, integrated system. This is, broadly, how the situation in the Buddha's day may be interpreted. The old Vedic society of the Aryans was in a state of dissolution as a consequence of the movement of Aryan peoples into a new geographical environment (that of the middle Gangetic plain), and as a result of their having settled into a new kind of economy, one which was predominantly agricultural rather than pastoral and nomadic. The brahman priests had emerged as a distinct social class and were, consciously or unconsciously, engaged in redefining their own position in society, and the position of other classes in relation to their own. The reconstituted civilization which was centred on kingship, brahmanically consecrated and legitimized, was only just beginning to emerge. Religion, as a phenomenon of the transitional period of flux between one civilization and another, a vestigial remnant of the old which had not yet been reintegrated in a new, emerging culture, seems to have existed in the Buddha's day in a number of characteristic forms.

With regard to these, and to the religious element in classical Hindu civilization[1] it may be useful at this point to correct a fairly common Western misconception. One of its best-known exponents was Albert Schweitzer. He worked out a broad contrast between Eastern and Western religions, using as a basis for differentiation their respective attitudes to the empirical world. Western religion, declared Schweitzer, was, in general, world- and life-affirming, while Eastern religion was world- and life-negating. Like all generalizations of such magnitude, Schweitzer's is open to many objections and qualifications. For instance, there are and have been examples of Western religious belief and practice which are very good candidates for inclusion in Schweitzer's world- and life-negating category. It is true that there are and have been some minor systems of thought and practice in Asia, especially in India, which do virtually deny the reality of the life of the senses and the physical, historical world, and which do direct men's attention away from the realm of sensory existence, which is regarded as ultimately unreal, to a realm of pure bliss which is to be attained through the realization of the idea that this world and its life are illusion.

But in the Buddha's time, however, such a world- and life-negating attitude was *not* a prominent characteristic of religious belief in India. It was not entirely unheard-of however, and was found in embryonic form in a few places in the Upanishadic literature. The Upanishads can be described in the most general way as philosophical writings. Most of the principal Upanishads are regarded as products of the period between about 800 BC and the time of the Buddha. The name 'Upanishad' indicates teaching which is given to a few select initiates, those who are 'sitting round, near': that is, near to the teacher who is imparting his esoteric doctrines to them. This interpretation of the title is confirmed by the contents and the style; the language used is often cryptic, requiring the possession of some kind of key for its elucidation, one which is not now always available. The reason for its cryptic nature appears to have been that the teaching was given only to those whom the teacher regarded as sufficiently mature spiritually. Unlike the later Sutra literature, the

85

Upanishads are not systematic treatises; they contain a variety of ideas, some of which are, in fact, in contradiction to one another. But certain central themes may be said to be common to all the Upanishadic literature. Of these the most outstanding is the idea that 'underlying the exterior world of change there is an unchangeable reality which is identical with that which underlies the essence in man.'[2] This identity is obscured from the vast generality of men, each of whom follows the devices and desires of what he imagines to be his 'true' self: namely, the empirical ego, which is subject to all the conflicting impressions and impulses that make for confusion and turmoil rather than peace. Deceived as he is by the passing, illusory world of the physical senses, each man's 'true' welfare is, rather, the realization of the identity of his own inner, essential being (*atman*) with the world-soul (*brāhman*). It was in connection with this teaching of the Upanishads that there developed a view of the material world as something to be rejected and renounced in the interests of the *atman*, or true self. In any case, however, the Upanishads represent the attitude of an elite few, and at the time of the Buddha such teaching was still largely esoteric.[3]

In order not to neglect anything which could conceivably be included under the heading of 'religion' at the time of the Buddha, it is appropriate to consider all phenomena which may possibly be relevant, even borderline candidates from the realm of the ideologies of the time. Three major areas can be identified: first, there was the sacrificial *cultus* of the hereditary priestly class, the brahmans; second, there was the vast range of popular cults and beliefs of the ordinary people, mostly villagers, who constituted the majority of the population; and third, there was the variety of ideas and practices expounded by various non-brahmanical teachers, who were known collectively as *shramaṇas*.

THE SACRIFICIAL SYSTEM OF THE BRAHMANS

The brahman or, properly, *brāhmaṇa*, was so called because of his claim to be the specialist in dealing with *brāhman*, the impersonal absolute which was held to be the source of the world and its life. The word *brāhman* referred also to the sacred word, the chant, which was the essence of the sacrificial ceremony. The knowledge of this sacred chanting was confined strictly to the priestly class, its guardians and preservers. In brahman theory, the world had come into existence through a primeval sacrifice, and was maintained in existence by the further performance of sacrifices by the brahmans. Although brahmanistic theology envisaged a large number of deities, prominent among whom were Agni and Indra, even these were held to be subject to the power of the sacrifice, and thus, ultimately, to the controller of the sacrifice, the brahman priest. The stage of development which had been reached by the early Buddhist period was one in which, as S. N. Dasgupta puts it, 'sacrifice is not offered to a god with a view to propitiate him or to obtain from him welfare on earth or bliss in Heaven; these rewards are directly produced by the sacrifice itself through the correct performance of complicated and interconnected ceremonials which constitute the sacrifice.'[4] Thus, in the time with which we are concerned, the sacrifice, which the brahman controlled, had come to be regarded 'as possessing a mystical potency superior even to the gods'.[5]

With this claim for the mystical supremacy of the sacrifice, in which the brahmans were specialists, went a corresponding claim for the social supremacy of the specialists themselves. The line of argument which the brahmans used was simple, and if the first claim were accepted, the second had to be, inevitably. The world, ran the argument, was kept in existence, and the important aims of human life were achieved, by the operation of the sacrifice; the brahmans were the sole possessors of the knowledge of how the sacrifice was to be performed, and it was their dharma, or duty, and theirs only, to perform it. The second claim was that the brahmans, consequently, were the most essential class in society. By their due and wise control of *brāhman*, the sacred force, the world continues in existence.

Both these claims were rejected by the Buddha, according to the early tradition of the Buddhists. The Buddha's attitude to the brahmanical sacrifice is evident in many of the early texts, and is set out in detail in a discourse known as the *Kūṭadanta Sutta*, which deals explicitly with this subject. It recounts a conversation which is supposed to have taken place between the Buddha and a brahman named Kūṭadanta or 'Sharp-tooth', who lived at a place called Khānumata, where he owned some land which had been presented to him by the king. T. W. Rhys Davids captures the spirit of the situation by rendering this brahman's title as 'the Very Reverend Sir Goldstick Sharptooth, lord of the manor of Khānumata'.[6] In this rather ironical story he is 'represented as doing the very last thing any brahman of position, under similar circumstances, would think of doing. He goes to the Samana Gotama for advice....' This highly improbable action on the part of the brahman is a device which enables the storyteller to set forth the Buddhist attitude to sacrifice in the words of the Buddha to this imaginary brahman. In what the Buddha says to him there is no direct criticism of the brahmanical theory of sacrifice; only an indirect allusion to its practical aspects. Kūṭadanta asks the Buddha how a sacrifice should be performed, and in reply the Buddha tells an ironical story of a great sacrifice that had once been offered by the brahman chaplain of a very prosperous king. 'At that sacrifice neither were any oxen slain, neither goats, nor fowls, nor fatted pigs, nor were any kinds of living creatures put to death. No trees were cut down to be used as posts, no dabbha grasses mown to strew around the sacrificial spot. And the slaves and messengers and workmen there employed were driven neither by rods nor fear, nor carried on their work weeping with tears upon their faces.... With ghee, and oil, and butter, and milk, and honey, and sugar only was that sacrifice accomplished.'[7] The irony consists in the fact that nothing could be more unlike a brahmanical sacrifice of the late Vedic period. The descriptive details are precisely the reverse of what would in fact have happened at a normal sacrifice. As Rhys Davids comments, all 'the muttering of mystic verses over each article used and over mangled and bleeding bodies of unhappy victims, verses on which all the magic efficacy of a sacrifice had been supposed to depend, is quietly ignored'.[8] The narrative continues with an account of the surprising decision of the king who had ordered the sacrifice not to make a levy on the people of his realm to pay for it, but to use his own wealth. This, moreover, after the people had asked to be taxed for the purpose. 'Sufficient wealth have I, my friends, laid up, the produce of taxation that is just. Do you keep yours, and take away more with you!' Thereupon the people, baulked in their desire to be taxed, made voluntary contributions which were to pay for the performance of three other great sacrifices, as well as that offered by the king. The tale is, of course, entirely ludicrous, and one can imagine the delight with which the Buddha's contemporaries would have responded to its humor. What emerges as the point of the story is a critique of brahmanical sacrifice on the grounds of economic wastefulness, cruelty to animals, forced labor, with harsh treatment of the laborers, and oppressive taxation of the people in order to pay for it all. It is clear, too, that the supposed efficacy of the sacrifice is being quietly dismissed. By implication, this heightens the objection to the lavish expenditure, cruelty and social oppression.

That there are, however forms of 'sacrifice' which are worth making, in the Buddhist view, is made clear in the second part of the narrative. Kūṭadanta asks the Buddha, 'Is there, O Gotama, any other sacrifice less difficult and less troublesome, with more fruit and more advantage than this?' The Buddha replies that there is. In fact there are six other preferable forms of sacrifice, and these the Buddha describes to Kūṭadanta. The first five are all 'sacrifices' which are open to ordinary householders. Better than the offering of the brahmanical sacrifice is an offering of alms to wandering holy men (*shramaṇas*). The second form of sacrifice, which is open to all, and better than the first, is to build a dwelling place, a *Vihāra*, for members of the Buddhist Order. Even better than this is the third kind of sacrifice, which is to go with a trusting heart to the Buddha as guide, and to the Doctrine which he teaches, and to the Order which he founded and in which the Doctrine is preserved. Such devotion is referred to in the regularly-repeated formula which anyone making the humblest claim to be a Buddhist still uses, in private and in public: 'To the Buddha I go for refuge, to the Dhamma I go for refuge, to the *Sangha* I go for refuge.' Even better than this, however, is to take the five precepts of Buddhist morality upon oneself. 'When a man with trusting heart takes upon himself the precepts—abstinence from destroying life; abstinence from taking what has not been given; abstinence from evil conduct in respect of lusts; abstinence from lying words; abstinence from strong, intoxicating, maddening drinks, the root of carelessness—that is a sacrifice better than open largesse, better than perpetual alms, better than the gift of dwelling places, better than accepting guidance.'[9] This is the fifth and highest form of 'sacrifice' for a householder, in the

Buddhist view. Beyond this there is only the sixth and greatest sacrifice, namely to give up the household life and become a member of the Buddhist Order, the *Sangha* (see chapter 7).

POPULAR CULTS AND BELIEFS

The significance of such teaching on the subject of sacrifice has to be seen in the context of the times when it was first given. For, as we have said, the Vedic sacrificial system was something which concerned the specialist, the brahman priest, and the man who was, at the very least, fairly well-to-do and able to meet the cost of such sacrificial offerings. For the common people, the villager, the peasant, the craftsman and the tradesman, there was a great variety of popular magic to which they might have resort for comfort, guidance, peace of mind, protection from evil, and so on. A list of these magical practices is given in one of the discourses of the Buddha.[10] They are described by the Buddha as 'low arts', and are of the kind practiced by certain of the brahmans and *shramanas*. They included, apparently, such activities as palmistry and fortunetelling; determining lucky sites for houses by a knowledge of the spirits of the place and how to propitiate them; prophecies of various kinds, concerning such matters as rainfall, the nature of the harvest, pestilences, disturbances, famines and so on; divining, by the use of signs, omens and celestial portents; the provision of charms and spells; the obtaining of oracular answers from gods by various means; the interpretation of dreams; the propitiation of demons; and the offerings of oblations of various kinds, such as grain or butter, to Agni the god of fire. That such practices are forbidden to members of the Buddha's Order is emphasized in a number of places. 'You are not, O *bhikkhus*, to learn or to teach the low arts [literally 'the brutish wisdom'] of divination, spells, omens, astrology, sacrifices to gods, witchcraft and quackery', the Buddha is reputed to have charged the members of the Order.[11] On another occasion, in answer to the question of how a member of the Buddhist Order is to achieve perfection and be entirely unattached to any worldly thing, the Buddha lists the many requirements; one of these is as follows: 'Let him not use Atharva-Vedic spells, nor things foretell from dreams or signs or stars; let not my follower predict from cries, cure barrenness, nor practice quackery.'[12]

The account of these magical practices or 'low arts' given in the Buddhist texts agrees well with the picture of priestly magic practiced mostly on behalf of the common people which is found in the brahmanical text compiled probably a little before the time of the Buddha, known as the *Atharva-Veda*. This is the fourth of the Vedic collection of hymns, and the last to be accorded official recognition. It stands somewhat apart from the other three Vedic hymn-collections[13] on account of the very much more popular, local, indigenous material which it contains, compared with the more Aryan and priestly-class concerns of the earlier collections. Nevertheless, it did eventually gain general recognition as a brahmanically composed text,[14] and this fact is itself further evidence that some brahmans were engaged in this kind of popular magical activity, possibly having taken over the role of earlier, pre-Aryan, non-brahmanical priests; in return for the provision of priestly-magical services the brahmans would expect from the villager recognition of their authority, and of the Vedic tradition they represented.

For our purpose the *Atharva-Veda* is important as evidence of popular attitudes and practices with regard to such matters as sorcery and magic at the time of the Buddha. A mention of some of its contents will illustrate the point. By far the greater part of the text consists of charms. These include charms against various diseases, and disease-causing demons; the diseases range from fever in general, through coughs, headaches, jaundice, excessive bodily discharges, constipation and internal pain, to heart disease and leprosy. There are charms against snake-poison, charms to promote the growth of hair, or virility, or long life, or for general exemption from disease. Another section contains imprecations to be used against sorcerers, demons and enemies. Yet another is devoted to the needs of men and women—charms for such varied purposes as obtaining a husband, or a child, or to prevent miscarriage, or to obtain easy childbirth, charms by which a man may secure a woman's love, or arouse her passion, or allay jealousy, or deprive a rival of his virility. One whole section consists of charms pertaining to the needs of a king: for his success as a ruler, for victory in battle and so on. Yet another contains charms to ensure political and social harmony while other sections are devoted to domestic and mercantile affairs. There is, significantly for the status of the text as Vedic, a section devoted to prayers and imprecations in the interests of the brahmans. The collection ends with a group of hymns to various gods and goddesses, such as Mother Earth, Kāma (the god of sexual love) and Kāla (time personified as a deity).

These, then, were the popular magical practices which had come within the sphere of interest of some brahman priests, sufficiently so for them to be regarded as at least marginally 'Vedic', once the Atharvan collection had gained recognition. It is interesting that the Buddha's attitude to these practices, in which brahmans had taken an interest, and which had thus passed, at least partially, under the aegis of the priests, was one of only moderate disapproval. His criticism of practices which were partly popular, partly priestly, was not so vigorous as his criticism of the brahmanical animal sacrifices, but it is clear enough that he wished to discourage the members of his own order from any interest in them.

More ambiguous is the Buddha's attitude to a popular-priestly form of belief, namely, in Brahma, the supreme creator-deity. At a later period of Indian religious history, Brahma as Creator became the somewhat shadowy first figure in the Hindu theistic trinity, the other two great deities being Vishnu the Preserver, and Shiva the Destroyer. But at the time of the Buddha, Brahma had recently emerged as the spirit of the universe (*Brāhman*) conceived of as a personal god. In the priestly texts called the *Brāhmaṇas*, which belong to a period some centuries before the time of the Buddha, the creator-deity, to whom sacrifice is offered, is known as Prajapati. In the Upanishadic literature, the supreme reality is represented as impersonal, and is referred to by the neuter noun *brāhman*. But in the popular epic-poem, the *Mahabharata*, the composition of which can be dated a century or so after the time of the Buddha (that is, from about the third century BC onwards), we find that Brahma (masculine) appears as a divine personal being, the god of creation. The earlier creator-deity, Prajapati, had it seems, come to be identified with the impersonal world-soul (*brāhman*) of the Upanishads,[15] and been given the new name, Brahma. It is uncertain just how important belief in Brahma had become by the time of the Buddha, or what place this creator-god held in the religious ideas and practices of the people. Some have argued that Brahma was never a very important god in popular belief. This is the view of the Indian historian, R. C. Majumdar: 'Although Brahma is theoretically acknowledged to be the creator of man and even of gods he never occupies a prominent place in the actual religious devotion of the people. Vishnu and Shiva overshadow him from the very beginning....'[16] On the other hand, it has been argued that the worship of Brahma, the creator-god, was in pre-Buddhist times very important and widespread, and that it only subsequently suffered eclipse, partly because of the rise of the rival cults of Vishnu and Shiva, and partly because of the spread of Buddhist and Jain belief and practice.[17]

What is clear from the early Buddhist sources is that Brahma was, so far as the Buddha was concerned, a fairly prominent feature of the celestial scenery of the time, and a figure whom one should not take too seriously. The notion that Brahma is the prime being, and creator of all other beings was treated with somewhat less than respect by the Buddha. A story attributed to him, tells how in the course of time this world-system passes away. Then, after a further period, it begins to re-evolve. At an early stage in this process Brahma's 'palace' (that is, his abode, or place in the celestial set-up) happens to be vacant. It is, however, soon filled by some being or other who, until then, had been living in the superior 'World of Radiance' but who finds himself, his merit having been exhausted, descending to the lower realm and coming to rebirth as Brahma. Newly arrived, and feeling lonely there in Brahma's palace, he wishes that he had some companions. It so happens that some more beings whose merit has run out just at that moment also descend from the World of Radiance and appear in Brahma's realm, as though in response to his wish. At this, the one who was first reborn thinks to himself, 'I am Brahma, the Great Brahma, the Supreme One, the Mighty, the All-seeing, The Ruler, the Lord of all, the Maker, the Creator, the Chief of all, appointing to each his place, the Ancient of Days, the Father of all that are and are to be. These other beings are of my creation. And why is that so? A while ago I thought, "Would that they might come!" And on my mental aspiration, behold the beings came.'[18] In a similar fashion the new arrivals conclude that the one who was there first must be their creator: 'This must be Brahma, the Great Brahma, the Supreme [etc.]. And we must have been created by him. And why? Because, as we see, it was he who was here first, and we came after that.' Finally, the Buddha suggests that when one of the beings in Brahma's realm, by reason of his poor stock of merit, suffers yet a further fall and arrives on earth, he reflects that while he is a fallen being, Brahma dwells forever in his heaven: 'He by whom we were created, he is steadfast, immutable, eternal, of a nature that knows no change, and he will remain so for ever and ever.'

One can safely assume that the Buddha was making light of contemporary belief in an eternal creator-god called Brahma. There would be no point in making fun of a belief which nobody held. In another of the discourses, Brahma, in the midst of his great retinue of subordinates, is represented as being asked a question by a member of the Buddhist Order: 'Where do the four great elements—earth, water, fire and wind—cease, leaving no trace behind?' In reply Brahma answers, 'I, brother, am the Great Brahma, the Supreme, the Mighty, the All seeing ... the Ancient of Days, the Father of all that are and are to be!' 'But', replies the Buddhist, 'I did not ask you whether you are indeed all that you now say. I asked you where the four great elements cease, leaving no trace behind.'[19] The fact is, of course, that this is a question Brahma cannot answer. In order to save face, and not display his ignorance before all his retinue, Brahma takes the Buddhist brother by the arm, leads him aside and says, in effect: 'I didn't wish to say so in front of them, for they think I know everything, but I don't know the answer. You really should not come to me with a question like that. You should ask the Buddha. I'm sure he will be able to tell you!' The attitude of deference towards the Buddha which is attributed to the god Brahma in this instance is shown elsewhere in Buddhist literature. The most famous example, perhaps, is the occasion when the Buddha, immediately after his Enlightenment, was pondering whether the *dhamma*, or truth, to which he had won could possibly be made known to other men. Brahma, perceiving what the Buddha was thinking, lamented the possible great loss to the world that might ensue if the Buddha did not proclaim to men his *dhamma*. He then left the Brahma-realm and immediately manifested himself before the

Buddha, and having saluted him with joined palms, said 'Lord, let the Lord teach *dhamma*; let the well-farer teach *dhamma*; there are beings with little dust in their eyes who, not hearing *dhamma* are decaying, but if they are learners of *dhamma* they will grow.'[20]

The contemporary view of Brahma which is reflected in these and other references in the early Buddhist writings is that he was the Creator of the universe, the highest of all beings, union with whom, through prayer and sacrifice, was the highest possible good for men. It is a view which is gently and ironically set aside in the Buddhist sources. The god who was the product of brahmanism mixed with popular mythology is represented as by no means the supreme being that his devotees believed him to be, but as deluded, somewhat ignorant, slightly pompous but nevertheless benevolent, and on the whole well-intentioned—a slightly larger-than-life-size human being. In fact Brahma is, in the Buddhist view, a type of being, rather than a single unique being; there are many Brahmas; they inhabit the heavenly region known as the Brahma-world, and rebirth in this realm is quite favorably regarded, even though, in the cosmic hierarchy, it is considerably inferior to the supreme state of *Nirvāna*, just as the Brahmas are in all things subordinate to the Buddha.

Just as tolerant on the whole is the Buddha's attitude towards belief in the many supernatural beings who were respected, venerated, propitiated or worshiped by the mass of the common people; such beliefs and practices have remained, throughout the centuries, major elements in the folklore of village India. Buddhist tolerance towards folk beliefs (shown by the Buddha himself and subsequently by Buddhist monks) may be seen to have had educative effects; it made easier a gradual and gentle infusion of Buddhist notions, in such a way that the original folk-beliefs were, over a long period, imperceptibly transformed and made to nourish Buddhist attitudes and to serve Buddhist religious goals.

Belief in evil spirits provides a good illustration of this process. There was at the time of the Buddha widespread belief in numerous demons, evil spirits, ogres, goblins and the like. These were thought of as acting capriciously and at random, and mostly in ways that were inimical to human welfare. They were often referred to as 'flesh-devourers', and this suggests that they were

95

thought of as horrific beings, akin to beasts of prey, cannibals, or as agents of wasting diseases. They were frequently, though not always, creatures of the night, or of lonely places, who by their wild, weird or loud cries caused alarm or dread to humans who encountered them. They could in their malice assume all sorts of deceptive shapes and disguises in order to seduce men or lead them astray. According to popular belief, one of the ways they could be placated was by offering of sacrifices.

Beliefs of this kind appear to have been tolerated by the Buddha, and it is this kind of imagery which is used in some of his discourses to the more unsophisticated of his hearers. Some of the members of the Order, monks and nuns, are recorded as using such popular notions to describe their own experiences, in the *Songs of the Brethren* and the *Songs of the Sisters*, for example.[21] The Buddha, however, appears to have made a new contribution to the demonology of his day. Out of the notion of the commonplace hostile demon, in conjunction with one or two other major concepts, such as that of *Mrtyu* (Death, personified) and *Namuci*, another great demon hostile to human welfare, there emerges in the teaching of the Buddha, the figure of Mara, the Evil One, the supreme head of all the forces that militated against human well-being and holy living. Instead of the experiences of evil being regarded as happening at random, they now begin to be seen as all part of the total evil in human experience which is brought into focus as having a unitary character. That is to say, all human experience of evil is seen as having a common root and source, and as having common, shared effects. To put it in these terms, however, is already to have moved on into the realm of abstract thinking and analysis. And this is precisely how the Buddhist notion of Mara, the Evil One, was used—to serve as a bridge-concept, a transition from the popular demonology on the one hand, which saw only chaos and random evil attacks from demons, to the idea of a common moral root for the ills which all humanity suffers, on the other. The importance of the concept lay in its use in religious practice. Whereas a peasant woman who encountered something terrifying in the darkness of the night might exclaim: 'How terrible for me! There is a demon after me!'[22] a Buddhist sister would in similar circumstances react by saying:

'Now who is this ...? It is that foolish Mara!' (for Mara's power, as every Buddhist knew, had been conquered once for all by the Buddha). As the present writer has dealt with this subject at length elsewhere it will be sufficient at this point to quote briefly from that other source certain words which have a bearing on the Buddha's attitude to popular, unsophisticated beliefs: '[The teaching of the Buddha] does not close the frontier of thought where it touches animism and popular demonology; it allows it to remain open, but controls it from the Buddhist side, and for Buddhist purposes.'[23]

So it can be seen that there is something of a contrast between the Buddha's attitude towards the brahmanical system of costly sacrifices on the one hand, and the popular beliefs and practices of the common people on the other, with a middle ground of moderate disapproval of popular magical practices, which had been adopted as 'Vedic' by some at least of the brahman priests. There were, however, at that time others beside the Buddha who were opposed to or indifferent to the priestly sacrificial system. But this was not enough in itself to provide a guarantee of any further common ground among them; there were, in fact, considerable differences between these various other teachers and their schools, and to these we must now turn our attention.

THE MENDICANT PHILOSOPHERS

It was mainly opposition to the brahmanical sacrificial and social system which the Buddha shared with other contemporary Indian teachers, or *shramanas*. The term *shramana* refers mainly to non-brahmans, but among these 'non-conformist' mendicant philosophers there were some brahmans by birth who also rejected the authority of the Vedic scriptures and the caste system of their day. Each *shramana* with his disciples constituted what may be loosely referred to as a 'sect' and between them these sects covered a variety of views, or philosophical positions, from materialism to mysticism. There seems, however, to have been an earlier stage, when there was practically no sectarian organization, but only a large number of individual ascetic, homeless wanderers, known in a broad sense as *ājīvakas*. This later became the name of a particular sect, but in the earlier period, just before

97

the time of the Buddha, the term can be applied to all who had adopted the *ājīva*, or 'special way of life which was the alternative to an ordinary trade'.[24] This alternative way of life was embraced, says A. K. Warder, 'by many who wished to escape the need to work, or the responsibility of family life, not to speak of conscription, forced labor or slavery, and was a carefree existence very different from the life of strenuous asceticism, complicated discipline, and intensive study required of members of most of the organized sects afterwards'.[25] This opting-out of the social and economic life of the time seems to have been the one feature common to men of otherwise widely varying viewpoints, all of whom, however, were sceptical or critical of the accepted religious philosophy of the brahmans. As individuals such men were known also as 'homeless ones', or *Parivrajakas*, men who had 'gone forth', forth, that is, from the life of the ordinary householder. There was, apparently, a recognized ritual connected with the initial act of 'going forth', a ritual which demonstrated the man's complete renunciation 'of the whole system of Vedic social practice and religious culture and all its signs and symbols'.[26] All external signs or marks which a man possessed, indicating his householder's status, kinship, and caste he ceremonially removed, and the implements and symbols of the Vedic brahmanical sacrifice were consigned to the fire.[27] By the time of the Buddha, wandering, mendicant ascetics in considerable numbers were a familiar feature of the social scene.[28]

After a while, however, their originally anarchic way of life came to be modified in the direction of rudimentary forms of organization. One of the factors which aided this development was the need, which such homeless wanderers could not avoid, for some kind of temporary shelter during the period of the monsoon rains. At about the beginning or the middle of June the thunderclouds gather and torrential rain beats down for long periods at a time; river channels, which in the dry weather a few weeks earlier are 'broad expanses of sand with small streams trickling down the center', become full rivers, broad and deep, rising every hour until they over-top their banks and inundate the surrounding countryside.'[29] Rivers everywhere throughout the Gangetic plain become wide, rapidly flowing torrents, which it is very difficult, if not impossible, to cross by ferry; so, since bridges are in most cases out of the question, and cross-country roads are either washed away or have become morasses of mud when any use is made of them, traveling is difficult and hazardous, as well as unpleasant. This state of affairs continues in most parts of northern and eastern India until the latter part of September. During this season of the year, therefore, the almsmen had to give up their wandering life for about three months and congregate in various temporary retreats from the rains—possibly caves or forest-shelters made especially for the purpose.

The other factor in the development of some degree of organization was the increasing power of the state. The monarchies of Koshala and Magadha, in particular, were extending their bounds and also intensifying the degree of control which was exercised over the lives of the people within their territories. If the wandering almsmen were not as a class to become objects of the king's displeasure and hostility they would have to organize themselves, and then, as organized schools of 'philosophers', show that they had some contribution to make to the public good. It became necessary for them to find leaders who would be able, as Warder says to 'confront the kings as powerful and respected heads of organized sects ... and convince them of the importance and usefulness of the *Shramanas* in the new society (in comparison with other occupations)'.[30]

THE ĀJĪVAKAS

So, out of what was possibly in the beginning a very broad category of homeless wanderers, 'drop-outs', or men of the 'alternative life' (*ājīvakas*), there developed a number of separate and distinct philosophical schools, committed to various different viewpoints. One of the best known of these inherited the name Ājīvakas as a special designation; the school so named adhered to the teaching of a man named Makkhali Gosala, who was one of the most prominent of the earlier leaders in the process of systematization. The doctrines of the Ājīvakas may, however, have been taught somewhat earlier by two other wandering philosophers whose names have been preserved, Purana Kassapa and Pakudha Kaccayana, and then have been coordinated or further developed by Gosala.

These doctrines are known to us mainly from the criticisms of them which are found in Buddhist and Jain literature. The Ājīvakas appear to have denied the notion of *karma*, namely, that a man's lot in his present existence is held to be the consequence of actions performed in previous existences and that his actions in this existence will determine his condition in future existences. The Buddhist understanding of the doctrine of *karma* carries with it the implication that a man can affect his own destiny for better or worse by his moral choices, and by the performance of morally wholesome or unwholesome acts. This principle the Ājīvakas rejected. In their view, it seems, the supposed choice of action had no real effect whatever on men's condition of life, here or hereafter. All that happened within the universe took place within a totally closed causal system in which all events were completely and unalterably determined by cosmic principles over which there was no control. The doctrine that men do not act in any real sense seems to have been the contribution of Purana; what appears as the act of a man, who is the supposed actor, is no act at all, and there is therefore no question of choice of action and, therefore, no moral choice.

The teaching of Purana Kassapa is represented in the Buddhist Pāli Canon in the following terms: 'To him who acts, O king, or causes another to act, to him who mutilates or causes another to mutilate, to him who punishes or causes another to punish, to him who causes grief or torment, to him who trembles or causes others to tremble, to him who kills a living creature, who takes what is not given, who breaks into houses, who commits dacoity, or robbery, or highway robbery, or adultery, or who speaks lies, to him thus acting there is no guilt. If with a discus with an edge sharp as a razor he should make all the living creatures on the earth one heap, one mass of flesh, there would be no guilt thence resulting, no increase of guilt would ensue. Were he to go along the south bank of the Ganges striking and slaying, mutilating and having men mutilated, oppressing and having men oppressed, there would be no guilt thence resulting, no increase of guilt would ensue. Were he to go along the north bank of the Ganges giving alms or causing them to be offered, there would be no merit thence resulting, no increase of merit. In generosity, in self-mastery, in control of the senses, in speaking truth, there is neither merit nor increase of merit.'[31]

Nevertheless, the Ājīvakas practiced an ascetic life. This fact they explained as being due, like everything else, to the wholly impersonal mechanism by which the universe operates. One of the inevitable stages in human destiny was the practice of asceticism. Every individual's destiny was unalterably fixed; men must pass through innumerable different kinds of existences, and last of all the ascetic life of the Ājīvaka wanderer. Then came final peace. The whole process had an unimaginably long duration; the number of years for its completion was reckoned as 'thirty million million million multiplied by the number of the grains of sand in the bed of the River Ganges'.[32]

The Ājīvaka doctrine would appear to be that 'all beings, all lives, all existent things, all living substances attain, and must attain, perfection in course of time.'[33] There is a fixed, orderly mode of progression through which all beings must pass, and through this transformation and constant change all, in the end, reach perfection. In the Ājīvaka scheme it was laid down that there were fixed numbers of beings in the various categories of existence at any one time: there were, for instance, fourteen hundred thousands of species of being, six classes of men, forty-nine hundred kinds of occupation, forty-nine hundred Ājīvakas, and forty-nine hundred (other) homeless wanderers.[34]

By such arguments the Ājīvakas would assert the necessity of their mode of existence to any enquiring monarch. Such questioning of *shramana* teachers and ascetics by Ajatashatru, the King of Magadha, who was contemporary with the Buddha, is described in the Pāli *sutta* entitled 'The Fruits of the Life of a Recluse'.[35] The king takes the line that since every other known occupation is profitable to society generally, as well as to the man who practices it, it is appropriate to ask what contribution is made by the life of the *shramana*.

The attempted justification by the leader of the Ājīvakas of their position does not appear to have impressed King Ajatashatru greatly: 'I neither applauded nor blamed what he said', recalls the king, 'and though dissatisfied I gave utterance to no expression of dissatisfaction, and neither accepting nor rejecting that answer of his, I arose from my seat and departed thence.'[36] One has to bear in mind, of course, that this is the Buddhist version of the matter.

THE JAINS

A somewhat similar position was maintained by the Jains. Mahavira, the leader of the Jain community at the time of the Buddha, appears to have been associated originally with Gosala, the leader of the Ājīvakas. Which of the two was the 'pupil' seems uncertain; possibly each was indebted to the other in certain respects. The tradition is that they were associates for six years and then parted company. They met again, sixteen years later, only to disagree with one another. The major point on which the Jains differed from the Ājīvakas was with regard to the freedom of the will. In opposition to the Ājīvakas they asserted that every living being (human and non-human) was a transmigrating soul, and that by choosing morally wholesome actions it was possible for the soul to wear out its bad *karma* and eventually, after sustained moral improvement of this sort, to gain release altogether from the mortal realm into the highest heaven, a pure, eternal, non-material state of being. Like the Ājīvakas, the Jains practiced very severe austerities, but in their case as a means of neutralizing bad *karma*, and of their own free choice.[37] They laid great emphasis also on the necessity to avoid the acquisition of further bad *karma* through violent deeds, and they therefore made it a principle to avoid taking life in any form.

THE MATERIALISTS

A completely different philosophical position was maintained by the school of *shramanas* known as Lokayatas, or materialists. Their name indicates that their principal concern was with *loka*, the material, common, or natural world. In the light of a long list of references to the Lokayatas in Indian literature from the time of the Buddha to the fourteenth century, T. W. Rhys Davids came to the conclusion that 'the best working hypothesis ... seems to be that about 500 BC the word Lokayata was used in a complimentary way as the name of a branch of Brahman learning, and probably meant *Nature-lore*—wise sayings, riddles, rhymes, and theories handed down by tradition as to cosmogony, the elements, the stars, the weather, scraps of astronomy, of elementary physics, even of anatomy, and knowledge of the nature of precious stones, and of birds and beasts and plants.'[38] On the basis of this rudimentary, folk-loristic view of the natural world there appears to have developed a theory of life whose principal exponent at the time of the Buddha was a man named Ajita of the hair-blanket (*kesa-kambalin*). In his own words, as they are represented in the Buddhist source, 'A human being is built up of the four elements [earth, air, fire and water]. When he dies the earthy in him returns and relapses to the earth, the fluid to the water, the heat to the fire, the windy to the air, and his faculties pass into space [by the 'faculties' are meant the five senses, and the mind]. The four bearers ... take his dead body away; till they reach the burning-ground men utter forth eulogies, but there his bones are bleached, and his offerings end in ashes.... Fools and wise alike, on the dissolution of the body, are cut off, annihilated, and after death they are not.'[39] A Buddhist commentator, Candrakirti, asserted that in the Lokayata view, consciousness was the product of the chemical interaction of the four elements of which the human body was composed, just as alcohol, with its inebriating power, is the product of ingredients which separately and by themselves are not inebriating. The Lokayatas appear to have rejected the idea of any moral causation: that is to say, the view that moral action produces one kind of consequence, and immoral action another kind of consequence. Every substance has its 'own nature' (*sva-bhava*)— it is self-determined. Translated into the realm of human action, this meant a doctrine of complete freedom of will. In the Lokayata view men were entirely free to act as they chose. The only proper criterion of action, in their view, was whether it increased human pleasure. By 'pleasure' was meant both the pleasures of the senses, and the mental pleasure of human relationships. Their ethic was therefore characterized as that of 'do-as-you-like' (*yadrccha*). On balance, life was potentially more full of pleasure than of pain; what was needed was the discrimination to seek pleasure in the ways in which it could most profitably be found, and this, no doubt, provided the Lokayata wanderers with the justification for their adoption of the 'alternative life'.

THE SCEPTICS

Finally, there was among the *shramaṇas* one more major position or school, generally known as the Agnostics, or Sceptics. These appear to have been men who rejected the traditional way of life, the Vedic doctrines, and the priestly system on the grounds that the speculative doctrines of priests and teachers were contradictory of one another, and that no final position of 'truth' could ever be reached. They avoided all argumentativeness, which, they said, was productive only of ill-temper. Their positive emphasis was on the cultivation of friendship and of peace of mind. These agnostics were criticized in the Buddhist sources as 'eel-wrigglers' because they wriggled out of every question that was put to them and refused to give any firm answer. Their leader, Sanjaya, is represented as saying, 'If you ask me whether there is another world—well, if I thought there were I would say so. But I don't say so. And I don't think it is thus or thus. And I don't think it is otherwise. And I don't deny it. And I don't say there neither is, nor is not, another world. And if you ask me about the beings produced by chance; or whether there is any fruit, any result, of good or bad actions; or whether a man who has won the truth continues, or not, after death—to each or any of these questions I give the same reply.'[40]

What was common to these various schools of thought found among the *shramaṇas*, of whom the Buddha also was one, was their rejection of the practices, beliefs and social system of the hereditary Vedic priesthood. But, as we have seen, they differed among themselves, and the Buddhists certainly differed, to greater or less degree, from all of them. We shall be in a better position to appreciate the points of difference between the doctrines of these other *shramaṇas* and the doctrine of the Buddha when we have considered the circumstances of the Buddha's life. It will then be possible to evaluate his role in relation to the religious, ideological, political and economic conditions of the time.

Part 3

Buddhist Civilization in Principle

6   Profile of the Buddha

THE BUDDHA'S HISTORICITY

Evidently, the Buddha belongs in the company of the *shramanas*, the non-brahman teachers who were critical of the brahmanical sacrificial system and who rejected the religious and social claims of the brahmans. How the Buddha's teaching differed from the other non-brahman schools of thought is considered later (see chapter 7). Meanwhile, there are other questions to be answered. We have to enquire about the characteristic concerns of the Buddha, the nature of his public activity, what kind of people he met with and what his relations with them were, how he was regarded by others, and so on. In this way, as the pattern of the Buddha's life is examined, and some sort of a profile emerges, it may be possible to determine a little more closely how he is to be characterized: that is, as religious innovator, or reformer, or as philosopher, or what.

First, we have to note that for the earliest Buddhists it was the word of the Buddha rather than the *life* of the Buddha which seems to have been of paramount importance. It was the discourses which were remembered, rehearsed at his death, and carefully preserved and transmitted in the community of his followers. His life-story was not in itself a matter of such intrinsic interest apparently, since the canon of scripture of the Theravadin school, which is representative of early or 'primitive' Buddhism (though not necessarily exclusively representative) contains no continuous narrative of his life. It was not until later in Buddhist history that full-length biographies of the Buddha were produced, such as the Sanskrit work of perhaps (at the earliest) the second century BC, entitled *The Great Event* (*Mahavastu*) or the more elaborate work by the Sanskrit poet of the second century AD, Ashvaghosha, entitled *The Acts of the Buddha* (*Buddhacarita*). Because of this apparent preoccupation of the earliest followers of the Buddha with his doctrines rather than his life, the idea has been suggested by some Buddhists that possibly the doctrine is all that matters. It is the doctrine, they urge, which has eternal validity; the disciples' concern is to accept it, apprehend it and practice it; the Buddha-figure is simply the personification of a spiritual principle. 'The existence of Gotama as an individual', writes Edward Conze, 'is, in any case a matter of little importance to Buddhist faith.'[1] To some extent this attitude may have been provoked by the suggestions of Western scholars (at a time when it was fashionable to question the historical existence of any cult hero) that the Buddha who is described in even the earliest Buddhist literature is pure invention. H. H. Wilson, for instance, argued that the Buddha's life as it has come down in the traditions, is nothing more than an allegorical version of the Sankhya philosophy; others, such as E. Senart and H. Kern, suggested that the Buddha was a solar symbol and the story of his life a solar myth.[2] The Indian scholar, T. R. V. Murti, while not denying the historical existence of Gotama, regards it as unimportant for the Mahayana form of Buddhist religion—that is, the form which he regards as the most fully developed and most adequate as a religion. 'The Mahayana religion escapes the predicament of having to depend on any particular historical person as the founder.'[3]

It is worth noting, in passing, that the late-nineteenth-century wave of scepticism about the historicity of the Buddha has now receded. As Andre Bareau has said, nowadays, as a result of greater knowledge of the philological and archaeological sources, scientific study admits that in the case of the Buddha there really existed an historical personage the principal traits of whose life and personality can be known.[4] It is important to notice, too, that while the Buddha's earliest disciples seem to have had no interest in recounting the entire life of the Buddha *seriatim*, they were nevertheless concerned to record carefully what they appear to have considered the most important events, events relating to certain crucial or significant moments in the pattern of the Buddha's life, such as his renunciation of the life of a prince, his enlightenment, the inauguration of his public activity as a teacher, and his decease.

These four events provide a convenient framework within which to examine the personality and role of the Buddha; they indicate four historically important aspects of the Buddha's relation to the life of his time: (1) his particular social and cultural milieu; (2) the experience of spiritual unrest, and subsequent enlightenment which he underwent; (3) the nature of his public activity; and (4) the significance of the ceremonies connected with his decease.

GOTAMA'S SOCIAL AND CULTURAL MILIEU

The man who was to become known as the Buddha (and who until his enlightenment at Bodh-Gaya is properly known as the *Bodhisattva*, or one who has the essence of Buddhahood, or enlightenment) was, says the tradition, the son of Suddhodana, the leading citizen of Kapilavastu. This was a busy town on the north-west to south-east trade route which ran along the foot of the Himalayan mountains, amid the thick forests at the extreme northern edge of the Gangetic plain. It lay due north of Banaras, and a few miles within the border of what is now Nepal. The town was the capital of the Shakyas, a people who had, as we have seen, an aristocratic republican form of government. Their territory probably extended about fifty miles from east to west, and about thirty or forty from north to south, from the foot of the Himalayas.[5] Apart from Kapilavastu, the capital, the region contained a number of market towns. The Buddha-to-be belonged to the clan of the Gotamas, and it is by this name that he is often known, as if it were a surname. His given, or personal name was Siddhartha. Later Buddhist literature magnifies the position of his father to that of a very great king and depicts the life-style of the young prince as one of extreme grandeur, luxury and wealth. It is more probable that his father was the elected head of an aristocratic hereditary ruling class, having some of the rank, status and prestige of the ruler of a small kingdom, but nothing more. As might be expected, the Buddhist sources provide a certain amount of information about the Shakyas, although it is mostly of the kind that has to be pieced together from scattered references. With regard to the ancestry of the Shakyas, for example, there is an interesting allusion to the progenitors of their tribe having had their dwelling 'on the slopes of the Himalayas'.[6] In the present form of the story, as it is told in the Pāli Canon, although it is explained that these progenitors *went* to the Himalayas when they were banished from the court of their father, a legendary Indian *rājā* of ancient times, named Okkaka, the explanation could well be a device to account for the fact that the ancestors of what was now a north-Indian tribe had at an earlier period lived in the Himalayas, if this were a strongly established tradition among them. It would, in fact, be more in accordance with the natural course of migration for a Himalayan tribe to have moved southwards towards the sun and the plains than *vice versa*, for, in general, this has been the predominant direction in which migration of peoples occurred throughout north India and continental South-East Asia. The *Ambaṭṭha Sutta*, in which the story occurs, suggests that the Shakyas were a non-brahman tribe. The brahman Ambattha, in conversation with the Buddha, referring to the division of society into those who were brahmans and those who were not, reminded the Buddha that it was the duty of the latter to serve the former, and to honor them. The Shakyas, he complained, appeared to be lacking in this sense of respect for brahmans. 'Once, Gotama, I had to go to Kapilavastu on some business or other ... and went into the Shakya's Congress Hall (*Santhāgāra-sālā*). Now at that time there were a number of Shakyas, old and young, seated in the hall on grand seats, making merry and joking together, nudging one another with their fingers; and for a truth, methinks, it was I myself that was the subject of their jokes; and not one of them even offered me a seat. That, Gotama, is neither fitting, nor is it seemly, that the Shakyas, menials as they are, mere menials, should neither venerate, nor value, nor esteem, nor give gifts to, nor pay honour to Brahmans.'[7]

Such lack of respect for brahmans which is attributed to the Shakyas in this tale may possibly reflect the attitude of the developed Buddhist community towards the brahmans. It is also possible that this was known by the Buddhists to have been the attitude of the Shakya people. If the Shakyas were Himalayan hill people who had migrated to the edge of the plains, it is likely that they would have been of a sturdy independent spirit, and well disposed to reject the social pretensions of the Aryan brahman class. That they were of such a spirit is suggested by one or two other casual references.[8] Their sturdy spirit is shown too in their relations with the neighboring great monarchy of Koshala (see chapter 3, p. 62 ff.). The king of Koshala, Pasenadi, a great admirer of the Buddha, and benefactor of the Buddhist Order, wished to strengthen his relationship with the Shakyas. He sent to the Shakyan elders a polite request that he might be allowed to marry one of their daughters. They, however, considered that such a marriage would be degrading to them; it would, they said, destroy the purity of their race and be contrary to their tradition. But they could not afford to risk the anger of this very powerful neighboring king, so they sent him the illegitimate daughter of one of the chiefs, born of a slave-woman, passing her off as pure Shakyan. The attitude of the Shakyans is referred to in the course of the story, (the *Bhadda-Sāla Jātaka*) in the words of king Pasenadi's messengers: 'These Shakyas are desperately proud, in matters of birth!'[9] Another interesting fact about the Shakyas is that they were fond of sports, and especially archery. They had an established school of archery, run by a family who specialized in this sport.'[10] It is said, too, that the Buddha, as a young man, had to prove his prowess as an archer before any Shakyan nobleman would consider him as a future son-in-law.[11] While Kapilavastu, the capital of the Shakyan republic, was not one of the recognized six great cities (*mahānagara*) of the time, it was certainly a place of importance and some affluence. It is described as a city where there were crowds of people and plenty of food, a place whose streets were full of traffic, in the form of elephants, horses, chariots, carts and pedestrians, and where, with their hubbub and jingle and clatter, was mingled the sound of street musicians, singers and traders.[12] The general pattern of Indian cities of this period has already been described (see chapter 3, p. 62 ff.), and Kapilavastu would, no doubt have conformed generally to this pattern. The Buddhist sources mention the council hall, the *Santhāgāra-sālā*, which stood at the center of the town, and where public business, administrative and judicial, was carried out. Mention is made, too, of the massive ramparts surrounding the city, said to have been eighteen cubits high. It was as the leading citizen of such a city, and as one who carried the responsibility for presiding over the affairs of the small state of which Kapilavastu was the capital, that we have to see the father of the Bodhisattva. It is appropriate to think, not so much in terms of the idle ostentation of the court of some great oriental emperor, as of the material comfort and well-being of a cultured upper-class townsman in a prosperous commercial and administrative center:

of urbanity and sophistication, rather than of luxurious imperial grandeur.

The background of the Buddha's youth and early manhood is represented, therefore, as having been one of urban life, comfortable and easy by the standards of the time, and made more so by the privileges that went with superior social class; Shakyan society was certainly not classless, as the story of king Pasenadi's bride makes clear. The fact that the Shakyan state was not a monarchy may be significant in connection with the problem which was raised in chapter 4, namely, which came first—individualism, monarchy, or urbanism? Gotama's milieu, to the time of his manhood, was that of urban life, but it did not include experience of a developed monarchical society. The problem which he seems to have felt most keenly and which set him on his spiritual quest, was that of the suffering of *the individual*. This suggests that it was primarily urban life which precipitated individualism, rather than monarchy, or, at any rate, that this is how it was understood by the early Buddhist community. Moreover, it was a concern with the pain and the unsatisfactoriness of ordinary, common mortal existence which stirred Gotama; this can be seen as both a consequence of his upbringing and a determining factor in the shape of the solution which he discovered for the ills of human existence. For the milieu in which he probably grew up is that of a traditional ruling class, one occupied with the practical aspects of public life, with the smooth functioning of the machinery of society and perhaps at least some general concern with, and feeling of responsibility for, human welfare.

It is meaningless to say, as some have done[13] that the Buddha, a child of his time, was heir to the Hindu religious tradition. In the first place, it is an anachronism to ascribe a Hindu religious tradition to this early period; the characteristic set of beliefs and practices which came to be known as 'Hindu' (the word itself being a product of the Muslim period) was yet to be developed. Moreover, it is difficult to see how the Buddha can be described as an heir to the brahman religious tradition. One who did not believe in God, nor in theories of creation, and who did not accept the authority of the Veda, was about as much an heir to the Hindu tradition as Karl Marx was a Zionist.

It has been suggested that if Gotama was indebted to any earlier figure in the cultural history of India, the most likely candidate is Kapila, to whom is attributed the atheistic Sankhya doctrine. It is very likely, writes R. C. Majumdar, that Gotama, since he came from Kapilavastu, 'had some knowledge of the Sankhya doctrine'.[14]

The affinity between the teaching of the Buddha and the Sankhya philosophy was hinted at by Ashvaghosha (the Buddhist writer mentioned on page 93) in his full-length biography of the Buddha, the *Buddhacarita*. Those who hold the view that the Buddha was influenced by Sankhya attitudes point to the fact that one of the teachers to whom he resorted in the course of his wanderings, before his own 'awakenment' at Bodh-Gaya, was Āḷāra (or Āṛāda) Kālāma. Āḷāra's philosophy seems to have borne some slight resemblance to the Sankhya system, although there seem also to have been significant differences. The fact that Gotama stayed only a short while with Āḷāra and then left him, because he was not satisfied with his teaching,[15] could mean that Gotama found Āḷāra either insufficiently Sankhyan in his views, or too much so. A modern Indian writer takes the view that it would be a serious error to overlook the major similarity between the Sankyha system and Buddhism—the atheistic position which is common to them: 'since the Sankhya was undoubtedly much older than the rise of Buddhism, we are left with the strong presumption that at least for his atheism the Buddha was directly indebted to the Sankhya, though he evidently differed much from Kapila in his main interest.'[16] But this is to assume that Gotama was incapable by himself of arriving at an atheistic view, or adopting an atheistic premise as his starting-point. The likelihood that Gotama, living in Kapilavastu, might have been familiar with the Sankhya view, has to be taken in conjunction with the suggestion of Dandekar that the origin of the Sankhya is to be found in a 'pre-Vedic, non-Aryan thought complex'.[17] So it is an open possibility that Gotama's atheism also had its origin in the pre-Vedic, non-Aryan, non-Brahmanical culture of north-eastern India in general, and of the Shakya people in particular.

The notion that Gotama was a 'religious' man evidently needs careful scrutiny. That he has come to be so regarded may be partly because of the assimilation of Buddhism with theistic systems of

113

belief and practice as a 'religion', and partly because of the ill-founded idea that the inhabitants of India are, and always have been, more religiously inclined than the peoples of the West. In this way the Buddha has been subsumed under the general category of religious teachers or leaders. The Buddha's teaching, and the life of the early Buddhists is often regarded as an answer to personal spiritual *malaise*, a doctrine of personal salvation. The possibility which is being raised here is that it was something other than this. It has to be admitted, however, that the story of Gotama's enlightenment does, on the face of it, look very like a personal salvation story of a purely religious kind. But this may be because the modern understanding of 'religion' is being projected back into the time of the Buddha and made the criterion of his experience. We need to enquire what is said in the tradition of early Buddhism about the whole complex of events leading to the enlightenment at Bodh-Gaya.

THE ENLIGHTENMENT

According to tradition, Gotama was twenty-nine years of age when the decisive events occurred which led to his enlightenment. Various accounts are available, and they differ considerably, especially with regard to the circumstances of the renunciation. According to the later, more elaborate accounts, written in Sanskrit, the Bodhisattva, while he was out driving his chariot, was confronted successively by a very old man, then by a very sick man, and finally by a corpse being carried out to the burning *ghat*. These sights disturbed him profoundly, for they raised questions which he had apparently not considered before. Finally, the sight of a holy man stirred in him the desire to live the ascetic life and strive for spiritual enlightenment.

On the other hand, an early Pāli text gives an account which suggests that it was as a result of long reflection upon the human condition that Gotama decided to devote himself to a disciplined quest for spiritual satisfaction. In this account of the matter, the Buddha, some years after the event, makes known to his followers the two possible ends to which men may devote their lives, in terms of his own earlier experience. He identifies these two ends as the noble or holy quest (*ariya-pariyesanā*) and the ignoble or unholy quest. Briefly, the human situation is seen as one in which, because of belief in self (*atta* or *atman*), men are vulnerable to the process of ageing, decay and dying, and hence to sorrow. The word translated as sorrow (*dukkha*) in fact carries a much deeper and stronger connotation than the English word, and implies a sense of the utter unsatisfactoriness, weariness and pain of mortal existence. The ignoble quest, to which many devote their lives, consists in seeking after things which are liable to ageing, decay and death, the very conditions from which deliverance is needed.

'And what, monks, is the noble quest? That someone, being liable to birth because of self, and knowing the peril in whatever is liable to birth, seeks the unborn, the uttermost security from bonds—*nibbāna*.' The same formula is then repeated for each of the other conditions of mortal existence. The noble quest is that in which someone, who because of self is vulnerable to ageing, decaying, dying, stain and sorrow, and who knows the peril in whatever is liable to the same things, seeks the unageing, the undecaying, the undying, the stainless, the unsorrowing—that which is itself freedom from all constraints: *nibbāna*. The Buddha then goes on to say that when he was still the Bodhisattva, it was considerations such as these which stirred him, and made him ask 'Why do I seek what is liable to birth ... to ageing ... to decay ... to death ... to stain ... to sorrow? Being myself liable to birth, to ageing, to decay, to death, to stain, to sorrow, I should seek the unborn, the unageing, the undecaying, the undying, the stainless, the unsorrowing.'[18] It is understandable, as E. J. Thomas pointed out, that this kind of account of personal experience and reflection should have been developed into the story of encounters with an old man, a sick man, and a corpse; it is less understandable, on the other hand, how, if these encounters had been real events the story could subsequently 'have been converted into this abstract form'.[19] On the day on which he saw these three manifestations of the human condition, so the tradition asserts, another event took place—the birth of Bodhisattva's son. On hearing the news, he pronounced his son's name, 'Rahula'. The commentators suggest the presence of a pun: the word 'rahula' means, they say, 'a bond', and so the Bodhisattva's utterance had a double meaning: 'Rahula is born. A bond is born.' Thus, it is very interesting to notice that of the six conditions of human existence mentioned in the Buddha's discourse—birth, ageing, decay, dying, stain and sorrow—four illustrative examples have been found in what are represented as the events surrounding the great renunciation. Finally, there is the further curious incident concerning a Shakya maiden named Kisagotami. It is said that from her balcony she saw Gotama returning home in his chariot after the news of his son's birth had been announced to him. She saw Gotama's 'beauty and glory' and 'she was filled with joy and delight', and began to sing: 'Happy is the mother, happy is the father, happy is the wife who has such a husband!' The word which she used for 'happy' (*nibbuta*) meant also 'cool' or 'healthy'. The Bodhisattva, upon hearing her song took the word to mean 'cool', and, says the tradition, 'with aversion in his heart for lusts, he thought, "When the fire of passion is cooled, the heart is happy; when the fire of illusion, pride, false views and all the lusts and pains are extinguished it is happy".' In gratitude for the lesson she had taught him, the story continues, he sent the maiden a very costly pearl necklace. 'She thought that prince Siddhattha (Gotama) was in love with her, and had sent her a present, and she was filled with delight.' But a few hours later, in the quietness of the night, awakening to the sight of the dancers who had been entertaining him, and were now asleep in all kinds of disgusting and unseemly postures, he renounced the life of sensual pleasures, and took the crucial step of leaving his home, to set out on the life of the homeless wanderer, in search of spiritual peace.

Perhaps both the abstract analysis of the human situation, and the picturesque account, with its various personal illustrations, of the kind of 'fetters' or constraints from which Gotama felt he had to escape, indicate in their contrasting ways the nature of his quest. The abstract version emphasizes that it is 'the self', the *atman*, which is the ultimate root of the human experience of sorrow. It is because of the idea of 'self' that men are vulnerable to birth, ageing, decay, death, stain, and sorrow; it is this notion of 'self' which causes men to experience life as sorrowful. The stories of Gotama's encounters with old age, disease, death, birth and the taint of passion may have been the kind of characteristic experiences which brought a young man to see that it is the unending search for the satisfaction of the desires of the individual which leads to spiritual disenchantment. It was from this condition, from these constraints, that he sought some way of deliverance.

We return, therefore, to the point which was made earlier, that it was the ultimate unsatisfactoriness, the sorrowfulness of life, which set Gotama on his spiritual quest. How this quest was fulfilled, what was the nature of the 'salvation' which he found, we shall consider in detail in the next chapter. What we now have to take account of is the typical environment, the locale for his public activity after the enlightenment, after the great discovery had been made.

THE NATURE OF THE BUDDHA'S PUBLIC ACTIVITY

If we are correct in thinking that the problems of human life with which the Buddha was primarily concerned were the kind of problems which arise with the development of individualism, and if this was a feature which was more characteristic of urban than of rural life, then it is reasonable to expect that those in greatest need of his teaching, of his prescription for freedom and peace, would be found in the urban centers rather than in the countryside. It was, in fact, precisely there, in the cities, that most of the Buddha's public activity took place.

The profound experience he underwent at Bodh-Gaya was his awakening to the truth; it was itself an end of all the constraints of which he had previously been aware, and it was therefore described as *vimutti*, release, or *nibbāna*, the state of 'coolness' or 'health after fever'. The tradition represents him as at first uncertain whether this truth which he had apprehended could ever be conveyed to other men. 'This *dhamma*, attained to by me is deep, difficult to see, difficult to understand, tranquil, excellent, beyond dialectic, subtle, intelligible to the learned. But this is a creation delighting in sensual pleasure, rejoicing in sensual pleasure ... [and for them] this were a matter difficult to see....' The Buddha recalls that, as he was pondering and deciding against the attempt to communicate his discovery of truth to the generality of men, it occurred to the god Brahma that the world would be lost, would be destroyed, if the Buddha now refrained from teaching his doctrines (*dhamma*). He thereupon manifested himself to the Buddha in the way we have already seen.[20] The intention of this story may have been to show that even the gods were dependent on the eternal *dhamma* which the Buddha had perceived, and were therefore subordinate both to the *dhamma* and to him who was its bearer. The story has the effect, too, of showing that the relationship between the Buddha and the gods of popular belief was one of tolerant co-existence.

Now that he was persuaded that he should attempt to communicate the truth to others, the Buddha began to consider how this might most effectively be done. It is significant that the place he then made for was Varanasi, or Banaras, which, as we have seen, was at that time the intellectual and philosophical metropolis of northern India (see p. 65 f.). To some extent this significant fact is concealed by the ostensible reason given for his choice of Banaras—that he knew that he would meet there a group of five men whom he had known earlier, when he and they had been seeking spiritual satisfaction. It was to them that he now hoped to make known the truth. What has to be noticed is that their spiritual quest had led them to Banaras: it is almost as though, in ancient India, it was the case that all religious and philosophical seekers must at some time or other find their way to that ancient and holy center of worship and philosophy. There, in a park a little way outside the city, he found them; and there he expounded to them in systematic, developed order, the *dhamma*, the truth by which release from the problems and constraints of mortal existence might be gained.

The account of this exposition is the famous *Dhamma-cakkappavattana Sutta*—the discourse (or Sutta) concerning the putting into motion of the wheel of *dhamma*. The Buddha remained with the five at Banaras and, a few days later, after another session of teaching, the five achieved the state of wisdom, dispassion, and release from all the bonds of empirical mortal existence, a state known technically in Buddhism as *arahant*-ship, a term which will be explained later. It is appropriate to call the occasion 'a session of teaching', for this is the nearest, in the writer's view, that one can get to a satisfactory description of the method used by the Buddha. To say that he preached a sermon (although this terminology has been used by Western writers to describe the Buddha's activity) would be rather misleading, for, to Western ears at least, it suggests a wholly passive role for the hearers, and for the preacher a position which is sometimes described as 'six feet above contradiction'. This was not so in the kind of teaching-sessions which are recorded in early Buddhist literature. The hearers frequently interject, or raise questions, or supply answers to questions addressed to them by the Buddha, and sometimes the Buddha engages them in what is almost a catechism. Even 'discourses' suggests something rather stilted, formal, and humorless, and it is clear that they were far from being addresses of that sort. It was, in fact, almost always a session of teaching, with the Buddha suiting his words to the occasion, and taking advantage of incidents happening at the time, adapting himself to the mood or condition of the hearers and allowing them to take a good deal of the initiative. In some ways these sessions might suggest, as the closest parallel, an academic seminar or tutorial, but the resemblance is only partial. On occasions the Buddha was addressing very large numbers of people, and apart from the fact that one is unlikely to meet tutors of his quality, there seems, in addition, to have been something of what today would be called a 'charismatic' quality about his teaching.

At Banaras the Buddha remained throughout the rainy season which then followed: that is to say, for about four months. His teaching won further adherents. The first was Yasa, a young man who, according to the Pāli sources, came to the Buddha by night, feeling distress and disgust at the sordid sight presented by his own attendants who were asleep in unseemly postures. This disgust at the physically sordid aspects of human life was only the occasion for his flight from home; other, earlier experiences had conditioned him for it. He is represented as having been, like Gotama, one who had enjoyed a comfortable life; his father was one of the most wealthy financiers of Banaras. The Buddha, seeing his distressed state, called him and said 'Come, Yasa, here you will find neither distress nor danger.' There followed a session of teaching, as with the five, and at the end of it Yasa, too, apprehended the truth which the Buddha had been expounding and achieved the state of release, or *arahant*-ship. His father, alarmed by his absence, had followed the marks of Yasa's slippers, and now he, too, arrived on the scene. Not seeing Yasa at first, but only the Buddha, the father engaged him in conversation.

119

After a time the father also came under the power of the Buddha's words, and there and then declared himself a follower. He is remembered in Buddhist tradition as the first lay-follower, or *upāsaka*. The next day Yasa's mother and another woman became the first female lay-followers, when the Buddha, in response to an invitation from Yasa's father, visited the family at home and had a meal with them. Four of Yasa's companions, sons of leading families in Banaras, also became disciples of the Buddha. These, with the five former associates of the Buddha who had been the first to receive his teaching, now constituted the nucleus of what was to become the *Sangha*, or assembly of disciples, sometimes called the Buddhist Order. Later, fifty more citizens of Banaras, who had heard the Buddha's teaching, became *arahants* and entered the Order. So there came into being at Banaras a community of disciples of some size. Its members, having understood the doctrine taught by the Buddha, were sent out in different directions to teach the *dhamma* to others. The result is represented as having been a great number of further candidates who were, from this time onwards, ordained into the Order by the monks, rather than by the Buddha himself.[21]

THE BUDDHA IN RAJAGRIHA AND SHRAVASTI

At the end of the rainy season the Buddha set out from Banaras eastwards, towards another of the six great cities of the time, Rajagriha, the Magadhan capital. On the way he visited the site of his enlightenment, staying there for a while and making converts to his doctrine. At Rajagriha more converts were made, including Sariputta and Moggallana, who later became, with Ananda, the most prominent members of the Order. The then king of Magadha, Bimbisara, became interested in the Buddha's teaching; he, too, was convinced of its value, and became a lay-follower.

No consecutive narrative of the public activity of the Buddha was constructed by the early Buddhists, but from the account of the travels and teaching which is contained in the Pāli Canon, it is possible to suggest, as Malalasekere has done,[22] an outline for at least the first twenty years. Then comes a period of a further twenty-five years when it is impossible to trace any consecutive chronology, until the last few weeks of the Buddha's life, when there is the very detailed account of the last journey in the *Mahā Parinibbāna Sutta*, the *Sutta* concerning the great event of the entry by the Buddha into complete *nirvāna* (*pari-nibbāna*).

What is significant, however, from the evidence contained in the vast collection of discourses of the Buddha in the Pāli Canon, is the large proportion of these which were delivered in two major cities, Rajagriha and Shravasti. In almost all cases the discourse is introduced by a short note, indicating the place where it was delivered, and the occasion. From the evidence of these contextual notes it is possible to see that the Buddha lived more in the city of Shravasti than anywhere else. Until the later part of his life, when it lost its pride of place to Rajagriha, Shravasti, the capital of Koshala, was the most important city of the Gangetic plain, commercially and politically. The Buddha first went there at the invitation of a rich merchant named Anathapindika, whom he met at Rajagriha on the visit which has just been described. Anathapindika was visiting Rajagriha on business, and like so many others in the city, came to hear of the new doctrine which was being taught by the Shakya-sage. He, too, was converted and became a lay-follower. He invited the Buddha to spend the next rainy season at Shravasti, and when the invitation was accepted, he set off back to the Koshalan capital. Having arrived, he bought a piece of land on the outskirts of the city, at considerable cost, and had a suitable *vihāra*, or retreat-house, built in readiness for occupation by the Buddha and his company.

From the time when the Buddha and his companions first went to live in Shravasti it became virtually their headquarters. Twenty-five rainy seasons were spent there by the Buddha; the remaining twenty were spent in various other towns and cities, mainly Rajagriha. Of the discourses of the Buddha which go to make up the *Sutta-Piṭaka*, 871 are said to have been delivered in Shravasti. Of 498 canonical *Jātaka* stories, the telling of which is attributed to the Buddha, 416 are said to have been told in Shravasti.

Kapilavastu, the Buddha's home city, was visited by him more than once in the course of the years. On the first visit, in the year of his enlightenment, Gotama's little son, Rahula, was ordained as a novice. Thirteen years later, when he had come of age, Rahula was given *upasampadā*, or higher ordination, this time in the city of Shravasti.[23]

Rajagriha, the other major city with which the Buddha's work was most closely associated, was the capital of the Magadhan kingdom, which was increasing in power and prestige throughout the Buddha's lifetime. The expansion of the city beyond its old bounds during this period was a sign of its increasing population. Its king, Bimbisara (see p. 120), remained a firm friend and supporter of the Buddha throughout his life. He entertained the Buddha and his companions and presented them with a place of residence. Even during the years when Shravasti was mainly his headquarters, the Buddha seems to have paid frequent visits to Rajagriha. Many important discourses are connected with the Magadhan capital, and it was from here that the Buddha set out on his last journey. By that time there were in Rajagriha eighteen large monasteries for members of the Buddhist Order.[24] This concentration of Buddhist houses in a large capital city shows the kind of milieu in which early Buddhism flourished and was most at home.

THE BUDDHA'S LAST JOURNEY

The Buddha's last journey is described in some detail in one of the longest of the Pāli texts, the *Sutta of the Great Decease* (*Mahā Parinibbāna Sutta*). The events which are related cover a period of some months, and the narrative has many facets, each having its special value to this or that reader or hearer. What is unmistakable is the portrait of the Buddha which emerges: the portrait of the discoverer, initiator and exponent of a social, psychological and political philosophy, who takes his place among the great leaders and rulers of the world (a *Chakravartin*, or *world-ruler*).

The narrative of the *Sutta* begins in the city of Rajagriha. Bimbisara, the Buddha's helper and admirer, is no longer king of Magadha; he has been succeeded by his son, Ajatashatru. We are told that he was about to launch an attack on one of the remaining republican federations, the Vajjians, whose territory was to the north of Magadha, across the Ganges. He is represented, rather curiously, as sending a messenger to the Buddha, who at that time was in Rajagriha, to ask his advice on the matter. 'Tell him', the king instructs his brahman messenger, 'that Ajatashatru, the king

122

of Magadha ... has resolved, "I will strike at these Vajjians, mighty and powerful though they be, I will root out these Vajjians, I will destroy these Vajjians, I will bring these Vajjians to utter ruin!""[25] The messenger is instructed to listen carefully to what the Buddha has to say by way of comment, and to come and repeat it to the king. The Buddha's comment turns out to be rather cryptic. He declares that so long as the Vajjians continue to observe their traditions properly, and to meet regularly in their republican assembly, seeking agreement in all matters, so long as they honor their elders, and maintain their customary rites and ceremonies as a republic, no harm can come to them; their prosperity is assured. The brahman messenger takes the meaning of the prediction to be that the Vajjians cannot be overcome in battle; they will be overcome only by diplomacy and internal dissension. Having drawn this conclusion, he hurries back to his royal master.

The Buddha then repeats to his companions word for word what he had said concerning the Vajjians, but applying his prediction, now, to the Buddhist *Sangha*. So long as the *Sangha* members continue to observe their traditions properly, and to meet regularly in their assembly, seeking agreement in all matters, and so on, no harm can come to the *Sangha*: it can only prosper. The crucial fact in the interpretation of this utterance of the Buddha is that the Vajjians were destroyed very shortly after this incident. According to tradition, spies and infiltrators succeeded in sowing the seeds of suspicion among the leaders and elders of the ruling assembly, and soon there was a rich crop of dissension and internal conflict which Ajatashatru was able to turn to his advantage. The Vajjian republic was conquered, and absorbed into the Magadhan monarchy. So, by the time this prediction of the Buddha was being repeated and transmitted in the oral tradition of the monks, it was known that, as a fact of history, the Vajjians had not succeeded in meeting the conditions required for their survival. It would have been clear to the monks who passed on these words of the Buddha that there must be some other, more permanent value in this utterance than simply an oblique prediction of the ruin of a people who were now only of historical interest. The point of the discourse lay in the application to the Buddhist *Sangha* of the same conditions for survival. The old republican *Sanghas* or assemblies had now almost all disappeared, victims of historical circumstances in the form of expanding monarchical power. If that were a matter for regret, it had to be remembered that the *Sangha* tradition was nevertheless being perpetuated and preserved in a new form—in the life of the Buddhist community, the new *Sangha*; we shall take up this point again later, when we come to examine the life of the *Sangha* (chapter 8). Meanwhile, what emerges from this opening section of the *Sutta of the Great Decease* is the evident and real interest of the Buddha in forms of social and political structure.

Soon after the incident concerning the Vajjians, according to the narrative, the Buddha and his companions left Rajagriha and began traveling northwards. They reached the southern shore of the Ganges at a place which at that time was called Pataligama, but which a century or so later was to be known as Pataliputra, when it became the new capital city of the expanding kingdom of Magadha; today it is Patna, the chief city of Bihar State. At this place the Buddha talked through the night with some local people who had assembled specially at the rest-house for travelers, where the Buddha was staying. These were lay-followers, who, while acknowledging the outstanding value of the Buddha's teaching, still continued their household life. In the Buddha's view, they too had an important place in the scheme of things, and it was for this reason that he undertook to instruct them in detail in the matters of social morality, pointing out to them the various advantages of moral uprightness and integrity. The morning after he had spoken with these householders, the Buddha observed that some ministers of the Magadhan state were supervising the construction of a new fortress at Pataligama. He then, it is said, uttered a prediction concerning this new stronghold. 'As far, Ananda, as Aryan people resort, as far as merchants travel, this will become the chief city, Pataliputra, a center for the interchange of all kinds of wares. But three dangers will hang over Pataliputra, that of fire, that of water, and that of dissension among friends.'[26] The event referred to, the transfer of the royal capital of Magadha to Pataliputra, took place probably during the reign of Ajatashatru's son; the significance of the reference for our present purpose lies in the fact that the Buddha is represented as being keenly interested in a matter of this sort—the founding and growth of what was to become a great city.

After crossing the Ganges, and passing through two smaller towns, the Buddha and his companions came to the city of Vaishali, the capital of the Licchavi republic. Here the Buddha accepted the invitation of Ambapali, the chief courtesan of the city, to take a meal at her house after she had heard him teaching and been gladdened by his words. The chief citizens of Licchavi, hearing of the acceptance from Ambapali herself, asked her to be so good as to give way in deference to them, so that they might entertain the Buddha. But although they offered her a large sum of money, on this occasion her favor was not to be bought. 'My lords', she replied, 'were you to offer all Vaishali with its subject territory, I would not give up so honourable a feast!'[27]

The Buddha remained in Vaishali for some time. It was a place which he had visited several times before in his travels, and for which he seems to have had a special liking. It contained a number of splendid shrines dedicated to popular local deities, and the Buddha particularly enjoyed their beauty. 'How delightful a spot, Ananda, is Vaishali. How charming the Udena Shrine, and the Gotamaka Shrine, and the Shrine of the Seven Mangoes, and the Shrine of Many Sons, and the Sarandada Shrine, and the Chapala Shrine.'[28] The Sutta tells that after this visit, when the time came for him to leave the city, knowing that it would be the last time he would see Vaishali before he died, the Buddha turned and took a long, full look at the city, and then continued on his journey.

THE VILLAGE OF KUSHINARA

The place in which his entry into final *nibbāna* occurred was a small, insignificant village called Kushinara. A little while before, it had become clear to the Buddha's companions that the end of his mortal existence was now very near; not only was he eighty years of age, but he had become physically very weak. They had asked what ceremonies would be appropriate after his death, and had been instructed that the remains of a *Tathāgata*, or Buddha, should be treated in the same way as it was customary to treat the remains of a *Chakravartin*, a universal emperor. They were to be wrapped in cloth, and soaked in oil, placed on a funeral pyre made of all kinds of fragrant wood, and burned; the relics were then to be enshrined in a great memorial cairn, or *stūpa*, built at the center of a crossroads. This was how the funeral rites of a *Chakravartin* were carried out; the memorial cairn would be built at some important crossing of routes, in a major city.

The Buddha's companions were surprised when they realized, from their master's severely weakened condition that it was in Kushinara that his life was to end. Ananda expressed their feeling: 'Let not the Exalted One die in this little wattle-and-daub town, in this town in the midst of the jungle, in this branch township. For, lord, there are other great cities, such as Champa, Rajagriha, Shravasti, Shaketa, Kaushambi and Banaras. Let the Exalted One die in one of them. There there are many wealthy nobles and heads of houses, believers in the *Tathāgata*, who will pay due honour to the remains of the *Tathāgata*.'[29]

Perhaps Ananda really did feel such dismay at the prospect of the Buddha's life ending in Kushinara and of the cremation of his remains having to be carried out in so remote a spot. Perhaps Buddhists of a later age were embarrassed by, or at least surprised at, the lowliness of the place where, as a matter of historical fact, the death of the Buddha had occurred. The word which is used here to describe Kushinara as a town 'in the midst of the jungle' (*ujjangala*) may mean what in India would be called a 'jungly' place: that is, as the commentator Buddhaghosa understood it, a lawless, heathen, pagan sort of place; or it may mean simply a barren, waste place. In either case, Ananda's objection seems to indicate that the appropriate place for the Buddha to end his life would be a great city, an urbane and civilized place, the kind of place with which he was most properly associated.

An attempt to remove the objection and the embarrassment is made by the insertion at this point in the narrative of a tale of the ancient splendors of Kushinara in some former age when it was the capital city of a great emperor, Maha Sudassana. In those days the royal city, Kushavasti (as it was then known) 'was mighty and prosperous and full of people, crowded with men and provided with all things for food'. This description of the former glories of Kushinara is elsewhere expanded into a full-length discourse, contained in a separate *Sutta*, called the *Maha Sudassana Sutta*,[30] and it is found also as a *Jātaka* story.[31] The account of the city which is given in these longer versions is highly idealistic; even if no such city ever quite existed in Indian history, the description allows us to see what was obviously the Buddhist notion of an ideal city, and to this aspect of the matter we shall return later on (see chapter 8, p. 165 ff.).

THE URBANITY OF THE BUDDHA

Whether appropriately or inappropriately, then, it was in this little town in the jungle that the Buddha's life ended. There his body was cremated, and the relics were divided, a portion being given to each of eight legitimate claimants: the king of Magadha, the people of Vaishali, the people of Kapilavastu, the people of Kushinara, three other tribes, and a brahman named Vethadipaka. In each of the respective towns or cities to which the relics were taken a memorial cairn was built. Over the vessel in which the remains had been collected another cairn was built, and yet another over the remaining embers. According to the tradition, therefore, ten *stūpas*, or places where the Buddha was remembered and honored, came into being immediately after his death. Some of these were in great cities —Rajagriha, Vaishali, and Kapilavastu—and so the dishonor which Ananda felt was incurred in the Buddha's life ending outside a great city, where no worthy memorial could be maintained, was removed.

This brief survey of the pattern of the Buddha's life, the milieu from which he came, and the characteristic features of his public activities, shows that the setting of his life, from the first to the last days, was predominantly urban. It was a life spent in great centers where people came together to trade and to deliberate, to study and to practice their special crafts and industries, to discuss and to be entertained, to seek justice, to make money, or to find the truth. The appeal of his doctrines was primarily to men of an urban background. Among the things which, tradition suggests, might be said in praise of him was that he abstained from 'village ways' (*gamādhamma*),[32] a term which could also be translated 'vile conduct'.

T. W. Rhys Davids suggests that the phrase means 'the practice of country folk ... the opposite of *pori*, urbane'.[33] Later in

127

the same passage it is said, in fact, that the words of the Buddha are 'pleasant to the ear, reaching to the heart, urbane *(pori)*'. The point here seems to be that the Buddha's urbanity of speech was consistent with the rational quality of the ideas which he expressed.

Towards contemporary forms of religion, it is clear that the Buddha adopted a generally tolerant attitude, with the exception of his criticism of the brahman hereditary priesthood and the sacrificial system. Towards folk beliefs and practices, except for those which came within the scope of priestly magic, he showed the urbane man's understanding of the proper place which mythology and ritual hold in the lives of unsophisticated people. He was not a religious reformer of the iconoclastic kind. Nor was he a prophet, if by that is understood one who comes as the messenger, servant or spokesman of the deity, for to the extent that Brahma may be taken as the supreme deity for the men of the sixth century BC in north India, the Buddha's relation to him is certainly not that of a servant, but rather that of one who has superior knowledge and insight. The Buddha's insight is represented as being, not that of the dogmatist, who asserts that such and such is the case and demands men's acceptance of his assertion in faith, but rather that of the analyst. And the analysis which is offered is both logical and psychological; its appeal is in its self-authenticating quality. Urbanity of manner and speech were wholly consistent with the rationality of what was expressed. It is to an examination of the doctrines themselves that we must now turn, in order to demonstrate this consistency.

7   The New Wisdom

The nature of the change which took place when Gotama sat meditating under the bodhi* tree on the bank of the Nairanjana river is traditionally described by saying that he became the Buddha, that is, the Awakened. In later Buddhist literature, the transition is described in terms which make it literally an earth-shaking event, but the earlier literature gives a more prosaic and analytical account, and one which makes the event described extremely difficult to fit into the categories of 'religious' or 'spiritual' experience. This was no 'inaugural vision', such as the prophets of Israel underwent. There was no sense of awe at the realization of the presence of the divine being, such as Isaiah felt; no ecstatic experience like that of Jeremiah; no voice from heaven accompanying the descent of the holy spirit as Christian tradition represents happening in the case of Jesus; no archangel as in the case of Muhammad, coming down to announce 'Thou art God's apostle', making the chosen one to fall upon his knees and tremble. The account given in a Pāli Sutta called *Discourse on the Ariyan Quest*[1] is represented as being the Buddha's own version of the matter given years later to some of his disciples at Shravasti. Having described his wanderings in search of the truth, he tells them how in due course he arrived at Uruvela (the ancient name for the place that has become known as Bodh-Gaya). 'There I saw a delightful stretch of land and a lovely woodland grove, and a clear flowing river with a delightful ford, and a village for support nearby.' Seeing what a suitable place this was for earnest and strenuous meditation, he sat down there.[2] What follows is an account of the intellectual penetration into the nature of the human situation which the Buddha then achieved, in which the

---

* *Ficus religiosus*, the sacred tree of India. The tradition that it was beneath such a tree that Gotama enlightenment gained has no strong historical foundation. See the article, 'Bodhi-tree' by T. O. Ling, in A Dictionary of Comparative Religion ed. by S. O. F. Brandon, (1970) p. 145.

notion of the individual 'self' (*atman*) is seen as the root of mankind's troubles (see chapter 6, p. 115).

DISCOVERY BASED ON ANALYSIS

Another early Buddhist text from the same collection describes in rather more detail the process by which the Buddha became 'awakened' to the truth. This consisted first of his entry into and progress through four successively deeper stages of meditation; the emphasis here lies upon the purification of the mind which was necessary. In this way he is said to have achieved concentration, equanimity and dispassion. There then followed three further stages, one in each of the three watches of the night. First, says the Buddha, 'with the mind composed, quite purified, quite clarified, without blemish, without defilement ... I directed my mind to the knowledge and recollection of my former habitations [existences].' In the second watch of the night, 'with the mind composed ... I directed my mind to the knowledge of the passing hence and the arising of beings', that is, to the working of the law of Karma, or moral retribution. 'I comprehended that beings are mean, excellent, comely, ugly, well-destined, ill-going, according to the consequences of their deeds.' Finally, in the third watch, he discovered the four noble truths concerning the human situation. 'I understood it as it really is: suffering, the arising of suffering, the stopping of suffering, and the course leading to the stopping of suffering.' Knowing this, he says, his mind became free. 'In freedom the knowledge came to be: I am freed; and I comprehended: Destroyed is birth, brought to a close is the Brahma-faring, done is what was to be done, there is no more of being thus. This was the third knowledge attained by me in the last watch of the night; ignorance was dispelled, knowledge arose, darkness was dispelled, light arose even as I abided diligent, ardent, self-resolute.'[3]

In yet other versions of these events is was the theory of 'Conditioned Origination' (*Paṭicca Samuppāda*) which the Buddha is said to have discovered during this critical night, and so became fully 'awakened' to the truth of human existence. This is a basic Buddhist doctrine which has become best known, perhaps, through its pictorial representation, particularly in Tibetan art, as the Wheel of Existence. In its verbal form it is found, with slight differences, in various places in early Buddhist literature. It is regarded as so fundamental a truth that it is represented as being the vital discovery made by all 'Buddhas'. Its discovery by a former Buddha, Vipassi, is described in the *Mahāpadāna Sutta.*[4] We are told that he was meditating in seclusion (at the point in his life story which Gotama had reached in his when he sat down on the bank of the Nairanjana river), and reflected thus: 'Verily this world has fallen upon trouble; one is born, and grows old, and dies, and falls from one state, and springs up in another. And from this suffering, moreover, no one knows of any way of escape, even from decay and death. When shall a way of escape from this suffering be made known, from decay and from death?'[5] He then went on to seek an answer to the question: What is the antecedent cause or condition of decay and dying? The answer he reached was that birth was the antecedent cause. What then, he asked, conditions birth? The answer to this, he found, was that 'becoming' conditions birth. Similarly, the antecedent cause was sought for each link in the chain of causation: becoming was conditioned by the attitude and activity of 'grasping'; grasping arose out of craving; craving out of feeling; feeling out of sense-contact; sense-contact out of the six-fold field of the senses;[6] the six-fold field of the senses arose out of the physical body, or 'name and form'; and the physical body is conditioned by, or arises out of cognition. At this point the recession ends in the particular text; elsewhere in Buddhist literature there are two more antecedent causes: the impulses, and ignorance.

The significance of this relentlessly pursued analysis is found when the series is reversed, and it is affirmed that when ignorance ceases, the impulses cease; when the impulses cease, cognition ceases; and so on, to the final stage—when birth (*i.e.*, rebirth) ceases, then 'decay and dying, grief, lamentation, ill, sorrow and despair cease'. As D. L. Snellgrove has commented, 'Attempts have been made to discover a logical sequence of ideas from this ill-sorted list, both by early commentators and by European scholars. But no general relationship between the terms can be found which will relate in the same manner any two consecutive terms. The list is best understood as it is first presented to us, as a spontaneous searching back and back into the origins of death and rebirth.'[7] A further difficulty lies in the fact that the English translations of the various terms are in some cases little more than attempts to put a name to what, even in the original, is somewhat obscure. But although we may have to be content with an imperfect understanding of the series itself, we can at any rate perceive the nature of the Buddha's approach to the problem of the human condition. It was based on analytical reasoning; what was discovered was discovered by strenuous effort of the mind. But it was in the Buddhist view no 'ordinary' mind which put forth this almost super-human effort of understanding; it was essentially a mind purified, calmed, and cooled from all evil passion. It would be incorrect to say that this was *merely* an intellectual approach, for moral values obviously play a primary and absolutely indispensable part, too. Even so, in the last resort, Buddhist wisdom is to be regarded as a discovery of the human mind; it is in no sense a revelation to Gotama given by a non-human spirit or divine being.

There are a number of ways in which the Buddha's analysis of human existence can be set out. There is, as we have seen, the twelvefold causal chain, or circle of causes and effects. There is also the presentation of the essentials in the form of the 'four noble truths'. Again, there is a well-known and frequently used characterization of all life in terms of the 'three marks of existence—suffering, impermanence and non-individuality. In every case the starting-point, the datum, is *dukkha*, the suffering, pain or grief which is the common lot of *all living beings*. For the Buddha, this is what constituted the problem to be solved; it was from here that all his thinking started and it was to the curing of this condition that all his effort was directed.

THE THREE MARKS OF EXISTENCE

Of the three 'marks' or characteristics of existence the first, then, is suffering; this is the most immediately obvious of the three, and possibly the one which is most readily comprehended. According to the Buddhist view, however, even this aspect of existence is not always fully apparent; men may be deluded by temporary and superficial experiences of pleasure into thinking that through the pursuit of selfish interests, pleasure can be a permanent possession. The teaching of the Buddha consisted in showing how the life of the unenlightened individual was permeated by suffering. This is emphasized in the exposition of the first of the 'four noble truths', the truth concerning suffering: 'Birth is suffering (*dukkha*), decay is suffering, death is suffering; sorrow, lamentation, pain, grief and despair are suffering.' This means, as a modern Buddhist writer comments, 'that all forms of existence whatsoever are unsatisfactory and subject to suffering (*dukkha*)'.[8] The same writer adds that this does not refer only to actual suffering—suffering which is felt as such, but 'in consequence of the universal law of impermanency, all the phenomena of existence whatsoever, even the sublimest states of existence; are subject to change and dissolution, and hence are miserable and unsatisfactory: and that thus, without exception, they all contain in themselves the germ of suffering'.[9]

The second mark or characteristic of existence is *anicca*, or impermanence. 'Impermanency of things is the rising, passing and changing of things, or the disappearance of things that have become or arisen. The meaning is that these things never persist in the same way, but that they are vanishing and dissolving from moment to moment.'[10] At the physical level continual flux is not difficult to discern: the human body is a continual flowing in and out of various substances; dead skin is constantly being removed and new skin forms; old cells are worn out and replaced by new cells; the waste products of the body's metabolism are disposed of in various ways. What is more, the physical pattern or structure is itself subject to constant, though slower, change: from infancy to childhood, through youth and adolescence to maturity, and then on into middle and old age, the physical size and shape of the components which go by the name of John Smith do not remain the same for long. According to Buddhist thought, even more impermanent are states of mind or consciousness. But this all-pervading impermanency may not always be discerned; the workings of 'commonsense' may serve to obscure it. 'The characteristic of impermanence does not become apparent because, when rise and fall are not given attention, it is concealed by continuity.... However, when continuity is disrupted by discerning rise and fall, the characteristic of impermanence becomes apparent in its true nature.'[11]

Related to this second mark of existence, according to the Buddha, is the third—*anattā*: that the idea of a permanent, unchanging ego as the basis of individual personality is a fiction. Nevertheless, it is this idea that there is a permanent ego whose interests must be served and protected, and whose power must be magnified, which ensures that suffering will continue to characterize existence.

THE FOUR NOBLE TRUTHS

The other method used by the Buddha in setting forth his analysis of the human situation was that of the four noble truths. Here again, the universal fact of suffering, or the unsatisfactoriness of life, its pain, its *malaise*, its inherent 'ill'-ness, is the starting-point. This is the first noble truth. The second identifies what is, so to speak, the motive power which keeps this universal suffering going, the fuel which prevents the fire from going out, and that is craving or desire. This same factor has occurred in another connection: it is one of the twelve links in the chain of conditioned origination which has already been mentioned. In that context it is seen as arising out of feeling, and in its turn giving rise to the activity of selfish 'grasping'. The third noble truth concerns cessation (*nirodha*), and it is that the cessation of suffering is a consequence of the cessation of craving. The word used in this connection—*nirodha*—is a synonym of *nibbāna* (in Sanskrit, *nirvāna*), the best-known name for the goal which Buddhist teaching has in view. *Nirvāna* is the cessation of all evil passion, and because evil passion is regarded in Buddhist thought as a kind of fever, its cessation may be thought of as a 'cooling' after fever, a recovery of health. In fact, in the Buddha's time the associated adjective *nibbuta* seems to have been an everyday term to describe one who is well again after an illness. It is evident from this that the original Buddhist goal, *nirvāna*, was the restoration of healthy conditions of life *here and now*, rather than in some remote and transcendent realm beyond this life. It will be seen that the Buddhist way is essentially a therapy. But the subject of the cure is not the individual. It would be more accurate to say that individualism is the disease for which a cure is needed. To this point we shall return later.

The fourth noble truth was the declaration that a way existed through which the cure might be achieved; this was the way delineated by the Buddha, which consisted of morality, meditation and the attainment of wisdom. These three constituents of the Buddhist way are all essential. There is an amplified description of the way in terms of eight rather than three constituent features. In this, the single item 'morality' becomes right speech, right bodily action, and right means of livelihood.[12]

This insistence on morality, and the giving of specific guidance on morality, are wholly characteristic of the Buddha's teaching. Morality is not a secondary matter; in the prescription offered by the Buddha it is a *sine qua non*. And just as the single requirement, 'morality', was given fuller expression, in terms of the three major forms of moral conduct which have just been mentioned, so these three are also given fuller expression in other contexts. One of the most commonly used summaries of what moral living meant for Buddhists, from the earliest days, is the list of five precepts: to abstain from taking the life of any being; to abstain from stealing; from unlawful sexual intercourse; from speaking falsely; and from the use of drugs, including alcohol. These are the basic moral precepts for the whole of human society, as we shall see in connection with actual societies or civilizations of Asia which reckon themselves to be Buddhist. For members of the professional order, the *Sangha* there is a more elaborate code of morality (see chapter 8, note 23) but this, with its two hundred and seventy or so rules, is also an elaboration of those same basic principles of morality, and has the same aim and intention as the five precepts.

INDIVIDUALITY AND THE HUMAN *MALAISE*

In its simplest form, the intention of Buddhist morality can be said to be the undermining, erosion or withering of the idea of one's own permanent individuality. For each human being commonly feels this to be supremely important to him, and since it was this attachment of importance to individuality which, in the Buddha's view, was the root of human *malaise*, its destruction was the essential feature in the cure of that *malaise*. Of the three characteristic marks of existence, suffering, impermanence, and the fictional quality of the ego, the first two are relatively easy to comprehend, even if they are not accepted; in any case, Buddhism shares them to some extent with other systems of thought. But the third, the assertion that the individual ego is a pure fiction or illusion, is one which will ordinarily be found more difficult to accept because it seems to run counter to commonsense. It is, moreover, an assertion which Buddhism does not share with any other system of the time; indeed it belongs almost wholly and uniquely to early Buddhism, at least until recent times and the development of modern psychological theory. It was the one feature of Buddhism which other Indian philosophers regarded as its characteristic *par excellence* for they labeled it 'the no-soul doctrine' (*nairyatmavāda*).

MORALITY, MEDITATION AND WISDOM

Since this popular notion of a permanent individual ego has so firm a hold generally, special measures are required to deal with it. These are connected with the Buddhist practice of meditation. The purpose of this, in the earliest period at least, seems to have been to enable others to follow the Buddha along the path of release from the confined consciousness of being an individual, an ego, to consciousness of a wider, fuller kind. Step by step with meditational practices aimed at the cooling down of the passions which kept the notion of the ego alive went the practice of intellectual analysis of human existence. One 'practiced' the analysis which the Buddha had set forth, even though at first it was very difficult. With continual practice, accompanied by constant moral purification, came a degree of mastery of this way of seeing things. The moral purification was of necessity impersonal, since it was the notion of individuality which was being dissolved; what was happening was described as the encouragement of morally good states of being (states which were, however, not confined to any one individual center of consciousness) and the discouragement of morally unwholesome states of being. It follows that meditation, in its intention and scope, ranged over a much wider area of being than the one encapsulated within one human body.

More than this concerning Buddhist meditation it is not appropriate or even profitable to say in the present context. It is hoped, however, that this will give the reader sufficient understanding of the general point of view and method of early Buddhism to enable him to decide to what extent and in what sense it was a religion.

When the practice had been faithfully followed then, there would follow, almost immediately in the case of some people, or more slowly in the case of others, that realization of the truth which the Buddha himself had first won. This was the third and final state of the Buddhist schema, after morality and meditation, and was characterized either as 'wisdom', or as the state of enlightenment, or liberation from the state of being bound to the ego-idea. The notion of the individual ego having been dissolved, with it inevitably disappeared the whole burden of individual *karma* or retribution and the prospect of the continually repeated experience of the sufferings of the individual ego. This, however, was only the negative aspect of the matter, the condition of ill from which human existence needed to be cured. There was also the positive aspect, the new, wider, fuller consciousness of being which was opened up when the walls of individualism were broken down. This was the new community, and without careful examination of what this entailed, any attempt to understand early Buddhism is bound to be unsuccessful. It is because some Western descriptions of early Buddhism have left out this social dimension that they have failed to make sense. We must examine the new community which Buddhism entailed very soon, but first, however, it is appropriate to consider the nature of the Buddhist analysis in relation to other systems of thought.

EARLY BUDDHIST DOCTRINE IN THE CONTEXT OF THE TIMES

One way of characterizing the Buddhist system is to say that it is a form of rationalism. 'By rejecting animism and ritualism and emphasizing a rational outlook which treats reality as a causally and functionally determined system of plural synergies (*saṃskaras*), the emergence of Buddhism marks an important event in the history of Indian thought. The most distinctive feature of Buddhist ethics is its freedom from theism, which leaves room for rationalism and rules out submission to some superhuman power controlling the world-process.'[13]

The 'rational outlook' which was certainly a very marked feature of early Buddhism had, as G. S. P. Misra's words imply, two aspects. On the one hand there was the rejection of dogmatic theistic presuppositions. On the other, there was the attempt to analyze, that is to reveal, the basic data of human existence. The Buddha himself is represented as making a clear distinction between these two contrasting attitudes: 'I am', he said 'an analyst, not a dogmatist.'[14] By dogmatist he meant one who made categorical statements which were to be accepted simply on the authority of the one who made them. The Buddha insisted that all propositions must be tested, including his own. The testing of these had to take the form of the living out of the disciplined life of morality, meditation and the systematic cultivation of insight. The propositions, as such, were not to become objects of attachment, any more than anything else in life, but were to be regarded simply as pointers or guides.

One of the most important characteristics of the Buddha's teaching, therefore, was the attitude of non-acceptance of traditional orthodoxy of any kind and, instead, a very marked 'intellectualism' as Max Weber called it.[15] This differentiates Buddhism from the orthodox theistic religion of the brahmans of his day, but it does not, of course, mark off the Buddha's teaching in any distinct way from the teachings of other *shramanas*, who likewise rejected traditional orthodoxy. What most clearly differentiated the Buddha's teaching from theirs was his theory of the absolute impermanence of all things (*anitya*) and, above all, his denial of permanent individuality (*anattā*). The Jains, for instance, reacted very strongly to the latter aspect of the Buddha's teaching; it was, they said, a 'pernicious view'.[16]

On the other hand, the Buddha's insistence on the real possibility of human choice and freedom of action, and his opposition to fatalism differentiate his teaching from that of the Ajivakas. His rejection of asceticism, and his constant avowal of the importance of the middle way between it and hedonism mark his teaching off from that of the Jains and the Ajivakas (see pp. 99 ff.) on the one hand, and the materialists, the Lokayatas (see p. 102) on the other.

It is not necessary to go farther in indicating the general outlines of the Buddha's teaching, and in pointing to those features of it which are indisputable and unmistakable. The main purpose has been to show, first, that the teaching of the Buddha cannot justifiably be described as 'religious', if by that we mean having reference to or depending on belief in any superhuman being or spirit. Such beliefs are not affirmed in the teaching of the Buddha, nor are they seen to be a necessary part of his scheme of thought. How is this view of life to be characterized, if not as a religion? We are left with only one possibility. In its original form Buddhism is best described as a theory of existence, an ideology, or possibly as a philosophy. But even in the simplest form known to us, it is, by its own terms of reference, not a *personal* philosophy. This point is important, and calls for a little elaboration.

EARLY BUDDHISM AS A PSYCHO-SOCIAL PHILOSOPHY

The Buddha, it was acknowledged in the early Buddhist tradition, was a *shramaṇa*. The nearest equivalent which modern English can give us is, perhaps, 'philosopher', although this is not altogether satisfactory, as the basic meaning of the word, which its usage preserves, is 'one who strives, or labors hard'. Karl Marx observed that 'The philosophers have only interpreted the world, in various ways; the point, however, is to change it',[17] and one imagines that the Buddha would have agreed with the observation. What is certain, on the other hand, is that the Buddha was not regarded by the earliest generation of Buddhists as a superhuman figure of any kind. He had no religious role, such as that of the chosen revealer of divine truth, nor was he regarded by the early Buddhists as in any sense a superhuman savior. As a modern Buddhist writer puts it 'The Buddha exhorts his followers to depend on themselves for their deliverance, since both defilement and purity depend on oneself. One cannot directly purify or defile another. Clarifying his relationship with his followers and emphasizing the importance of self-reliance and individual striving the Buddha plainly states: You yourselves should make the exertion. The *Tathāgatas* are only teachers (*Dhammapada*, v. 276).'[18] The Buddha, or *Tathāgata*, does not

139

direct the attention of his disciples away from himself to some higher, holier being; he directs their attention to human nature, with which he is concerned and with which they, too, must be concerned. His words are in the spirit of the philosopher, whose attention is upon the human condition, and the right ordering of human affairs. As the son of the leading citizen of Kapilavastu, Gotama had the equality of status which enabled him throughout his long public life to meet with the kings of northern India on equal terms, but he did so also as one whose philosophy was of particular interest to those who dealt with the ordering of human affairs. The city with its royal court was the characteristic locus for his teaching activities. When he died we are told that he was honored and his mortal remains disposed of after the manner of a king. If one asked whether the Buddha had the greater affinity with the priest or with the king, and whether it was to religion or to secular affairs that his characteristic concerns were closer, there can be no doubt about the answers which would have to be given.

The rigorously logical and scientific method of the discourses which are preserved in the Pāli Canon has been fully and competently expounded by other writers.[19] G. S. P. Misra concludes his account of the matter with these words: 'It can truly be said that Buddhism appeared in the intellectual arena as a harbinger of a new trend in the realm of thinking. The empirical and analytical outlook of the Buddhists led them to found a system of psychology and logic which had great influence on Indian thought as a whole.'[20] The early Buddhist period in India was, writes A. K. Warder, 'one of the supreme ages of rationalism in human history', and he adds that 'we have not yet outlived its repercussions'.[21]

This, then, was the new wisdom; it can hardly be called a religion. What has to be asked, therefore, is why, before many centuries had passed, it had begun to assume the characteristics of a religion (in the terms in which religion has been defined in chapter 1), with the result that in modern Asia it is unequivocally as a religion that Buddhism appears in the analyses of social scientists.

It is possible, even from what has been discovered so far in the course of our investigation, to see how this came about. The Buddha was not hostile to the religious ideas and practices of the ordinary people. He did not endorse these ideas and practices, but neither did he, in general, oppose them. From his time and throughout the subsequent history of the tradition, the Buddhist attitude appears to have been based, whether consciously or not, on the recognition that a man's view of the world can only be modified, not radically changed. That is all that can be expected immediately, and in the short run. In the long run it is possible that a radical shift of viewpoint may take place, but with the generality of men it will be a very long run before this happens. A distinction is sometimes made between men of traditional, or pre-industrial, societies and men of modern, industrialized ones in terms of a contrast between irrationality and rationality. It is assumed that in pre-industrial societies the processes of thought are a-rational or non-rational, or even, it has been suggested, follow a different kind of rationality from the one characteristic of men of Westernized, industrial society. But, as Malinowski pointed out with reference to the rationality of primitive people, 'a moment's reflection is sufficient to show that no art or craft however primitive could have been invented or maintained, no organized form of hunting, fishing, tilling or search for food could be carried out without the careful observation of natural processes and a firm belief in its regularity, without the power of reasoning and without confidence in the power of reason; that is without the rudiments of science.'[22] The process of reasoning will in principle be the same for men of primitive and of more advanced societies; in both cases it will be a systematic tracing out of causal sequences. The significant difference between the two will be in the premises from which each respectively starts. Given certain premises, the logical development will be one line of thought; given different premises, it will be another. What, therefore, distinguishes one man's world-view from another's is not necessarily the rationality or irrationality of his processes of thought but the premises from which his reflections upon the world begin. They are usually bequeathed to him in a general way by his culture; they may be determined more particularly by his economic circumstances, or perhaps by his social status, or his role-relationships, and so on. If the conditioning factors are changed, then it is conceivable that a man will abandon one premise and adopt another. The rationality of a man when he is a wholehearted Protestant may not differ in any significant way from his rationality when he decides to convert and become a Catholic; what is likely to have happened is that he has come to adopt a different premise as the basis for his reasoning about the world and about his part in the whole scheme of things. Rationality, remaining constant throughout, may have a part to play in convincing him that the explanatory value of a process of reasoning based on premise A is superior to the explanatory value of the process which is based on premise B. He may therefore change his premise, from B to A. Or the change may be due to rational choices less evident and conscious, to more indirect and unconscious influences, like a change in any of the other determining factors which have been mentioned—economic or social status, role-relationships, and so on.

The Buddhist method appears to have been not to make a frontal attack on the premise which was responsible for a man's world-view. The approach was rather one or other of the two which have been outlined: that is to say, either the use of rational means to persuade men to alter their premises, by a demonstration of the evidently superior explanatory value of basing thought on premise A rather than premise B; or by conditioning them through a new regime of life. In this latter case, men were to adopt the new way of life because of certain evident, inherent attractions which it had for them. At this stage, however, the premises on which they based their world-view were still those, let us say, of the artisan of a north Indian city in the sixth century BC. Buddhist monks do not all become masters of the Buddha's philosophy overnight, by the act of entering the Order. But in the course of following out the day-to-day and year-to-year requirements of life in the Buddhist Order, there ensues for such monks a slow and subtle shift in their view of the world. The adoption of this kind of policy might seem to leave Buddhism open to too great a danger of corruption. To some observers this is how it has seemed; for Buddhism has been tolerant, and has countenanced beliefs and practices which are fundamentally alien to its own central affirmations, beliefs, for instance of a polytheistic nature. Nevertheless, the principle has never altogether been lost sight of, that the Buddhist world-view is not dependent in any way upon belief in a god or gods or upon practices associated with such beliefs.

The phrase 'Buddhist world-view' has just been used, but only in the sense of a general view of human life and of the human situation, and not in the more technical sense of a systematically worked-out cosmology or cosmic geography. Such a world-view can, however, be found in Buddhism as it developed after the lifetime of Gotama; to be more accurate, there were three main Buddhist variations of Indian cosmology.[23] In all of these the major features of general Indian cosmology appear. There are sufficient references in the discourses of the Buddha to suggest that he is to be regarded as making use of traditional ideas about cosmic geography, although sometimes in a light-hearted and sometimes in a noncommittal way. It certainly does not appear to be a subject which, in the view of the early tradition, he regarded as of sufficient importance to deserve serious attention, or the elaborate systematic formulation which it received later on, in the *Abhidhamma* literature,[24] produced mostly after the Buddha's death.

We are now nearer to being able to offer at least a tentative answer to the question which was raised at the outset of this study: What is Buddhism? It will be evident that Buddhism is essentially *a theory of existence*. It is, however, a theory which consists of both diagnosis (of the human *malaise*) and prescription for a cure. Since the practical steps which need to be taken to put the prescription into effect are also part of Buddhism, it is certainly more than a theory. And it is more than a theory of *human* existence only, since the whole of life, human and non-human, comes within the range of its scrutiny and analysis. It is a theory of existence which is principally characterized and distinguished from other theories by the fact that it discountenances and discourages the concept of the individual, and regards the boundaries between one so-called 'individual' and others as artificial. Moreover, it is a theory of existence which is in no way dependent on the idea of a divine revelation to which, ultimately, all men must submit in faith. Although it is a view of life which the Buddha is said to have gained at his enlightenment, that event is not thought of as having been brought about by some supra-human or supra-natural power; nor is it thought of as being beyond the ability of any other human being to achieve. True, the achievement does not come through intellectual effort alone; it presupposes great moral striving and purification, but this, too, is something which men are regarded as able to achieve without needing to resort to supernatural aid.

Buddhism is, therefore, in a certain sense, secular. It is certainly secular, if the sacred is defined in theistic terms, for neither the Buddhist diagnosis, or the putting into effect of the Buddhist prescription—morality and meditation—is in any way dependent on belief in a god or gods, or in a personal power of any kind, and Buddhism does not necessarily or in principle entail any practices of a traditional religious kind, cultic or ritualistic, such as sacrifices to the gods, reading the holy scriptures, sacred meals, prayers and so on. Indeed, in such matters, it was in origin anti-religious if anything. In matters of dogma it was non-theistic, except in the sense that the gods were accepted as part of the cosmic scenery; but they were also regarded as having no ultimate priority or significance. However, if the new wisdom had a certain relative secularity it was not secular in an absolute sense, for there appears to have been, from the earliest stage that can be identified, an awareness of a transcendental dimension, a sense of that which is sacred, although it is not expressed in terms of belief in a god. There is, in the early formulation of Buddhist teaching, a sense of necessary loyalty to that which transcends immediate personal gain or satisfaction, to values which lie beyond the interests of human individuals or the interests of the contemporary societies and political organizations of India in the sixth century BC. In broad terms, the new wisdom consisted of an invitation to men, even an appeal to them, to discover and recognize that the structure of being was different from what was commonly supposed, and that the human individual was *not* the key concept to the understanding of the human situation. It was an appeal also to realize this in the actual reorganization of human affairs, a reorganization directed towards a new, non-individualistic society. It is this aspect of early Buddhism which has often been ignored in modern, Western accounts, and it is to this, the social dimension of Buddhism, that we must now turn our attention.

8   The New Society

In the words of a great Indian of modern times, Rabindranath Tagore, the way of the Buddha is 'the elimination of all limits of love', it is 'the sublimation of self in a truth which is love itself'.[1] Tagore has, in these words, identified the essence of what has come to be called Buddhism. For Buddhism is not, as so many Westerners have imagined, a private cult of escape from the real world. The word 'imagined' is used deliberately because such a view of Buddhism can proceed only from the exercise of the imagination, not from knowledge of the Buddha's teaching, or of the nature of the Buddhist community, the *Sangha*, or of Buddhist history. To speak of Buddhism as something concerned with the private salvation of the individual soul is to ignore entirely the basic Buddhist repudiation of the notion of the individual soul. The teaching of the Buddha was not concerned with the private destiny of the individual, but with something much wider, the whole realm of sentient being, the whole of consciousness. This inevitably entailed a concern with social and political matters, and these receive a large share of attention in the teaching of the Buddha as it is represented in the Pāli texts. Moreover, as we have seen, the context of the Buddha's own spiritual quest was the increasing individualism which accompanied the growth of cities and monarchies, and the problems attendant upon this growth. To attempt to understand Buddhism apart from its social dimension is futile. Individualism places limits on love, and if Buddhism is an attempt to deal with what it sees as the disease of individualism, and is primarily a method of eliminating these limits, as Tagore realized, then it will entail a concern with the social and political dimension.

The primary form which this process takes is the life of the Buddhist community, the *Sangha*. The members of this community were in India called *bhikkhus* (Pāli) or *bhikshus* (Sanskrit). In Western languages they are most usually referred to as 'monks' or the equivalent, and the *ārāmas*, or local institutions which provide the physical setting for their common life are often

145

referred to as 'monasteries'. But this terminology, borrowed from European practice, is misleading.[2] The word 'monk', derived from the word *monachus*, 'originally meant a religious hermit or solitary'; later on it came to mean 'a member of a community or brotherhood living apart from the world'.[3] In neither of these senses can the word be applied appropriately to a member of the Buddhist *Sangha*.

The word *bhikkhu* means, literally, a 'sharesman', that is, one who receives a share of something. The Buddhist *bhikkhus* were, in fact, a special case of what had been a common feature of Indian civilization from a very early period. In general, as Sukumar Dutt has pointed out, the almsman or sharesman in India is 'differentiated from an ordinary beggar by the sacramental character of his begging. His begging is not just a means of subsistence but an outward token'[4]—an outward token of his renunciation of private or personal sources of livelihood or ownership of wealth, and his dependence instead on the 'common wealth', the public resources of the society in which he lives. Certainly, the Buddhist 'sharesman', has not contracted out of society. The life he leads and the goal he seeks is not for his own private benefit, for this would be directly contrary to the Buddhist repudiation of individualism. By being what he is and by following the life he does, society will benefit. The nature of the role-relationship between the *bhikkhu* and the householders clearly demonstrates that the Buddhist professional is integrally involved in society.

The 'share' which the *bhikkhu* received and which gave him his name was, primarily, the portion of food which was set aside for him by those householders who supported him. But it was more than this that he received; the share of food was representative of other things—the robes he wore, the shelter in which he lived, and the other material necessities of life, all of which were provided by the lay-people of the neighborhood. His acceptance of these things from the 'common wealth' so to speak, was a symbol of his own renunciation of private property. In return the Buddhist *bhikkhus* had important contributions to make to the common life of society, as we shall see. These were not material or economic contributions but they were sufficiently important for the *bhikkhus* to be able to accept the material

The New Society

support which they were offered as something which was their proper 'share'. If what they received is sometimes referred to as 'alms', it must be remembered that these were offered in a spirit of deference and gratitude; the *bhikkhus* were not, and are not, 'beggars' in any sense of the word. The *bhikkhu* was certainly *not*, therefore, someone who lived apart from the world, like the Christian monk. One of the important achievements of early Buddhism was that it developed a new context for the spiritual quest. Traditionally in India, the search for salvation from the evils of human existence meant a life of solitude. For the Buddhist it meant a life in the community. For a time, however, in the earliest period of Buddhist history, the old idea seems to have survived. So strong a hold did the Indian tradition of solitude have that even among Buddhists there were those who tried to practice the Buddha's teaching by the old method and, as an ancient text puts it, 'fare lonely as rhinoceros'.[5] But it was among the Buddhists that there soon emerged, for the first time in Indian history, an ordered community of those who were seeking for salvation from the human *malaise* as they saw it.

THE BEGINNINGS OF THE BUDDHIST ORDER

The *reasons* for having an ordered community, organized in local settlements, in close touch with the neighborhood, are to be found in the nature of the new wisdom itself. The *occasion* for the actual coming into existence of such organized local settlements was, as it happens, a phenomenon peculiar to ancient India. We shall look at each of these aspects in turn.

The reason for the Buddhist community life is inherent in the nature of the Buddha's teaching. We have seen that this teaching consists of diagnosis and prescription: diagnosis of the human *malaise* as consisting essentially of the disease of individualism, and prescription for its cure as consisting primarily of the undermining or erosion of the notion that individuality is something permanent and of great importance. It is in the life of the *Sangha* that the prescription can most effectively be applied. Here is the community of being which comes into existence when the walls of individuality are completely and permanently broken down. And here, too, are found the optimum conditions for those

147

who are seeking to achieve that state of life and consciousness where individuality is no more, but who have not yet arrived at that state.

The process of meditation which is prescribed in the early texts gives something of a glimpse of the community of consciousness which was aimed at in the *Sangha*.[6] The method was one which began from the recognition that, in its normal state, the mind, and particularly the surface of the mind, is constantly being fretted and distracted; it is in a state of continual upheaval, like the surface of the sea, tossed into countless waves by the buffeting of the wind. The first stage of meditation, or the first *jhāna*, to give it its technical name, is the calming of the mind by detaching it from the bombardment of the senses, and from discursive thinking. This makes possible the second stage in the process, namely concentration: that is, the concentration of the consciousness upon one point. When this has been achieved, and only then, the next stage can begin, the stage of experiencing clarity and equanimity. Consciousness, thus purified and calmed, is then able to expand, and the experience becomes that of 'unbounded space'. The final stages of the process do not concern us here. What is of interest at this point is the sequence: a narrowing down of consciousness, followed by expansion. The underlying theory seems to be that when consciousness, normally restless, wild or even uncontrollable, is brought to a single point, it can then be dealt with effectively (like the bringing under control and harnessing of a wild horse). Thus controlled, by concentration, it then begins to exhibit the pure qualities which are always waiting to be manifested, namely joy and equanimity. In this way the concentration of consciousness produces, of itself, a subsequent broadening out into unbounded dimensions of the inherent qualities which are now given their rightful place.

Now, it is evident that the process of meditation carried on by more than one 'individual' will begin, in each case, from a state where each is conscious of a multiplicity of sense objects and desires, and that it will lead to a state where all are sharing in the same consciousness of joy and equanimity, which is infinite and the same for all. When the impurities have been removed, then there can be a fusion. Incidentally, this raises the question of the Buddhist view of the fundamental moral nature of man. In

Buddhist philosophy, human nature is seen as fundamentally good rather than evil. The discipline which the life of the *bhikkhu* entails is likened by the Buddha to the process of refining gold. Stage by stage impurities are purged away: first the coarse dust and sand, gravel and grit; then the finer grit, then the trifling impurities like the very fine sand and dust. At last 'the gold-dust alone remains', and this is placed in the crucible and melted together, until it can be run out of the crucible. 'Then that gold is melted, molten, flawless, done with, its impurities strained off. It is pliable, workable, glistening, no longer brittle; it is capable of perfect workmanship... Just in the same way in a monk who is given to developing the higher consciousness there are gross impurities of deed, word and thought.' These, too, are gradually purged out, first the coarser impurities, and then the finer, subtler impurities, until there comes a time when all this dross has been removed and the basic pure state of consciousness is reached.[7] According to the Buddha, this level of permanently pure consciousness is achieved when all the common distinctions and ways of differentiating human beings have been purged away— such considerations, for example, as family pride, national pride and personal reputation. 'We note here', writes a modern Buddhist, commenting on this passage, 'how our preoccupations with thoughts concerning our race or state are considered harmful to the concept of a common humanity.'[8]

The stage at which purified consciousness begins to broaden out has also a social structure: this is the life of the *Sangha*. The experience of new purified consciousness, beginning with the experience of the Buddha, is, in this theory, to expand continually through human society in the form of the new community, the *Sangha*. Moreover, it is not only that the *Sangha* provides the right conditions for the practice of meditation—the restructuring of consciousness along non-individualistic lines; it also provides the maximum facilities for continued conditioning of consciousness away from individualism in all the ordinary, everyday actions of life. Both Buddhist meditation and Buddhist ethics have the same end in view.

This can be seen in connection with the ownership of property. One who becomes a member of the *Sangha* ceases to own any private property whatsoever. This has been a feature of *Sangha* life from the earliest times. Even those few articles of personal use, the robe, the alms-bowl and one or two other requisites, were in theory vested in the *Sangha*, and made available for the use of its members.[9]

However, it is interesting to notice that while the *Sangha* was, from a juristic point of view, the corporate person in whom property was vested, and while no *bhikkhu* had legal property rights, nevertheless, as K. N. Jayatilleke pointed out, 'some rights such as the right to life, to free speech, to personal freedom, etc., cluster round the notion of individual personality'.[10] He acknowledged that this would seem to be an inconsistency, for the doctrine of *anattā* would appear to be incompatible with the notion of personal responsibility. But since the psycho-physical processes of human life maintain a relative and temporary 'individuality', it is useful to distinguish one of these relatively individual series of processes from another, and to refer to each by the term 'person'. Where the Buddhist analysis differs from most other views of human nature is in denying any absolute and permanent substratum, 'soul', or 'person', in these temporary psycho-physical processes. In the Buddhist view of things it seems that the concept of individuality which is primarily and most emphatically denied is that of the private-property-owning individual. This is a practical, institutional expression of the basic doctrine that greed or grasping (*taṇhā*) is the root of human ills.

The *Sangha*, therefore, provides the environment in which a new dimension of consciousness becomes possible as a result of the denial, not only in theory but also in practice, of the idea of absolute and permanent individuality.

In the earliest period of Buddhist history the *Sangha* seems to have existed as a wandering sect, a movement with which a man identified himself with the minimum of formal ceremony, 'a unitary organization of monks hailing from all quarters irrespective of regional provenance'.[11] If European terms are to be used at all, such a wandering brotherhood was more like an order of friars than of monks. But this very fluid stage of its history seems to have been brief and transitional. The nature of the doctrine combined with historical circumstances soon resulted in the development of settled, local communities of *bhikkhus*. We have already seen that it was necessary in the conditions which prevail in the monsoon period in India for wandering sects of all kinds to seek shelter during the rainy season (see chapter 5, p. 84). But where Jains, Brahmanical wanderers, and other such schools neither required nor (in the case of the Jains) allowed any specially set apart 'retreat-houses' or lodgings in which all the members of the school in a given locality were to reside together for the period of the rains, in the case of the Buddhists it was precisely this which came to be prescribed. 'The Buddhist idea of rain-retreat seems to have been not to live [just] anywhere, or alone and companionless, or in promiscuous company, but to settle in a congregation of fellow-monks.'[12] The fact that this was the practice of no other sect of *shramanas* may be connected with the other feature which was unique to the Buddhist order—their adherence to the doctrine of *anattā*, or non-individuality. Perhaps the local settled communities were bound to have come into existence, the Buddhist view of life being what it was. Nevertheless, it happened that historically it was a particular feature of Indian life which precipitated the matter, and provided the actual occasion for the formation of local communities.

It is noteworthy that these were not established in remote places, in the depths of the forest and far from the busy centers of travel and trade and government; this was the environment which Brahmanical ascetics sought,[13] but not the Buddhists. The latter, on the contrary, established their typical settlements on the edge of a town or city, partly, as we have already seen, because it was from among the growing urban population of the time that the Buddhists found most of their recruits, and partly, too, because the size of the Buddhist communities required a substantial number of householders near enough to provide the necessary economic support. This, therefore, soon became the normal location for a Buddhist *ārāma*, as the local institutional settlement was called, although there was a minority of *bhikkhus*, of more conservative disposition, who preferred to have their dwellings in forest glades, and who were known by the general designation, *Aranyakas* (Forest-dwellers). They were in this way conforming to the more traditional Indian view of the proper setting for a life of meditation; but the majority of Buddhist *bhikkhus* was characterized by the more radical attitude, one which was more consistent with the special nature of Buddhist ideas, and which recognized that close proximity to the important centers of the world's business was where the communities belonged.[14]

THE POLITICAL AFFINITIES OF THE *SANGHA*

One point which is frequently emphasized in the early tradition is that the Buddha had firmly rejected the notion of authoritarian rule in the new community which he had brought into existence. The Buddhist *Sangha*, whatever else it might resemble, would not resemble a monarchy. The Buddha himself was not in any sense a personal ruler, nor was any member of the community to think of himself in this way after the Buddha's death: 'Surely, Ananda, should there be anyone who harbors the thought, "It is I who will lead the brotherhood", or, "The Order is dependent upon me", it is he who should lay down instructions in any matter concerning the Order. Now the *Tathāgata* [the Buddha], Ananda, thinks not that it is he who should lead the brotherhood, or that the Order is dependent on him. Why then should he leave instructions in any matter concerning the Order?'[15] The implication for the members is clear: 'Therefore, O Ananda, be ye lamps unto yourselves.... Hold fast to the *Dhamma* as a lamp.'[16]

In this respect the Buddhist community was perpetuating the tradition of the tribal republican *Sanghas* (see chapter 4, pp. 68 f.), which, 'knew nothing of personal rule' as S. Dutt points out; 'they deliberated and acted together, were communistic in their property- relationships, republican in their conduct of affairs and had the tribal council as their organ of Government.'[17]

As another recent and more specialist study of the tribal republics of this period observes 'each member of the assembly was called a *rājā* (ruler), but none had the individual power to mould the decisions of the assembly.'[18]

It is clear that the Buddhist community inherited certain forms and methods of organization from the tribal republics. The question which was raised earlier must now be considered more fully, namely, whether the Buddhist *Sangha* was simply a reproduction of the old tribal collective or *Sangha*, or whether it was a conscious and deliberate improvement on the older model, which was in the Buddha's day disappearing before the advance of the great monarchies, Koshala and Magadha. Was the Buddhist

Sangha organized in imitation of the older political *Sanghas* for no other reason than that the Buddhists were politically behind the times, or was it done, perhaps, in order to preserve something which was felt to be of value but which could be preserved in no other way (just as private enthusiasts in Britain today get together to preserve as a going concern some local steam railway)? On the other hand, was the Buddhist community organized as a new-style *Sangha*, one in which the defects which had made the old political model obsolete were corrected; was it a new and improved version which was being put forward as a serious contribution to political experimentation and development? Was it a version which would remedy, too, the weaknesses and disadvantages apparent in the monarchical system (just as, to continue the analogy, a reorganized and rationalized railway system of diesel locomotion might be seen as the most effective solution to the traffic and transportation problems of a country which is being slowly stifled by private motor cars)?[19]

The questions resolve into two main issues. The first concerns the internal government of the Buddhist community, the *Sangha*. The second concerns what form of government was regarded by the Buddha as desirable for society in general, outside the *Sangha*.

The answer to the first part of the question is relatively straightforward. The pattern which is represented as being laid down by the Buddha for the regulation of the affairs of the new community was one which has been loosely described as 'democratic'. Democracy is an ancient word, but as it is now understood, it is, of course, a political concept which emerged somewhat later in history and implies the existence of certain political institutions. The *Buddha-Sangha* has been described as democratic largely because there was no monarchical head, no authoritarian chain of command and responsibility, and because a recognized procedure existed for decision-making by the whole community corporately. Certainly every member of the *Sangha* was regarded as having equality of rights in any deliberations concerning the life of the community.

K. N. Jayatilleke has argued that 'even the cosmic perspective is for the Buddhist democratic, for any man of his own free will may aspire to and attain to the status of a Buddha'[20], and that democracy was of the essence of the early community. The

Sangha has been described, also, as a 'system of government formed by the *Bhikkhus*, for the *Bhikkhus* and of the *Bhikkhus*'[21], and therefore a democracy. But the principles of government in the *Sangha* differed from those of a modern democratic state in one important respect, which needs to be carefully considered.

The ideal for the government of the new community is described by the Buddha, as we have seen, in connection with the Vajjian confederacy. 'So long, O *bhikkhus*, as the brethren foregather oft, and frequent the formal meetings of their *Sangha*, *so long as they meet together in concord, and carry out in concord the duties of the Sangha* ... so long may the brethren be expected not to decline but to prosper.'[22] It is expressly stated that 'concord' or unanimity is essential for the proper functioning of the *Sangha*, otherwise its life will decline. The corpus of rulings on its life and organization and the conduct and discipline of its members, known as the *Vinaya-piṭaka*,[23] contains similar injunctions for the community.[24] The principle which seems to have been regarded as of supreme importance was that of the maintenance of unity of view within each local company or *Sangha*. For as soon as permanent local settlements had been developed each of these was regarded as a *Sangha* in itself, a complete microcosm, so to speak, of the whole *Sangha*. And while it was accepted that differences of opinion were likely to develop, what was regarded as of greatest importance was that each local fellowship, which provided the actual, day-to-day experience of common life, was to be a unity, undivided by any controversial issues. If controversy did arise—and it was recognized that it could and would—the method laid down for dealing with the situation was that the dissenting group should remove itself and form a new settlement.[25] This 'law of schism'[26], as it was called, was a matter of discussion at the second Buddhist Council, held at Vaishali a century after the Buddha's death; it was very important that this procedure should be agreed upon because the maintenance of the essential principle of unity in the *Sangha* depended on it. It was recognized that honest differences of opinion had to be allowed for, but not at the expense of the structural unity of the local *Sangha*. As Sukumar Dutt has put it, the unitary character of the local *Sangha* was 'the basic principle of its functioning'.[27] All other considerations were subordinate to this basic principle of local structural unity.

In view of what was said earlier concerning the *Sangha* as the necessary context for living the new life of non-individualism, it will be easily understood why unity was so important. It is this aspect of the *Sangha's* constitution, therefore, which, in the final analysis, distinguishes it from a democratic body. A democratic organization is one in which the majority opinion is honored and prevails. The advantage of this method is that, if it can be followed consistently, the formation of schismatic, dissenting groups is avoided; but the price is the subordination of minority views. The Buddhist method is one which allows minority views to be held, and not disregarded, but the price to be paid is the multiplication of bodies with different points of view. The Buddhists, like others, had to choose between the two principles; that the choice was a very difficult one to make is seen from the fact that the matter was not settled until a hundred years after the Buddha's decease. However, once a principle has been agreed upon, allowances can be made for the fact that certain advantages accruing from the opposite decision have been surrendered. In this case, what was surrendered was ideological solidarity. Other political and religious institutions faced with a similar choice have sometimes chosen the totalitarian way: formal organizational unity has been maintained at the expense of the rights of self-expression on the part of minority groups. The history of Catholicism in Europe, which is as much a matter of politics as of religion, demonstrates what ensues when total institutional unity is evaluated more highly than arrangements for the tolerance of dissent. Any group which threatens the formal unity of the total organization has to be regarded as something alien to the true nature of the organization itself; it is a sect, rather than true church. In the Buddhist case, the inevitability of sectarian differences has been acknowledged, with the result that Buddhism has not experienced the internecine wars of religion that have characterized some other traditions, where dissent or 'heresy' has been something to be stamped out.

This should not be taken to imply that the Buddhist *Sangha* recognized no canons or orthodoxy. The matter is represented as having been explicitly dealt with by the Buddha himself, who set out certain criteria by which authentic Buddhist doctrine could be recognized.[28]

In the matter of the relationship between the *Sangha* of the Vajjian confederacy and the Buddhist *Sangha*, it emerges that the latter was modeled very closely on the former. It is not properly described as democratic in the modern sense; its characteristics were those of the old tribal republic, in which unanimity among the assembled elders was the supreme requirement. Now, it is clear that where this was the underlying principle of government, lack of unanimity would produce dysfunction of the system and possibly its breakdown, more quickly than any other single factor; the Buddha implied as much in the observations he made on the prospects for the Vajjian confederacy's continued well-being.[29] Events showed that the Vajjian system was fallible. The reason adduced for this, in the Buddhist view, was the disease of individualism, which had now spread to the tribal republics, and was proving too much for the strength of republican solidarity. J. P. Sharma sees the collapse of the tribal republics, which took place soon after the Buddha's decease, as due to the intrusion of individualism. The old understanding was that no individual member of the republican assembly had the power to mould the decisions of the assembly; nevertheless, by the time that the Buddha was called upon to give an opinion on the prospects of the republican *Sanghas*, a situation had developed in which it is probable, says Sharma, 'that some councilors or leaders of the republic either wished to rise above the rest and become virtual rulers ... or that some preferred to betray the republic for their selfish interests, thus becoming lieutenants of a king. The latter could offer these betrayers substantial rewards either in the form of material gains or by entrusting them with important state offices which they could not expect while the republic continued and prospered.'[30] The downfall of the republics was thus closely connected with the spread of monarchy and of the spirit of individualism, or, as Sharma describes it, of 'personal ambition'.

If the *malaise* which had afflicted the tribal republic system could be identified as individualism, then the remedy for individualism could serve as the remedy, or as means of reviving the *Sangha* system—assuming that in all other respects it was worth restoring. That it was appears to be the assumption implicit in the organization of the early Buddhist Community as a *Sangha*. What was being said, in effect, was this: 'The tribal republican system of organization is preferable to monarchy, but lately it has been infected by the spread of individualism; this is the evil factor in the situation. Buddhist practice can remedy this evil, and so the *Sangha* system of solid organization can and will be restored. The *Sangha* system which is needed now is the new *Buddha-Sangha*.'

The Buddhist *Sangha* might be seen, then, in the context of the fifth century BC, as the prototype social organization of the future. But there were serious difficulties in the way of such a prescription for the welfare of human society. Between the prototype, even as it could be seen in existence here and there, and the transformation of the whole of human society into a universal *Sangha*, there was, so to speak, a large practicability gap. To organize what was still a relatively small sect or cult-association as a republican *Sangha* was one thing; to propose that this form of politico-social organization could, by means of the therapy which Buddhism offered, become once again the norm for Indian society as a whole was quite another. Such a proposal would, in the circumstances of the time have been entirely impracticable, for a number of reasons. There is evidence to suggest that they were fully appreciated by the Buddha or at least in early Buddhist tradition, and that an interim scheme was envisaged which would make the best of the existing situation and encourage the development of a political and social climate more favourable to the full adoption of Buddhist attitudes and principles.

The two major reasons against the idea of the whole of contemporary Indian society becoming a universal Buddhist *Sangha* were, first, the existence of powerful monarchies, and second, the unreadiness of the mass of the people for participation in the kind of society envisaged in Buddhist teaching. The Buddhist mission to society, if one may call it that, appears to have had both of these problems in view, and to have developed appropriate policies in each case.

THE BUDDHIST ATTITUDE TO THE COMMON PEOPLE

The common people, or, more precisely, 'the ordinary man', is referred to by a word which occurs with relative frequency throughout the Pāli literature—*puthujjana*. The basic meaning of *puthu* is 'widespread' and this meaning is carried into the usage of the word composed from it by the addition of *jana*, a person or a man. The word has thus been translated appropriately into English as 'the ordinary man', 'the common man' or 'the average man'.[31] From the various occurrences of the word in the early literature, it appears that the Buddha used it to refer to the generality of man distinct from brahmans and recluses.[32] It has to be remembered that the Buddha gives the word 'brahman' a new meaning, apart from its technical caste connotation. The priestly class who had in the Buddha's day appropriated the term had no special, innate right to it, according to the Buddha. A brahman is a brahman by character, and not merely by some hereditary right. In the conversations of the Buddha with brahmans the latter are often represented as being led by the course of the argument to admit this point. Perhaps some real brahmans of the Buddha's day did so, in fact. In any case it is clear that this was the Buddhist view of the matter. So 'brahmans and *shramaṇas*' becomes a phrase virtually equivalent in meaning to those who, from a Buddhist point of view, are genuinely in pursuit of the truth and of a righteous life. The generality of men who are thus distinguished from them are, in effect, the mass of mankind who are not members of the Buddhist community.

It is possible to construct from the references in the Pāli texts a fairly detailed picture of the average man, or, literally, man as he is commonly found, from the point of view of the Buddha, or of the early Buddhists.

The ordinary man, we are told, 'is addicted to pleasure', and is at the mercy of his senses.[33] He is enthralled by the eye with objects that charm, by the tongue with savors that charm, etc.[34] He follows his natural desires, 'uncontrolled in the six-fold sense sphere, and eats his fill with ravenous delight among the five sensual pleasures'.[35] He welcomes personal fame and praise but resents obscurity and blame.[36] He is easily provoked to deeds of a morally unwholesome kind; he will murder his own father or his mother, inflict wounds on a saintly man, and cause dissension within the Buddhist *Sangha*.[37] He is greedy[38] and lustful.[39] On the other hand, he resents any ill fortune; when afflicted with pain he is distressed and overcome with bewilderment about it;[40] he finds that those things on which he sets his hopes frequently turn out to be a disappointment;[41] he dislikes the sight of disease, or old age or death;[42] when old age comes upon him he mourns and pines and is tormented by sorrow,[43] and finally he goes to Purgatory.[44] All this is because he is lacking in wisdom, and in knowledge of the truth. Not only does he adhere to popular superstitions,[45] but he knows not, he sees not things as they really are,[46] he takes no account of those who are holy, those who are true, he does not comprehend which thing should and which things should not be attended to;[47] he knows nothing of the origination of compounded things, and so is not set free from the power of ill;[48] he fails to reflect adequately and to understand the experiences of life for what they really are.[49]

The fact that he is described in the singular should not be allowed to disguise from us that this is the Buddha's view of the mass of mankind. Such being the case, J. P. Sharma is justified in his conclusion that the Buddhist *Sangha*, like the Greek oligarchies, was based on a belief in the 'unwisdom of the multitude'.[50]

BUDDHIST SOCIAL ETHICS FOR THE LAYMAN

Such belief did not lead, however, in the Buddhist case at least, to an attitude of cynicism towards the multitude. Far from it: the common people have an important part in the Buddhist scheme of things, for their present condition is not accepted as permanent or final. Indeed, between them and the *Sangha* there exists an important relationship, not of reciprocity exactly, but of complementariness. This relationship is set out formally in an early Buddhist text, the *Sigāla* homily,[51] which remains today one of the best-known portions of Buddhist literature among the Buddhists of Sri Lanka and South-East Asia.

The *Sigāla* homily is presented as being the extended answer given by the Buddha to a question from a young householder regarding his moral duties. The comprehensive nature of the advice which the Buddha gives him with regard to domestic and social relationships would by itself be sufficient to dispose of any assertion that the early Buddhist community's concerns were entirely 'otherworldly', 'spiritual' or 'selfish'. As a Buddhist of a later age, commenting on it, said 'nothing in the duties of a householder is left unmentioned'.[52] It was, added the same writer, for the householder what the *Vinaya*, or code of discipline, was for the members of the *Sangha*.

The duties are set out in an orderly way, intended, no doubt, as T. W. Rhys Davids observed, to assist the memory. Six sets of reciprocal role expectations, or duties, are enumerated: first, those between parents and children; next, between pupils and teachers; then, husband and wife; followed by friends and companions; masters and servants; and finally householders and members of the *Sangha*. In each category, five duties are enumerated, with the exception of the *Sangha's* duties to householders, and in this case there are six.

Children are to support their parents, who once supported them; they are to perform the proper family duties, to maintain the family line; to uphold the family tradition; (meaning, perhaps, not dissipating the family property and maintaining the family honour); and they are to show themselves worthy of their heritage. Parents are to restrain their child from wrongdoing, to inspire him to virtue; to train him for a profession, to contract a suitable marriage for him; and in due time to make over to him his inheritance.

Pupils are to serve their teachers by showing respect to them, by waiting upon them, by showing eagerness to learn, by supplying their needs, and by paying attention when they are being taught. Teachers in return are to give their pupils moral training, they are to inspire in them a love of learning, they are to instruct them in every subject, are to speak well of their pupils, and to protect them from any danger.

A husband is to cherish his wife by treating her with respect, by being kind to her, by being faithful, by allowing her her proper due rights, and by providing her with suitable ornaments. In return, a wife is to show her love for her husband by maintaining a well-ordered household, by being hospitable to their relatives and friends, by being faithful, by being thrifty, and by being diligent.

A man should recognize his obligations to his friends by making them gifts, by courtesy and benevolence towards them, by treating them as his equals, and by keeping his word to them. In return he may expect that they will take care of him or of his interests when he is unable to do so himself (for example, says the commentator, if he falls down in the street after too much drinking, his friend will stay with him until he sobers up, so that his clothes are not stolen), they will provide him with refuge when he needs it, they will stand by him in times of trouble, and will be kind to his family.

A good master (i.e., employer) is one who may be relied upon to show consideration towards his employees by allotting each one work suited to his capacity, by supplying them with good food and pay, by providing care for them when they are sick, by sharing with them any unusual delicacies which he receives, and by granting them regular time off from work. In return, employees or servants should show their affection for their master by being out of bed betimes and not going to bed until he has done so, by being contented with the fair treatment they receive, by doing their work cheerfully and thoroughly, and by speaking well of their master to others.

Finally, the reciprocal duties of householders and members of the *Sangha* are set out. A good householder ministers to the *bhikkhus* by showing affection for them in his actions, in his speech, and in his thoughts, by giving them a warm welcome and ample hospitality and by providing generally for their material needs. In return, the members of the *Sangha* are to show their affection for the householder by restraining him from evil courses of action, by exhorting him to do what is honorable, by entertaining kindly feelings towards him, by imparting knowledge to him, by dealing with his difficulties and doubts, and by revealing to him the way to heaven. The last is the sixth duty. Every other class of citizen named has been given five duties, but for the *bhikkhu* there is this one extra, which thus stands by itself in a position of special emphasis.

'We can realize', commented T. W. Rhys Davids, 'how happy would have been the village or the clan on the banks of the Ganges, where the people were full of kindly spirit of fellow-feeling, the noble spirit of justice, which breathes through these naive and simple sayings.'[53] Those who have been acquainted with the life of a country like Burma, where Buddhist culture was still a living force[54] will know that this is true, for the reality has existed. There is evidence that in India something approaching such a state of society existed wherever Buddhist culture or civilization was able to establish itself.

Here the crux of the matter is reached: the ability of Buddhism to establish and maintain itself. The 'practicability gap' which was mentioned a little earlier, between the Buddhist vision for human society and the realization of it in any actual society, was not quickly or easily bridged. There were, and are, certain essential conditions to be fulfilled before a Buddhist form of civilization can come into being anywhere. These necessary conditions have two primary focal points: (1) the *Sangha*, and (2) the governing power. In India at the time of the Buddha, the latter meant, of course, the monarchy. These will now be considered in a little more detail.

THE SOCIAL FUNCTION OF THE *SANGHA*

In the first place, it was essential that the *Sangha* should function within the wider society in the kind of way that was outlined in the *Sigāla* homily. The duties there envisaged for the *bhikkhu* in his relations with the householder require constant, day-to-day contacts between the two. That is why the word 'monk', if it means a man who lives apart from the world, is in the strict sense inappropriate as a translation of *bhikkhu*. The *bhikkhu* has to exhort the householder, restrain him when necessary, instruct him, clear up his doubts, and constantly direct his attention to the path he should follow in order to reach 'heaven'.[55] This he would do most effectively if he himself was following that path and was providing an example and an inspiration to the householder, who otherwise, as we have seen, was all too prone to aim at the short-term goal of sensual pleasure. From the point of view of an anthropological analysis of Buddhism in modern Sri Lanka, Obeyesekere points out a principle which is inherent in early

Buddhism also. The life of the *bhikkhu*, who has given up the comforts of household life as something which he no longer needs, has an important social function. His life 'exemplifies in exaggerated form the inhibition of natural drives, and such inhibition is a prerequisite for the conduct of all social life'. The effect of the example of an ascetic life was pointed out by Durkheim in terms which exactly fit the Buddhist situation: 'it is ... a good thing that the ascetic ideal be incarnated eminently in certain persons, whose specialty, so to speak, it is to represent, almost with excess, this aspect of the ritual life, for they are like so many models, inciting to effort. Such is the historic role of the great ascetics. When their deeds and acts are analyzed in detail, one asks himself what useful end they can have. He is struck by the fact that there is something excessive in the disdain they profess for all that ordinarily impassions men. But these exaggerations are necessary to sustain among the believers a sufficient disgust for an easy life and common pleasures. *It is necessary that an élite put the end too high, if the crowd is not to put it too low. It is necessary that some exaggerate, if the average is to remain at a fitting level.*'[56]

Whether these words of Durkheim are true for any other system or not, they are certainly true of early Buddhism. A passage from a canonical text reflects exactly the kind of attitude on the part of the lay-follower that Durkheim has depicted. 'As long as they live, the *Arahants* ... are abstainers from the slaying of creatures; ... they are modest, show kindness, they abide friendly and compassionate to all creatures, to all beings. So also do I abide this night and day ... abstaining from such actions, showing kindness to all beings. As long as they live the *Arahants* ... abstain from stealing ... they abide in purity free from theft. So also do I myself also abide....' The same formula is repeated for each of the eight precepts which were observed by those lay-followers or *upāsakas* who were aiming at a somewhat higher level of moral attainment, in imitation of the example of the *bhikkhus*, and especially of the *Arahants*, who were regarded as having fully conquered selfish passions. 'As long as they live the *Arahants* dwell observing chastity ... abstaining from falsehood ... abstaining from fermented liquor, which gives occasion to sloth ... living on one meal a day ... refraining from going to exhibitions of dancing ... from the use of luxurious beds.... So also do I abide. I also this night and day do likewise. By this observance I imitate the Arahants and I shall have kept the sabbath.'[57]

The particular occasion for the recital of these words was, as the last sentence indicates, the lay disciple's observance of a higher standard of moral discipline during the night and day of the Sabbath, a practice which is still followed in Buddhist countries today. The householder who, once or twice a month, undertook this somewhat stricter rule of life would naturally be more disposed to follow the normally required five basic precepts more carefully than if he were not disciplining himself from time to time at a more advanced level. And from his example other householders might also be encouraged to take the Buddhist moral code more seriously. There was thus a widening circle from each local Buddhist *Sangha*, a radiation of heightened morality, whose influence would, as time went by, penetrate more and more deeply into the surrounding society.

In this way, what was referred to above as the unreadiness of the mass of people to participate in, and make a success of, the kind of society envisaged in Buddhist teaching, would gradually diminish. Meanwhile, however, there would still be many who were not likely to respond to these influences, and whose attitudes and actions would have socially destructive effects if they were not held in check. In other words, there was the problem of how to deal with potentially violent or anti-social elements, even though it was only for an interim period while the Buddhist prescription became more widely effective in raising the level of moral life and eliminating social conflict and violence. There were, moreover, the monarchies, decreasing in numbers as the larger swallowed up the smaller, but not decreasing in the extent or degree of their power. These would constitute the most serious obstacle of all in the way of any hopes for the gradual establishment of a universal republic with the Buddhist *Sangha* as its heart.

It may be useful at this point to remind ourselves that the Buddha, when he had achieved Buddhahood, does not appear to have abandoned the interest, which his family tradition and milieu had given him, in public affairs and the concerns of government. We may remind ourselves, too, that it was perfectly natural that the public world should come within the scope of the Buddhist prescription. This was not due merely to the need to guarantee the *Sangha* with political freedom and a sound economic basis, necessary pre-conditions for its untrammeled existence and security though these were. It was due equally to the fact that the private world of the individual, as the 'real' or important world, was denied legitimacy in Buddhist doctrine. Salvation was the movement away from this private, separate and ultimately false existence to a wider, non-egotistical sphere of being. Here, then, we have three very important reasons why there developed in early Buddhism so strong a concern with the wise and beneficent government of human society: the Buddha's own background, the need to ensure optimum conditions for the Buddhist prescription for society to take effect, and—most important—the fact that by its very nature, unique among the ideologies of the time in its denial of the individual soul, Buddhism could never be a 'private' salvation, 'the flight of the alone to the Alone' or any other kind of world-rejecting escapism; by its very nature its concerns were with the public world.

THE BUDDHIST ATTITUDE TO MONARCHICAL GOVERNMENT

The *Sangha* was to provide the growth point, or, rather, a multiplicity of growth points, from which would spread the new pattern of humanity, the social restructuring of human life, which had as its aim the elimination of individualism with all its human ill effects. While this process was going on, it would be folly to disregard the large areas of society which were as yet untouched by the influence of the *Sangha*, for unchecked individualism and violence in these areas would threaten the peaceful growth of the *Sangha*, and of what may be called the Buddhistically oriented areas of society. Social stability appears to have been recognized by the Buddha as a necessary condition for the success of social and moral reconstruction. In the existing situation in north India in the fifth century BC the surest guarantee of social stability appeared to be in the direction of a strong and benevolent monarchy. Moreover, a really enlightened monarchy, sympathetic to Buddhism, might have the further important, positive function of providing those conditions and of helping to create those attitudes among the people which would facilitate the widespread acceptance of the Buddhist prescription. This appears to have been the logic underlying the attitude of the Buddha towards the contemporary monarchs of Koshala and Magadha, as it is represented in the Pāli Canon.

Throughout his life, as we have seen, the Buddha was closely associated with the royal courts of his day. Pasenadi, the king of Koshala, and Bimbisara, the king of Magadha, were his life-long personal friends and supporters. Pasenadi, it is said, frequently visited the Buddha to have discussions with him.[58] It may be recalled that it was in Pasenadi's capital, Shravasti, that the majority of the Buddha's discourses were delivered. Bimbisara, from the time when he first entertained the Buddha, in his palace at Rajagriha, until his death thirty-seven years later, was a firm supporter of the Buddhist *Sangha*, and himself a disciple or *upāsaka*, practicing the layman's higher eight-fold morality six times a month.[59] It may be recalled, too, that by this time Koshala and Magadha between them covered most of the territory of the lower Gangetic plain, that is, roughly the whole extent of the plain between the Himalaya and the Chotanagpur plateau, from modern Lucknow eastwards to Bhagalpur. The Buddha can hardly be said to have been out of contact with the important centers of political power of his day. He may justly be described as a social and political theorist, and indeed this aspect of his historical significance has been so generally ignored that it needs heavy emphasis. But he was not only a theorist; in addition to the familiarity with the concerns of government, which his upbringing in Kapilavastu would have given him, he was in constant touch with current problems of government, through the two kings who were his supporters and disciples. Nor was this indirect involvement simply a matter of *ad hoc* problem-solving; the early Buddhist literature represents the Buddha as one who frequently had something to say on matters of policy.

It is not surprising, therefore, to find one of the most outstanding of historians of Indian political thought, U. N. Ghoshal,[60] observing that 'the most important contribution of the early Buddhist canonists to the store of our ancient political thought consists in their "total" application of the principle of righteousness to the branches of the king's internal and foreign administration.'[61]

The unwisdom of the multitude, the need for social and economic stability as a prerequisite of the prescription to overcome this unwisdom, the emergence of powerful monarchically ruled states—these things together provide an explanation of why the Buddha, who seems to have regarded the republican *Sangha* as the ideal form of government, nevertheless gave a large place in his teaching to the important role of the righteous monarch. A number of the *Jātaka* stories contain descriptions of the ideal king, and exhortations concerning good government.[62] The realm of the wise king is one which is free from all oppression, not ruled arbitrarily but with equity, where good men are honoured[63] and where the king and his officials exhibit qualities of selflessness, rectitude, mercy, political wisdom and a sense of equal respect for all beings, including different classes of society, townsmen, countrymen, religious teachers, and even birds and beasts.[64] The importance of the personal righteousness of the king is strongly emphasized.[65] A figure of speech frequently used is the bull who leads the herd aright: 'so should a king to righteous ways be true; the common folk injustice will eschew, and through the realm shall holy peace ensue.'[66] 'When kings are righteous, the ministers of kings are righteous. When ministers are righteous, brahmans and householders also are righteous. Thus townsfolk and villagers are righteous. This being so, moon and sun go right in their courses. This being so, constellations and stars do likewise; days and nights, months and fortnights, seasons and years go on their courses regularly; winds blow regularly and in due season. Thus the *devas* are not annoyed and the sky-*deva* bestows sufficient rain. Rains falling seasonably, the crops ripen in due season. *Bhikkhus*, when crops ripen in due season, men who live on those crops are long-lived, well-favoured, strong and free from sickness.'[67]

Figs, oil, honey, molasses, root-crops, fruits all taste sweeter and better in a country where the king rules righteously, according to another *Jātaka* story.'[68]

The economic welfare of the people should, in the Buddhist view, be a special concern of the wise king, who is exhorted to take positive, specific measures which will benefit the country, together with or in addition to the effects of his own personal righteousness. In the *Kūṭadanta Sutta* (see chapter 5, p. 87) we are told of a great king who, conscious of his good fortune hitherto, thought it advisable to offer a great sacrifice, and thereby ensure the continuance of his prosperity. His chaplain, however, tried to dissuade him, and pointed out that there would be greater wisdom in taking preventive action against possible occurrences of crime. This could be done, suggested the chaplain, by removing the economic causes of discontent. To farmers the king should issue a subsidy of food and of seed-corn. To merchants and tradesmen he should make available sources of capital which they could invest in their businesses. To those in government service he should give adequate wages and supplies of food. If this were to be done there would be no danger of subversion of the state by malcontents, but on the contrary, 'the king's revenue will go up; the country will be quiet and at peace; and the populace, pleased one with another and happy, dancing their children in their arms, will dwell with open doors.'[69] The king followed his chaplain's advice and all happened as the chaplain had predicted. It will be noticed that the advice given by this 'chaplain' is of a kind that would be offered by a Buddhist rather than by a brahman. Sacrifice is a waste of time; the king should concern himself instead with ensuring full employment in the country. The same principle is emphasized in another well-known *Sutta*, which tells the story of the city of Kushinara in its former days of prosperity, under the Great King of Glory.[70]

On the other hand, another *Sutta*[71] tells of a king who failed to make provision for the poor, and of the serious consequences in the life of the state. This king, we are told, instead of going to a holy man to ask advice concerning the proper duty of a king, as his prosperous and wise predecessors had done, followed his own devices. 'By his own ideas he governed his people; and they so governed, differently from what they had been, did not prosper as they used to under former kings.'[72] The one thing he had failed to do, apparently, was to make provision to remedy the condition of the poor in his realm. 'And because this was not done, poverty became widespread.'[73] This led to cases of theft. At first the king had dealt with the offenders by making them grants of money, on the grounds that they had stolen because they were poor men and this was the best way to remedy the situation. But in a short time this suggested itself to others as an easy way of making money, and the incidence of theft increased rapidly. The king thereupon changed his policy, and began cutting off the heads of those who were caught stealing. But this violent measure only engendered further violence. Thieves now began to say among themselves, Let us also resort to violence: 'Let us also now have sharp swords made ready for ourselves, and [as for] them, from whom we take what is not given us—what they call theft—let us put a final stop to them, inflict on them the uttermost penalty, and cut their heads off.' And so, we are told, 'they got themselves sharp swords, and came forth to sack village and town and city, and to work highway robbery. And them whom they robbed they made an end of, cutting off their heads.'[74] Such also, was the sad end of the state itself, whose ruler had failed to make adequate and wise provision for the relief of poverty. From stealing and violence there followed murder, lying, evil-speaking, adultery, false opinions, incest, and perverted lust, until the physical condition of the people deteriorated to the point where their life span was only a fraction of what it had once been.[75]

In these and similar early Buddhist stories, a great responsibility is laid upon the sovereign ruler of the state to act righteously, as far as his own life and conduct of affairs is concerned, and wisely, too, in terms of a social and economic ethic concerning which, it is emphasized, he needs to take advice from 'brahmans'. In the Buddhist literature, as we have seen, 'brahmans' are classed with *shramanas* and are recognized as such by their character and holy life, not by any hereditary right from having been born of a priestly family. The advice the righteous king needs to take, in other words, is that which, ideally, he will be offered by the Buddhist *Sangha*.

There is a significant difference between the ethics of the state, with which the early Buddhist tradition was concerned, and the brahmanical idea of the moral responsibilities of the king. As U. N. Ghoshal has observed, the brahmanical royal ethic was the king's own personal *dharma* or duty, 'conceived in sufficiently elastic terms to provide for the needs of the kingdom and to permit in *Manu* and still more in the *Mahabharata* (after

Bhishma) the wholesale incorporation of the *Arthasastra* categories'. On the other hand, 'the Buddhist *dharma* in its relation to the king involves the application of the universal ethics of Buddhism to the state administration.'[76] The king, in brahmanical theory, is working out his own personal *moksha*, or salvation, by doing his proper duty, or *dharma*, as a king, just as any other man works out his salvation by doing his own proper duty. The performance of one's personal *dharma* is the dominating principle in the brahmanical theory. But in the Buddhist view, the king is the agent or instrument through which the eternal, universal *Dharma* is made effective.

The point is made explicitly in a collection of sayings concerning kings found in the Pāli *Aṅguttara-Nikāya*. The Buddha is represented as saying to the members of the *Sangha*, 'Bhikkhus, the king who rolls the wheel of state, a *Dhamma-man*, a *Dhamma-king*, rolls indeed no unroyal wheel.' One of the *bhikkhus* then asks, 'But who, Lord, is the king of the King?' The answer given by the Buddha is 'It is *Dhamma*, O *bhikkhu*!'[77] The Buddhist king—the *Dhamma-king* or *Dharma-rājā*— that is, the kind of king whose rule is envisaged as necessary for the implementing of the Buddhist scheme for society, is the king who rules in subordination to one power only—that of the eternal, universal *Dharma* (*Dhamma*). It is this which gives his rule a unique quality; in so far as he rules in accordance with universal *Dharma*, his rule itself has a quality of universalism; it is not appropriate to any one locality or region or period of time. The corollary of this would appear to be that neighboring *Dhamma-kings* will find themselves ruling by the same eternal universalist principles and therefore in harmony with one another. The notion of a single universal *Dharma-rājā* is already to be found in the early Buddhist tradition, as the idea of the one universal monarch, the *Chakravartin*. In Sanskrit literature *Dharma-rājā* is another name for the Buddha.

THE *CHAKRAVARTIN* AND THE BUDDHA

It is significant that in Pāli Buddhist literature also there is, in many of the references to the *Chakravartin*, a clear and conscious parallelism between this universal world-ruler and the *Tathāgata*, or Buddha. Beside or behind the *Chakravartin* there stands the Buddha: the two are so closely linked that they almost appear to be one and the same in different roles. There was a strong tradition that Gotama's Buddhahood was seen as an alternative to his being a *Chakravartin*. But there is also a suggestion, in many passages, that the Buddha is in every respect virtually identical with the *Chakravartin*. '*Bhikkhus*, these two persons born into the world are born to the profit and happiness of many, to the profit, happiness and welfare of many folk. What two? A *Tathāgata*, an arahant who is a fully Enlightened One (Buddha), and a world-ruling monarch ... *Bhikkhus*, these two persons born into the world are born as extraordinary men. What two? A *Tathāgata* ... and a world-ruling monarch. *Bhikkhus*, the death of two persons is regretted by many folk. Of what two? A *Tathāgata* ... and a world-ruling monarch. *Bhikkhus*, these two are worthy of a relic-shrine [*stūpa*]. What two? A *Tathāgata* ... and a world-ruling monarch.'[78] Ghoshal interprets the parallel drawn here and elsewhere in Buddhist canonical texts between the Buddha and the World-ruler as meaning that the World-ruler 'is the temporal counterpart of the spiritual World-teacher, resembling him not only in his outward bodily form (the so-called thirty-two bodily signs of the superman) and the extraordinary incidents of his birth, death, cremation and commemoration, but also in the jointly unique role as universal benefactors.'[79]

It is this close resemblance, amounting to virtual identity, between the World-ruler and the World-teacher which has the effect, by implication, of distinguishing the Buddhist conception of an emperor or world-ruler from the brahmanical conception of the emperor, as the latter is set out, for instance, in the *Arthasastra* of Kautilya. The political philosophy which this treatise embodies, and with which political practice corresponded fairly closely, is that might is right, or that what is expedient is right. The Buddhist political philosophy was founded, as K. N. Jayatilleke pointed out, on the principle that 'the wheel of might turns in dependence on the wheel of righteousness.'[80] The conflict between the two philosophies was one which, as we shall shortly see, was experienced as a conflict of conscience by the emperor Ashoka.

171

Certain clear inter-relationships can thus be seen within the structure of society envisaged in early Buddhist tradition and practice. Three major elements can be distinguished: the *Sangha*, the king, and the mass of the people. Three relationships can also be distinguished.

(1) The *Sangha*, as the realization in practice, or visible embodiment, of the new wisdom, stood in a special relationship to the king which was a continuation of the relationship which had existed between the Buddha in his day and the kings of Koshala and Magadha. This relationship was in principle of the same kind as that between the World-teacher and the World-ruler.

(2) In the other direction the *Sangha* was related to the mass of the people. The community of the *Sangha* arose out of the common people who both provided its recruits and ministered to its needs. Moreover, what the community of the *Sangha* was now, all humanity was eventually to become; proleptically, the common people were members of the *Sangha*.

(3) Meanwhile, it was necessary that until all should have fully apprehended the Buddha-Dhamma and have entered into the wider realm of consciousness to which life in the Sangha led, there should be a center of political power to bring an interim unity into what would otherwise be the chaos of multiple units, to maintain law and order and promote the common welfare. From the people, in the Buddhist view, the king derived his authority rather than from any divine source; in their name and for their good he exercised it (see chapter 4, p. 72 f). This triangular relationship, Sangha, king and people, provides the basic structure of Buddhist civilization. The introduction of Buddhism into a country meant, therefore, the attempt to establish this structure, and Buddhist civilization may be said to exist where this structure can be found. It will be the purpose of the second part of this book to trace the expansion of Buddhist civilization in these terms, first in India, and then, by way of confirmation, in Sri Lanka too.

Part 4

Buddhist Civilization in Practice

9   The Ashokan Buddhist State

The reordering of human consciousness, and the reordering of human society—these, we have seen, were the two complementary aspects of the Buddha's teaching. If, in the Pāli Canon, it is the reordering of human consciousness which receives greater emphasis and has the greater amount of teaching devoted to it, this is because it was the primary concern of the Buddhist Order, the *Sangha*, while the second was regarded as the proper concern of the enlightened political ruler, acting in accordance with the general principles of the Buddha's teaching, and in cooperation with the *Sangha*, in order to promote what can be called a Buddhistic society. These two complementary concerns constituted the Buddhist prescription for the curing of the ills of the human condition. Now, there is nothing to prevent anyone from using the word 'religion' to describe this program of action, just as there is nothing to prevent anyone from applying the same word to the philosophy, political and economic revolution proposed by Karl Marx, but in each case it would be a highly specialized and somewhat bizarre usage. The two ideologies, as it happens, are not dissimilar, in so far as both are prescriptions which owe nothing to supernatural or theological beliefs, and both are critical of contemporary religious practice. In the Buddhist case, this criticism is milder, and the general attitude, so far as popular beliefs and practices are concerned, is somewhat more tolerant, although even here there is a strong similarity between the early Buddhist attitude to popular religion and that of Karl Marx, expressed in his famous characterization of religion as 'the sigh of the oppressed creature, the heart of a heartless world, just as it is the spirit of the spiritless situation.'[1]

The Buddha's attitude to popular, as distinct from priestly, religion was one of mildly tolerant disapproval, coupled with an acknowledgement of the fact that unless other, basic, factors in the situation were changed, it was futile merely to try to argue people out of their prejudices and superstitions. The Buddhist prescription was a plan for dealing with those other factors, psychological, social and political. Similarly Karl Marx insisted that it was the disease of which nineteenth-century European religion was the symptom which had to be dealt with, not merely the symptoms themselves. Both Buddhism and Marxism are based on a philosophical rather than a theological view of the human situation,[2] and both envisage the solution in terms of 'cells' or growth-points, characterized by the respective principles of corporate existence which each sets out, and devoted to the dissemination of these principles in theory and in action. Both envisage a stage at which the growth of these revolutionary cells will enable the center of political and economic power to be brought within the revolutionary sphere. In the Marxist case this is a clearly defined aim and constitutes 'the revolution' *par excellence*, to be achieved if necessary by violence; in the Buddhist case it is less clearly defined as a conscious aim of the *Sangha's* existence and growth, but the conversion of the political ruler to the attitudes entailed in the Buddhist revolution is obviously regarded in the early texts as highly desirable.

THE ASHOKAN REALIZATION OF THE BUDDHIST STATE

It took about two and a half centuries from the decease of the Buddha for this to come about in India. It is true that the two great kings of the Buddha's own day, Pasenadi and Bimbisara, were very sympathetically inclined towards the Buddha, his teaching, and his new community, but there does not appear to have been, either in Koshala or Magadha, a serious and systematic effort during the Buddha's lifetime to make the life of the state conform to the principles of the *Dhamma* like that subsequently made in the Mauryan empire under the emperor Ashoka in the third century BC. For the *Sangha* so to grow in influence and public esteem that eventually a monarch was entirely convinced of the rightness of Buddhist social and ethical principles, and dedicated himself to their practical realization, took two and a half centuries, but this was, nevertheless, the logical and proper consummation of the *Sangha's* growth in popularity and influence during that period. Inherent in the Buddha's prescription for society was the Buddhistic world-ruler, or *Chakravartin*, and the adherence of Ashoka to Buddhism was not just an unexpected and unhoped-for stroke of luck; it had, since the Buddha's day, clearly been potential in the situation in north India, given the gradual growth and influence of the *Sangha*.

The intervening period had been for the Buddhist *Sangha* one of gradual expansion in spite of difficulties and, occasionally, hostility. In the kingdom of Magadha dynasty had succeeded dynasty, and the power and extent of the kingdom gradually increased. About a hundred and sixty years after the decease of the Buddha, a man named Chandragupta Maurya established himself as ruler of Magadha, displacing the Nanda dynasty.[3] The Nanda kings had, during the previous forty years, built up an empire in northern India that extended up to the frontiers of the Punjab.[4] The empire of Chandragupta was even more vast. He began by fighting a war of liberation in the north-west of India, to rid the Punjab and Sind of the Greek army of occupation left by Alexander the Great. He then marched south-eastwards to attack and slay the rich, proud and tyrannical king of Magadha, Dhana Nanda, in his capital at Pataliputra (Patna). Contemporary Greek writers testify to the vastness of the empire which Chandragupta established in India, from the borders of Persia to as far south as modern Goa, and as far east as the edge of the Ganges delta. This empire was inherited by his son, and later by his grandson, Ashoka. It was left to Ashoka during the early years of his reign, which began about the year 268 BC,[5] to extend the empire's boundaries south-eastwards to the Bay of Bengal by a violent campaign against Kalinga, an area roughly corresponding to modern Orissa.

Chandragupta had been guided and advised by a brahman minister, Chanakya. This brahman is identified with Kautilya, the author of the treatise on statecraft known as the *Arthasastra*. It was he who was the architect of the Mauryan empire. In the principles of government which he had laid down, and in which he had first instructed Chandragupta, the latter's son and grandson, Bindusara and Ashoka, were also trained. Ashoka thus entered upon his career as emperor of the greater part of the Indian sub-continent, heir to a brahman tradition of statecraft, in which he, as a young prince, had been educated, first in theory and then in practice, since the age of about ten.[6]

He was exposed, however, to other traditions. The new movements of thought and practice, of which Jainism and Buddhism were the two major representatives, were particularly strong in eastern India, and brahmanism as a social and ceremonial system was, as yet, correspondingly weaker. There is evidence that Chandragupta was an adherent of Jainism, at least towards the end of his life. Ashoka's mother, according to a Buddhist tradition, was strongly attracted to the doctrines of the Ajivakas. His first wife, Devi, was a lay supporter of the Buddhist *Sangha*, and the two children he had by her, Mahinda, his son, and Sanghamitra his daughter, entered the *Sangha* themselves, as *bhikkhu* and *bhikkhuni* respectively, in the sixth year of Ashoka's reign, according to the Pāli canonical tradition. It was inevitable, too, that Ashoka himself, as he grew up, would have become familiar with the doctrines and practices of the Buddhist fraternity, which had by then been in existence and growing steadily in eastern India for more than two hundred years.

The turning-point in Ashoka's life appears to have come immediately after the conquest of Kalinga, where victory had been gained only at the price of a great human slaughter, which in Ashoka's own account of it, ran into many thousands. In the Kautilyan theory of statecraft it was the monarch's duty to expand the bounds of his realm by military conquest. The difference between the bramanical concept of kingship and the Buddhist was, as we have already noticed (chapter 8, p. 169), that in brahmanical theory, the king was working out his own personal salvation or *moksha* by the correct and due performance of his own personal *dharma*, that which was proper to him personally as king, whereas in the Buddhist conception of monarchical government, the king was the necessary instrument through which universal *Dharma* or righteousness, found expression. The enlargement of his domain by violent conquest was not required of a king in the Buddhist conception of monarchy, but rather the cultivation of peace, both with his neighbors and within his own realm.

ASHOKA ADOPTS THE BUDDHIST VIEWPOINT

It was from the brahmanical, Kautilyan theory of statecraft to the Buddhist conception that Ashoka turned, after the awful human massacre which his campaign against Kalinga had entailed. Exactly how this change of heart came about is unclear. There is the possibility that this third-generation member of the Mauryan dynasty was already predisposed to react against the brahmanical statecraft of his father and grandfather by the time he succeeded to the throne. Other philosophies were prominent in his empire and, as we have seen, were probably well-known to him, personally and through his own family. It may therefore have been as the result of his own knowledge of the Buddhist social ethic that Ashoka, reflecting on the necessary consequences of the kind of statecraft in which he had been trained, came to the decision to forsake the path of violent conquest and personal royal aggrandizement and devote himself instead to the realization of the Buddhist ideal of the righteous and peaceful monarch. A recent study of Ashoka[7] suggests that, while he had fully mastered the Kautilyan theory of statecraft, he felt it to be inadequate for the needs of his own situation and his own time. 'For Ashoka the state was not an end in itself but rather a means to an end higher than the state itself, namely, *dharma*, or morality.... If for Kautilya the state was a primitive instrument, for Ashoka it was an educative institution. For the dichotomy between force and morality, between Kautilya and Buddha, had existed for a long time. Ashoka felt that his most glorious mission was to resolve this dichotomy and endow the mechanism of the Kautilyan state with a moral soul.'[8] Professor Gokhale has, in these words, indicated that the perspective in which the Buddha-Dharma is properly seen is that of a 'public' (that is, an ethical-political) philosophy rather than merely a private cult of religious satisfaction or 'salvation'. Exactly at what point in his career Ashoka consciously arrived at this decision is, however, difficult to establish. It is not impossible, or even improbable, that it was reached as the outcome of his own reflection.

On the other hand, we have to remember that while Ashoka may have found himself in the position of an emperor in search of a new ethic, there is also the fact that the Buddhist movement had been for two centuries a potential civilization, pragmatically oriented towards monarchy, but needing a Buddhist monarch to convert the potential into the actual. Circumstances until then had not been favourable. Chandragupta, in so far as he was not entirely of orthodox brahmanical outlook, had been inclined towards Jainism. What little is known about Bindusara suggests that he was conventionally brahmanical in his policies, although an enquiring mind may be indicated by the story told of him, that he wished to purchase a philosopher from Greece, but was told that it was not the Greek custom to sell philosophers. Ashoka may from the time of his accession have appeared to the Buddhist *Sangha* as an altogether more promising candidate for the role of Buddhist king. Certainly the traditions suggest that some initiative in the matter of securing Ashoka's adherence was taken by members of the Buddhist fraternity. According to the Theravada tradition preserved in Sri Lanka, Ashoka inherited from his father the practice of a daily distribution of food to large numbers of brahmans, 'versed in the Brahma-doctrine'. After a while, however, Ashoka became disgusted at the greedy manner in which they grabbed at the food and decided that in future he would find other, more worthy recipients. Standing at his window he saw a *bhikkhu*, Nigrodha, passing along the street, and, impressed by his grave and peaceful bearing, sent for him to come at once. Nigrodha came calmly into the king's presence. The king, still standing, invited the *bhikkhu* to sit down. Since there was no other *bhikkhu* present, says the narrator (that is, since there was no one present who was superior in rank to him) Nigrodha sat down on the royal throne. When he saw this, we are told, Ashoka was glad that he, being uncertain of the order of precedence for a king and a *bhikkhu*, had not made the mistake of offering Nigrodha an inferior seat. 'Seeing him seated there king Ashoka rejoiced greatly that he had honored him according to his rank.'[9] The episode is interesting as an illustration of the evidently accepted principle that any member of the *Sangha* takes precedence over the king, and that the king, therefore, is, in Buddhist theory, subordinate in status to the *Sangha*. The chronicler then goes on to tell how Nigrodha, after he had received the king's gift of food, was questioned by Ashoka concerning his doctrine, and how, in response, he expounded to Ashoka some verses on the subject of 'unwearying zeal'.[10] Ashoka was greatly impressed by this exposition of Buddhist doctrines and undertook to offer food regularly to Nigrodha. The next day, accompanied by other *bhikkhus*, Nigrodha again received food from the king, and again expounded the doctrine. As a result, Ashoka thereupon became a Buddhist lay follower.[11] Another account of the manner in which Ashoka became an adherent of Buddhism is found in a collection known as the *Divyavadana*; one of the sections of this is 'The Book of King Ashoka', a work which possibly originated in Mathura, in north India, in the second Century BC. According to this source, it was a *bhikkhu* named Upagupta who was the agent of Ashoka's conversion.

The evidence of the Buddhist Chronicles, in the form in which we now have them, however, dates from the sixth century AD.[12] They do, of course, embody material which had been transmitted from generation to generation of *bhikkhus* with that scrupulous accuracy which is characteristic of Indian memorizing. The tradition which is embodied in the Pāli chronicles may very well go back to within less than a century after Ashoka's time. But Ashoka himself provided contemporary evidence of the events of his life in the imperial edicts which he caused to be inscribed on rock faces and on specially erected stone pillars at various important centers throughout his realm. A number of such edicts were promulgated throughout the course of the reign, and each was inscribed in a number of different places.[13]

In one of the earliest of them, Ashoka expresses his desire that serious moral effort should be made by all his subjects: 'Thus speaks *Devanam-piya* [beloved of the gods], Ashoka: I have been an *upāsaka* [Buddhist lay-follower] for more than two-and-a-half years, but for a year I did not make much progress. Now for more than a year I have drawn closer to the *Sangha*, and have become more ardent. The gods, who in India up to this time did not associate with men, now mingle with them,'[14] and this is the result of my efforts. Moreover, this is not something to be obtained only by the great, but it is also open to the humble, if they are earnest; and they can even reach heaven easily. This is the reason for this announcement, that both humble and great should make progress and that the neighboring peoples also should know that the progress is lasting....'[15]

The inscription from which the above is an extract is known as the Minor Rock Edict, 'From Suvarnagiri' (the first words of the inscription), the southern provincial capital of the empire, in Hyderabad.[16] The inscription includes a reference to the wide extent of its publication: it is to be inscribed 'here and elsewhere on the hills, and wherever there is a stone pillar it is to be engraved on that pillar'. Moreover the officers of the state are directed to 'go out with [the text of] this throughout the whole of your district'. The words which have been quoted raise a number of interesting questions. Ashoka refers to himself here, as in every of the thirty-two inscriptions except three,[17] by the title *Devanam-piya*, 'Beloved of the gods'.[18] This might suggest that he was consciously asserting the importance of the gods in whom he believed and whose special instrument he felt himself to be. But it is unlikely that the title held this kind of significance; it was a conventional epithet, meaning roughly 'His Gracious Majesty', and was used by other kings of the time without apparently implying any distinctively religious attitude.[19] So far as Ashoka's moral attitude is concerned, this inscription is of interest in the present context for the evidence which it provides concerning his own progress towards his present state of moral zeal. What is not clear is whether the war of conquest which Ashoka waged against the Kalinga came after his first, rather formal, adherence to Buddhism as a lay-follower, (i.e., the first year, concerning which he says 'for a year I did not make much progress') or before it. If he had already become a lay-follower it might seem strange that he should then embark on such a violent and bloody campaign of conquest. On the other hand, if one adopted the view that he first became a lay-follower after the Kalingan war, out of a feeling of revulsion for war and an attraction towards Buddhism, some explanation would then be necessary for what would have to be regarded as the subsequent change in his attitude, from moral lukewarmness to zeal. No event is known to have occurred and no experience is mentioned by Ashoka which would account for the sudden zealousness. However, Ashoka has left a record of the profound moral impression made on him by the Kalinga campaign: 'When he had been consecrated eight years *Devanam-piya* Piyadassi[20] conquered Kalinga. A hundred and fifty thousand people were deported, a hundred thousand were killed and many times that number perished. Afterwards, now that Kalinga was annexed *Devanam-piya* very earnestly practiced *Dhamma*, and taught *Dhamma*. On conquering Kalinga *Devanam-piya* felt remorse, for, when an independent country is conquered, the slaughter, death and deportation of the people is extremely grievous to *Devanam-piya*, and weighs heavily on his mind. What is even more deplorable to *Devanam-piya*, is that those who dwell there, whether brahmans, *shramaṇas*, or those of other sects, or householders who show obedience to their superiors, obedience to mother and father, obedience to their teachers and behave well and devotedly towards their friends, acquaintances, colleagues, relatives, slaves, and servants all suffer violence, murder and separation from their loved ones. Even those who are fortunate to have escaped, whose love is undiminished [by the brutalizing effect of war], suffer from the misfortunes of their friends, acquaintances, colleagues and relatives. This participation of all men in suffering, weighs heavily on the mind of *Devanam-piya*. Except among the Greeks, there is no land where the religious orders of brahmans and *shramaṇas* are not to be found, and there is no land anywhere where men do not support one sect or another. Today if a hundredth or a thousandth part of those people who were killed or died or were deported when Kalinga was annexed were to suffer similarly, it would weigh heavily on the mind of *Devanam-piya*'[21]

Undoubtedly, the Kalingan war brought about a decisive change in Ashoka, and set him in active pursuit of the Buddhist goal of morality: 'afterwards ... he *very earnestly* practiced *Dhamma'* (emphasis added). This agrees well with the statement he makes in the Minor Rock Edict, quoted above, that after making no moral progress for a year (after he had become a Buddhist *upāsaka*), he has now 'for more than a year' been very ardent in his practice of morality. Since he tells us that the total length of time since he became an *upāsaka* was 'more than *two-and-a-half years'* (emphasis added), and his account of his 'lack of progress' followed by 'much progress' covers altogether ('a year' plus 'more than a year') something over *two* years, this leaves a period of about six months during which, presumably, he was engaged in the Kalingan war.

183

This reconstruction of the story from the evidence provided by Ashoka's own words carries with it the implication that his advance towards full and enthusiastic acceptance of what it entailed to be a Buddhist was gradual. This accords with what we have already observed concerning Ashoka's background. It is difficult to say that he was ever entirely ignorant of Buddhism; he did not suddenly turn to it after the Kalingan war, as to something unknown to him before; he had known of it, had been sufficiently attracted by it to become a lay-follower and to take the first steps in the direction of the renunciation of self and the interests of the self. But Buddhist teaching takes account of the fact that men usually advance by degrees towards this goal, even after they have set out in its pursuit; and so it was, apparently with Ashoka.

THE PUBLIC POLICIES OF ASHOKA AS A BUDDHIST RULER

What is presented to us in the evidence of most of the inscriptions, however, is the picture of an emperor who is now seriously, actively and effectively pursuing the kind of policies which are appropriate to a convinced Buddhist ruler.[22] It is interesting to notice where the emphasis was laid. In order of the frequency with which they are mentioned, Ashoka's principal preoccupations in the creation of a Buddhist realm appear to have been, first, exhortation of all the citizens of the state to moral effort, and, second, the implementing of measures designed to improve the quality of public life and facilitate the universal pursuit of Buddhist moral principles. Ashoka himself declares, in the Seventh Pillar Edict that 'The advancement of *Dhamma* amongst men has been achieved through two means, legislation and persuasion. But of these two, legislation has been less effective, and persuasion more so. I have proclaimed through legislation, for instance, that certain species of animals are not to be killed, and other such ideas. But men have increased their adherence to *Dhamma* by being persuaded not to injure living beings and not to take life.'[23]

'*Dhamma*' is mentioned frequently in Ashoka's edicts, and it is to this that he seems to be devoted. At an earlier stage of historical study of Ashoka's India, doubt was sometimes expressed whether the *Dhamma* to which he so often refers was identical with the Buddha-Dhamma, or Buddhist doctrine, as it is found in the canonical texts. The word *dhamma* was used widely, not only by Buddhists, and could bear a quite general meaning, such as 'piety'. But when the whole range of the Ashokan inscriptions is taken into account, there seems little room left for doubt that when Ashoka used the word he meant Buddha-Dhamma. In the First Minor Rock Edict he says, after greeting the *Sangha*, 'You know, Sirs, how deep is my respect for and faith in the *Buddha*, the *Dhamma*, and the *Sangha*. Sirs, whatever was spoken by the Buddha was well spoken. And, Sirs, allow me to tell you what I believe contributes to the long survival of the Buddhist Dhamma. These sermons on *Dhamma*, Sirs...', and then he gives a list of Buddhist discourses which he considers the most vital; 'These sermons on the *Dhamma*, Sirs, I desire that many *bhikkhus* and *bhikkhunis* should hear frequently and meditate upon, and likewise laymen and laywomen.'[24] His reverence for the Buddha is also clearly testified in the Second Minor Rock Edict, set up at Lumbini, the birthplace of Gotama, 'the Shakya-sage'; this edict records the fact that in the twentieth year of his reign, Ashoka 'came in person and reverenced the place where Buddha Shakyamuni was born', and how 'he caused a stone enclosure to be made and a stone pillar to be erected.'[25]

In view of the fact that it is very clearly the Buddha, Gotama, whom Ashoka regards as the great teacher, supremely to be reverenced, and the Buddhist *Sangha* to which he pays special and most frequent respect, it might seem surprising that, in his exposition of what he understands to be the essence of the *Dhamma*, which he mentions so much, there appears to be very little in the way of specifically Buddhist doctrine.

For the *Dhamma*, says Ashoka, is 'good behavior towards slaves and servants, obedience to mother and father, generosity towards friends, acquaintances and relatives, and towards *shramanas* and brahmans, and abstention from killing living beings.'[26] There are broadly two kinds of virtue mentioned here: first, various role- responsibilities: to servants, to parents, to friends and relatives, and to *shramanas* and brahmans; and second, abstention from killing. This basic pattern in the exposition of *Dhamma* occurs elsewhere in the inscriptions. For example: 'It is good to be obedient to one's mother and father, friends and relatives, to be generous to brahmans and *shramaṇas*; it is good not to kill living beings....' This is how the *Dhamma* is expounded in the Third Major Rock Edict. But in this instance, a further item is added, concerning economic activity: 'It is good not only to spend little, but to own the minimum of property.'[27] Again, in the Fourth Major Rock Edict, Ashoka reminds his subjects of the 'forms of the practice of *Dhamma*': they are, he says, 'abstention from killing, and non-injury to living beings, deference to relatives, brahmans and *shramaṇas*, obedience to mother and father, and obedience to elders'.[28] Non-injury of living beings, and abstention from killing are mentioned in the Seventh Pillar Edict as the characteristic ways in which public adherence to *Dhamma* has shown itself in Ashoka's realm: 'Men have increased their adherence to *Dhamma* by being persuaded not to injure living beings and not to take life.'[29] In two other contexts in the inscriptions Ashoka explains *Dhamma* in slightly different terms. The opening sentence of the Second Pillar Edict reads: 'Thus speaks *Devanam-piya*, the king *Piya-dassi*: *Dhamma* is good. And what is *Dhamma*? It is having few faults and many good deeds, mercy, charity, truthfulness, and purity.'[30] Again, in the Seventh Pillar Edict, he says, 'The glory of *Dhamma* will increase throughout the world, and it will be endorsed in the form of mercy, charity, truthfulness, purity, gentleness and virtue.' And he adds that 'Obedience to mother and father, obedience to teachers, deference to those advanced in age, and regard for brahmans and *shramaṇas*, the poor and the wretched, slaves and servants, have increased and will increase.'[31] If these various ways of expounding what Ashoka meant by *Dhamma* are set out synoptically,[32] it becomes clear that the item which occurs most frequently is abstention from killing; this is mentioned as a way of practicing *Dhamma* in four of the five inscriptions which explicitly explain what *Dhamma* is. The other most frequently occurring items are obedience to parents (four out of five), generosity towards *shramaṇas* and brahmans (four out of five) and good behavior towards friends and relatives (three out of five). Taken together, the catalogue of social responsibilities mentioned in the inscriptions corresponds closely to the well-known list in the 'layman's code of ethics' the *Sigāla-vada Sutta* of the Buddhist Pāli Canon (see chapter 8, p. 159). Together with the prominence of the injunction to avoid taking life, this gives an unmistakably Buddhist flavor to the Ashokan *Dhamma*. The important point to notice is that this is laymen's Buddhism; it is not *Dhamma* as doctrine, or philosophical analysis of the human situation, for that is the concern of the professionals, the *bhikkhus*. This, rather, is an ethical system whose primary characteristic principles are nonviolence and generosity. As we shall see later, this code of ethics has remained, down to modern times, the essence of Buddhism for lay people.

If non-violence and generosity are the essence of Buddhist morality for the common people, they are also, in the Buddhist state, the minimum requirements of morality for the king and for the corps of professional Buddhists, the *Sangha*. Buddhism has no clear-cut, two-fold standard of morality, one for laymen and one for religious orders or priests; such differences as are recognized are of levels of attainment, the transition from one level to another being gradual and imperceptible rather than clear and distinct. The over-all structure is one of progression through a continuum.

Certainly Ashoka himself appears to have accepted his own ethical obligations. Both in matters concerning himself and his court, and in those concerning the public welfare, he appears to have undertaken in various ways to fulfill his responsibilities as he understood them, as a Buddhist ruler.

Non-violence to living beings was interpreted to mean that, as far as possible, the slaughter of animals for food should cease. 'Formerly in the kitchens of *Devanam-piya Piya-dassi* [Ashoka] many hundreds of thousands of living animals were killed daily for meat. But now, at the time of writing this inscription on *Dhamma*, only three animals are killed, two peacocks and a deer, and the deer not invariably. Even these three animals will not be killed in future.'[33] In another inscription, he records that 'the king refrains from [eating] living beings, and indeed other men and whosoever [were] the king's huntsmen and fishermen have ceased from hunting....'[34] In yet another, much longer, inscription he records the ban which he has introduced on the killing of a wide variety of animals, birds, and fish, and even on the burning of forests without good reason.[35] As a result of his instructions to the people, 'abstention from killing and non-injury to living beings', as well as various forms of generosity and piety, 'have all

187

increased as never before for many centuries'.[36] The time which kings had formerly spent in hunting 'and other similar amusements' Ashoka devoted instead to the promotion of the moral condition of the realm. In the past, he records, kings used to go on pleasure tours. But in the tenth year of his reign, the year after he had begun to be a more ardent follower of the Buddhist way, he visited the scene of Gotama's Enlightenment at Bodh-Gaya. 'From that time arose the practice of tours connected with *Dhamma*, during which meetings are held with ascetics and brahmans, gifts are bestowed, meetings are arranged with aged folk, gold is distributed, meetings with the people of the countryside are held, instruction in *Dhamma* is given, and questions on *Dhamma* are answered.'[37] He adds that he finds this more enjoyable than any other kind of activity.

But as well as the royal entourage's use of time in this way, in the interests of public ethical instruction and philanthropy, the resources of the state were devoted to various public works for the common good. Throughout the entire realm, records the second Major Rock Edict, two medical services have been provided. 'These consist of the medical care of man, and the care of animals.' Moreover, 'medicinal herbs, whether useful to man or to beast, have been brought and planted wherever they did not grow.' Other public works mentioned in this inscription include the introduction of root crops and fruit trees where they were not grown formerly; the provision of wells at points along the roads, and the planting of trees for shade, to make travel easier for man and beast.[38] These things are recorded in the Seventh Pillar Edict too, where it is mentioned that provision of wells and of rest houses was made at regular intervals of eight kos[39] along the main roads, and the trees which were planted to provide shade are specified—banyan trees. The purpose of these public works is here said to have been 'that my people might conform to *Dhamma*'.[40] That is to say, it was considered that the improvement of the general quality of public life and health in these ways, and the enhanced trade that would follow, would help to create the conditions in which the Buddhist ethic could best be practiced. Another measure taken by Ashoka with this end in view was the appointment of welfare-officers, known as 'commissioners of *Dhamma*'.[41] This new office was instituted by

Ashoka in the twelfth year of his reign; appointments to the office were made throughout the whole realm. 'Among servants and nobles, brahmans and wealthy householders, among the poor and the aged, they are working for the welfare and happiness of those devoted to *Dhamma* and for the removal of their troubles. They are busy in promoting the welfare of prisoners should they have behaved irresponsibly, or releasing those that have children, are afflicted, or are aged.'[42]

ASHOKA'S ATTITUDE TO RELIGION

In the extracts from the Ashokan inscriptions which have been considered so far there has been virtually nothing that could unequivocally be called 'religious' in the emperor's concerns and policies. That is to say, there has been no mention of the sacred, or of sanctions for behavior derived from the sacred, unless *Dhamma* may be held to fill the place of the sacred. But we are not altogether without evidence of Ashoka's attitude to contemporary beliefs and practices associated with belief in gods and sacred beings. His total opposition to the sacrificial offering of any living being is clearly expressed in the First Major Rock Edict, and his disapproval of the kind of assemblies associated with such sacrifices.[43] In another of the rock edicts he deals with various kinds of rites, practiced by the common people on such occasions as the birth of a child, or at the start of a journey. Women, in particular, he says, 'perform a variety of ceremonies, which are trivial and useless'. The one 'ceremony' which is of great value is the practice of *Dhamma*.[44] The attitude which is revealed here—strong opposition to animal sacrifice, mild disapproval of useless and superstitious rites, together with commendation of the practice of the *Dhamma*—is characteristically Buddhist, and recalls, in particular, some of the Buddha's discourses in the *Dīgha Nikāya* (see chapter 5).

Ashoka appears to have shared contemporary cosmological belief, with notions of various layers of existence one upon the other. Below the earth were various hells; the surface of the earth was the abode of men, and above the surface of the earth were realms of increasingly refined and rarified atmosphere, the various heavens, where lived the spirit beings or devas, sometimes called 'gods'. These denizens of the upper regions were regarded as a 'natural' feature of the universe, as natural as any other beings, and subject to rebirth, but they enjoyed a more blissful present existence in heaven as a result of good karma in previous existences, according to the prevalent Indian view. Improvement in moral conditions on earth could attract them, however, and it was believed that in such happy circumstances the devas appeared from time to time among men. Such a condition of things Ashoka believed to have been brought about as a result of his strenuous efforts on behalf of *Dhamma*. Referring to his own increased moral ardour during the year that he had been a more active Buddhist he comments that 'The gods, who in India up to this time did not associate with men, now mingle with them.'[45] The same inscription endorses the contemporary popular idea that by living a good moral life any man could achieve a more blissful existence on some higher plane: 'This is not something to be obtained only by the great, but it is also open to the humble, if they are earnest; and they can even reach heaven easily.'

One further point of interest which arises from a study of the inscriptions is that Ashoka looked with strong disfavour upon sectarianism when it led to the disparagement of the views and attitudes of others. Like other rulers, before his time and since, Ashoka had a powerful interest in peace within his realm, in harmony among his subjects. True progress in essential truth, he says, will enable a man to control his speech 'so as not to extoll one's own sect or disparage another's on unsuitable occasions'; rather, 'one should honor another man's sect, for by doing so one increases the influence of one's own sect and benefits that of the other man; while by doing otherwise one diminishes the influence of one's own sect and harms the other man's.' In Ashoka's case, this concern with social harmony is all of a piece with his very evident and earnest concern for the general welfare of his subjects. He himself honored with gifts and attended to the affairs of Ajivakas, Jains, and brahmans as well as Buddhists.[46]

From this survey of the evidence of Ashoka's fairly numerous inscriptions, what emerges is the picture of a ruler who was converted from one ideology of government to another. He was, throughout his life, both before and after his adherence to Buddhism, first and foremost a king; he did not give up the affairs of government for the affairs of some other, spiritual realm. He became a Buddhist because it seemed to him that to do so was to become a better king; pursuit of the *Dhamma* would ensure that the realm over which he ruled was a better, happier and more peaceful place.

Ashoka has been compared to the Emperor Constantine, who made the Christian religion the official creed of the Roman Empire, and established the Church as the ecclesiastical arm of the state. If we start out with the idea that there is such a correspondence, that Ashoka was an Indian Constantine, then we soon find ourselves referring to the *Sangha* as the 'Buddhist Church',[47] and calling *bhikkhus* not merely 'monks', but even 'priests'. But what Ashoka promoted was a system of public morality and social welfare which was itself the logical working-out in the socio-political sphere of a sophisticated and radical analysis of the human situation. The basis of the appeal of this ideology was not to be found in any theistic sanctions, but in the self-evident attractiveness and value of the kind of life which it tended to produce when it was seriously adhered to and practiced over a sustained period. The corps of professionals set the ethical and existential goal so high (*nibbāna*) that in their pursuit of it, they enhanced the moral quality of the life of those around them. To support such men, to heed their philosophy, to facilitate the realization of their ideal by the proper ordering of society—this was Ashoka's primary concern from the time he became an enthusiastic Buddhist. As far as 'religion' was concerned, if by that were meant priesthood and sacrificial system, Ashoka was, like any other Buddhist, opposed to such institutions, as socially dangerous and intellectually deceptive. If by religion were meant popular rites and ceremonies other than sacrifice, he saw no great harm in these, nor any great usefulness either. Occasionally a ceremony or an ancient custom might have something to be said for it, as inculcating reverence for good traditions. But one should never be too dogmatic about such things, Ashoka held; certainly not if it were at the cost of fraternal goodwill and social harmony. Nevertheless, it was in the general area of mildly beneficial ancient customs that 'religious' forms of activity prospered in Ashoka's reign. The indigenous, non-brahmanical elements of popular belief were stimulated by the tolerance which they

191

enjoyed, and so, together with the growth and influence of Buddhism there went a growth of non-priestly beliefs and customs. Perhaps the most significant of these was the cult of veneration of *stūpas*, the stone or brick cairns in which were enshrined the reliquary remains of great men and heroes. The growth of this cult during Ashoka's time is clearly attested by the number of *stūpas* in India which have been identified as dating from this period. It was this, associated as it was with Buddhism, which more than anything else marks the beginning of the characterization of the Buddhist movement in religious terms. By Ashoka's time the seeds of the attitude of *bhakti*, or reverential, loving devotion, had been sown, seeds which in later centuries were to bloom luxuriantly in the worship by lay people not only of the Buddha, Gotama, but of countless other potential Buddhas, or Bodhisattvas, heavenly beings of such exalted and potent spirituality that they were in function and status indistinguishable from gods.

But in Ashoka's time all this lay in the future. Ashoka was no Constantine, discerning the growing popularity and power of the cult of a divine savior; nor did Ashoka, as Constantine did, hasten to identify himself and his realm with the name of a new god that before long would be above every divine name, throughout the Roman Empire. Nor did he, as Constantine, graft this new faith on to the old religion of the state, continuing himself to function as *pontifex maximus* of the old priesthood. In contrast to all this, Ashoka was attracted to a social philosophy, and was attracted all the more strongly as his awareness of the problems that attend an emperor's task grew. The more he was drawn to this philosophy of the restructured society and restructured consciousness, the farther he moved from the old, priestly statecraft of the brahmans, while still paying respect to popular traditions. If there is any useful historical parallel with the Buddhism of Ashokan India, it is not the Constantinism of imperial Rome but the Confucianism of imperial China. And it has long been doubted whether that can be called a religion.

THE EFFECT OF INDIAN RELIGIOSITY UPON BUDDHISM

The fact remains that by the end of Ashoka's reign, Buddhism had come to be very much more closely and intimately associated with popular religious practice than had formerly been the case. It may be useful at this point to remind ourselves that the essential features of Buddhist practice, as they are portrayed throughout the Pāli Canon, are morality and mental discipline, leading ultimately to wisdom, or enlightenment. At the higher levels of the Buddhist movement both morality and mental discipline were equally important and equally emphasized as the proper concerns of the Buddhist professional—the *bhikkhu*. But at the lower levels of engagement, among those who were living the lives of householders and workers, it was expected that the major preoccupation would be with morality. This is implied, too, in the Ashokan inscriptions, as we have seen. Morality, or, in Ashokan terminology, *Dhamma*, consisted of generosity, expressed in various social relations, of non-violence, and simplicity of life. So far as any *cultus* of worship is concerned, there would appear to be nothing in the nature of Buddhism itself to require it or justify it. It was on aesthetic grounds, apparently, that the Buddha admired the various shrines in the city of Vaishali[48]; his words to Ananda on each occasion when they visited these shrines had to do with the practice of mental discipline. The value of such shrines appears to have consisted in the opportunity which they provided, as the text of the *Mahā Parinibbāna Suttanta* has it, for developing, practicing, dwelling on, expanding and ascending to the very heights of the four paths to *iddhi*. *Iddhi* is a word which had various connotations, according to the context[49] for which the most general or comprehensive translation is 'glory' or 'majesty'. The 'glory' to which the 'four paths' here mentioned lead is that of the Buddhist who has attained the goal of emancipation from bondage to 'self-hood'. The four paths are those of will, moral effort, thought and analysis, in the context in each case of the struggle against evil.

So, while there was nothing in the nature of early Buddhism to require worship as an essential activity, as there is in theistic religions like Judaism, Christianity, Islam and Vaishnavism, there was a tendency, dating back apparently to the earliest period, to associate mental discipline, in certain circumstances, with the aesthetically helpful setting provided by an already existing shrine. Beyond this use of a shrine early Buddhism had no reason to go: certainly not in the direction of any kind of public ceremonial or *cultus*. So far as the *bhikkhus* were concerned, the Buddha was represented as having explicitly forbidden them to engage even in the reverencing of his mortal remains after his death. That, he said, could be left to pious men among the nobles and householders; *bhikkhus* should concentrate on making progress in moral and mental discipline.[50] It was for noblemen and householders who were supporters of the Buddhist movement to supply the land, the resources and the labor for the building of *stūpas*, so that the remains of the Buddha should be treated in the same way 'as men treat the remains of a *Chakravartin*',[51] or universal monarch. The cremation of the Buddha's body and the enshrinement of the bones and ashes was, as we saw earlier (chapter 6, p. 127), carried out in exactly the manner that was used for the cremation and enshrinement of the remains of a great emperor. We saw also (chapter 8, p. 170) that this was one of a number of ways in which the Buddha and the *Chakravartin* are regarded as counterparts, spiritual or philosophical on the one hand, and political on the other.

It has been suggested that the building of a mound or *stūpa* in which to enshrine relics was, in fact, an old custom put to new use in early Buddhism.[52] The old custom, says the exponent of this view, was the veneration of certain hemispherical mounds as sacred, and was a feature of ancient religious practice in a number of cultures. This custom was then given a new meaning by the use of such solid brick or stone mounds as receptacles for Buddhist relics; thus, what was originally simple *mound-worship* developed into *relic-worship*. There is no certainty about this, however, and the argument is based largely on the existence of 'traces of mound-worship in the Vedic age among the Aryans of India'.[53] While it is conceivable that *some* kind of cult of sacred mounds may have preceded their use in the early Buddhist period as reliquary shrines, there is no clear evidence of this. What is clear is that in the Ashokan period, large numbers of Buddhist *stūpas* were constructed, in the course of what appears to have been a widespread popular movement. What was expressed by this practice was devotion to the Buddha, and the desire to reverence him. It is possible that Ashoka himself was responsible for making the cult into a popular movement.[54] It must be emphasized that in the Ashokan period the 'Buddha-image' or 'Buddha-statue' (properly called a *Buddha-rūpa*) had not yet appeared on the scene; this was a devotional usage which did not develop until about the first century BC, somewhere in north-western India. Until then it was the *stūpa* which served as a focus of reverential feelings for the great man who had first gained supreme enlightenment, who had first taught the eternal truths of *Dhamma*, and had founded the Order of those who guarded, practiced and transmitted this eternal *Dhamma*. In India the tendency to pay elaborate respect and reverence to great men, to the point of deifying them, is well attested, from the modern period back to antiquity.[55] It combines with another well-attested and widespread emotional attitude—the desire to surrender oneself in self-abnegating adoration. In India this attitude is known as *bhakti*, well described as the experience in which 'mind and body are flooded with an overwhelming sweetness, the *Rasa* or *Raga*, which is the experience of being in love not with a human lover but a divine'.[56] This religious mood of utter surrender of the self to one who is thought of as savior or lord, makes its appearance in a variety of forms and in diverse cultures outside India, from the Amida-cults of medieval Japan to the Jesus-cults of modern America. In India the cult of the *bhagavatā*, the beloved or adored one, has often focused itself round an historical figure whom subsequent generations have invested with divine qualities.

This merging of various strands of folk-religion was made considerably easier by the encouragement which Ashoka gave to it by his insistence on the meeting and mingling of the adherents of different religious and philosophical sects; the Twelfth Major Rock Edict commands that different sects should listen to one another's principles, honor each other, and promote the essential doctrine of all sects, and adds that the carrying out of this policy was a special responsibility of the state-appointed 'commissioners of *Dhamma*'.[57]

That the Buddha had come to be the object of a popular *bhagavatā*-cult in the Ashokan period is clear from the opposition expressed by those *bhikkhus* who adhered to the earlier, simpler concept of the Buddha. The *Kathāvatthu*, one of the seven books of the Abhidhamma collection in the Pāli Canon, is generally regarded as having been compiled during Ashoka's reign. Its main purpose appears to have been the correction of various errors which had developed with regard to the Buddha, and the Buddhist way; the very production of such a work by the more orthodox *bkikkhus* of Ashoka's time is itself an important piece of evidence regarding Buddhist development during that period. As Sukumar Dutt has pointed out, there would have been no need for a work of this kind unless grave misconceptions regarding the Buddha and his teaching really had developed, and unless, too, there existed in the community a sense of the importance of preserving the earlier tradition in its pure form, and a feeling that this was now being seriously threatened.[58] Among the points dealt with in the *Kathāvatthu* was the idea that the Buddha had not really lived in the world of men, but in the 'heaven of bliss', appearing to men on earth in a specially created, temporary form to preach the Dhamma.[59] Together with this virtual deification of the Buddha there went also a tendency to deny him normal human characteristics,[60] and on the other hand to attribute to him unlimited magical power.[61]

Such views of the Buddha were still being refuted by the Theravadins when 'The Questions of King Milinda' was composed, probably in the first century of the Christian era.[62]

THE DEVELOPMENT OF A RELIGIOUS BUDDHISM

It is possible to see that during the Ashokan period a number of different but related factors were at work in Indian society, which, interacting upon one another, were tending to produce an amalgam of philosophy, meditational practice, ethics, devotional piety and folk-lore which can justifiably be described as 'religious Buddhism'. In this process the cult of the *stūpa* was possibly the crucial item. Royal support for the Buddhist movement meant the devotion of royal resources for the meritorious work of *stūpa*-building. The general economic prosperity which Ashoka's internal policies helped to foster, by providing a reasonable degree of peace within the empire and good facilities for communication and transport, meant that other prosperous citizens could afford to follow the royal example of *stūpa*-

building. The growth in the number of *stūpas* would, among the mass of the people, lead very easily in the Indian cultural atmosphere to a cult of the *bhagava*, the blessed one, the Buddha, in whose honor these *stūpas* had all been raised. Given this virtual deification of the Buddha as the blessed one, the Lord, there would be no difficulty at all in relating him to the pantheon of Indian folk-religion as one of the great beings, possibly the greatest, to whom adoration and worship were offered. Nor would the members of the *Sangha* be likely to discourage the building of *stūpas* and their use as popular shrines, since there was as we have seen, a tradition that the Buddha himself had spoken of the value of the shrines as places for fruitful mental discipline.

It is possible that it was the development of Buddhism from a socio-political philosophy to a popularly-based religious cult which was one of the chief causes of its eventual decline and virtual disappearance from India. Once it had come to be regarded as a religious system it could be thought of—and indeed was thought of—as a rival by those who adhered to, and whose interests were vested in, another religious ideology, notably the brahmans. Ashoka himself seems to have moved his position in this respect during the course of his roughly forty-year reign, from the earlier attitude of equal tolerance and encouragement of all sects and ideologies, to a more pronounced affinity for the Buddhist movement in his later years. His prohibition of the slaughter of animals would not have been altogether welcome to those who were the guardians of a tradition of sacrificial ritual. His measures aimed at restricting or banning popular festivals of which he did not approve would also have diminished to some extent his public image as a man of complete religious tolerance. When, in addition, during the latter part of his reign, it was seen that the emperor was increasingly associated with the Buddhist *Sangha* and its affairs, at a time when Buddhism was taking on the characteristics of another, rival religious system—rival, that is, to the system of ideas and practices which the brahmans believed it was their sacred duty to uphold and preserve—some kind of conflict between the two would appear inevitable. There has been some debate among scholars regarding the extent to which the opposition of the brahmans was responsible for the decline of the Ashokan Buddhist state.[63] Those who deny that there was such opposition have not, in the opinion of the author, produced reasons for this view sufficiently convincing to match the strength with which they appear to hold it.

Without doubt, Ashoka's rule was autocratic. The Ashokan state was in no sense a democracy. Within the *Sangha* itself there was, as we have noted, a democratic system of self-government, but so far as the general run of men were concerned the Buddhist view was that men who by nature were dominated by passion needed strong, morally wholesome, autocratic rule. It was such a rule that Ashoka saw it to be his duty to exercise. In doing so, while he must have had the tacit consent of the mass of the people, he would also have incurred the dislike and even enmity of any sections of the community whose interests were not compatible with the public promotion of *Dhamma*. Ashoka suppressed what he believed was not in accordance with *Dhamma*. In doing so, he incurred an intensified opposition to *Dhamma*, as well as to himself and his dynasty. The Mauryan dynasty declined rapidly after his death, and survived him by barely half a century before it was superseded by the re-established brahman state under the Sungas. Buddhism managed to survive, partly because of its now increasingly popular basis and its marriage to folk religion, and partly because the political power of brahmanism was not everywhere sufficiently great to allow the enforcement of that policy towards Buddhism which is stated clearly and unequivocally in what the Law of Manu has to say concerning the treatment of heretics: 'Men belonging to an heretical sect [classed here together with gamblers, dancers and singers, cruel men, those following forbidden occupations, and sellers of spirituous liquor] let him [the king] instantly banish from his town.'[64] Similarly, 'ascetics' (of heretical sects) are lumped together with 'those born of an illegal mixture of the castes', and 'those who have committed suicide' as classes of men to whom no honour should be given.[65]

By the end of Ashoka's reign, the structure of dual relationship which the *Sangha* had evolved, between the king on the one hand and the people on the other, was beginning to display some of the inherent disadvantages which it entailed, particularly in the Indian situation. The close ties between king and *Sangha* which Buddhist polity seemed to require had, as an inevitable effect, the antagonizing of the brahmans. In order to function properly, the Buddhist political arrangement which was pragmatically to be preferred, namely the securing of the king's adherence to Buddhist values, had also to exclude his adherence to brahman values and policies. By implication the scheme had to be exclusive to the *Sangha*. Ashoka's occasional declarations of goodwill towards the brahmans could not ultimately disguise the facts of the situation. The hostility of the brahmans, which exclusion from their former position of political influence would engender, gave the *Sangha* a vested interest in the continuance of royal patronage.

On the other hand, the *Sangha* did not and could not rely entirely on royal support, for this by itself was not sufficient. It is true that Ashoka, and after him, in a similar manner, Buddhist kings of Sri Lanka, gave generously for the supplying of the *Sangha's* needs, of food, clothing and housing. But these donations were, in the total perspective, symbolic and exemplary. Economically, the major support for the *Sangha*, on a day-to-day basis, would have come from the local people of the towns and cities of the Ashokan empire. Hence, there was a strong economic motive for an attitude of tolerance towards popular cults and beliefs, in order not to antagonize unnecessarily those on whom the *Sangha* depended for their daily needs. This attitude of tolerance was not difficult to accommodate for, as we have seen, it accorded well with the Buddhist view of the operation of reason and argument. But such an attitude towards popular belief and practices, arising out of both theory and economic requirement, had as its penalty the danger of the subversion of the *Sangha* by the all-pervasive popular cults of India, and particularly by the *bhagavatā*-cult.

The end of the Mauryan dynasty and the restoration of brahmanical statecraft of the Kautilyan kind to its former position of dominance might have seemed to signal the end of the Buddhist experiment to which Ashoka and, with less distinction, his successors, had devoted themselves. It might look as though Buddhism was now to survive in India merely as another of the many *bhagavatā*-cults of which India seems never to have had any shortage. Gotama the Buddha and his teaching, the quiet social and ideological revolution which had for three centuries been making steady progress in northern India and beyond, were now, it seemed, destined soon to be forgotten as men gave themselves instead to a cult of a heavenly lord, while brahman priests who advised the rulers of the state took good care that Buddhism should never again be allowed to achieve the political and social influence which it had under Ashoka.

That is how it might have seemed, and to some extent that is how it was; but not entirely so. For while, in some places, the *Sangha* was swayed by the increasingly influential cult of the heavenly lord and its diverse developments, in other places it maintained the tradition of Gotama, the Sage of the Shakyas, the man who had completely destroyed all attachment to the notion of the individual self, the man who was 'cooled' from all passion, and fully awakened, the *Samasambuddha*, who had also inaugurated the company, the *Sangha*, of those who followed him on this path, the company which, as the embodiment of that same selflessness, was to be the prototype for humanity as a whole. So long as there was a stream of *Sangha* life where this tradition was maintained, even though the actual structure of a Buddhist state had been dismantled, there was always the possibility that what had happened when Ashoka succeeded to the throne of Magadha could happen again, and that another monarch, adhering fully and confidently to the Buddhist tradition, might, in cooperation with the *Sangha*, bring back into being the Buddhist pattern of society. So long as the *Sangha* survived, somewhere, in its earlier form and with its earlier perspectives, that tradition would be preserved out of which the Buddhist state and the Buddhist ordering of the common life might once again emerge.

The *Sangha* did so survive, in the school of the Theravadins, or those who adhere to the doctrine of the elders, and it was this school which preserved the tradition of the Buddhist state, in south India, north-east India, and most notably and most continuously, in Sri Lanka. It is to the story of the planting of Buddhist civilization in Sri Lanka that we now turn our attention.

10   The Buddhist State in Sri Lanka

It has been suggested in the course of this outline of Buddhist civilization that the structure of Buddhism which is presupposed in the discourses of the Buddha and his public activities is that of a triangular relationship between the *Sangha*, the king and the people. It has been suggested further that this is precisely the structure of the Ashokan Buddhist state, the first sustained realization of the Buddhist ideal. The *Sangha*, the new community of those who have abandoned the individualistic notions which nourish so much 'commonsense' understanding of life, and which produce so much envy, hatred, sorrow and conflict, constitutes the growing point—or growing points— of the restructured humanity. Meanwhile, the large remaining area of society outside the *Sangha*, which is nevertheless proleptically *Sangha*, potential but not realized, must have its own appropriate forms of organization and control, which will both discourage the violent and morally unwholesome elements, and encourage the pursuit of peace and morally wholesome action. In ancient India this task had to be performed by a Buddhist king, and this is the task that Ashoka appears to have accepted and endeavored to fulfill, with notable success So long as the ordinary people of such a society are being schooled in Buddhist ways and Buddhist attitudes, particularly those of generosity in thought and action, and so long as they are as yet only at the elementary stage of schooling, so to speak, they are not to be harangued or castigated for holding ideas and practicing customs which belong to a pre-Buddhist stage of society. This appears to be the accepted Buddhist view, and so an open frontier is allowed, between Buddhist attitudes and practices and those of the earlier folk culture. In the Ashokan Buddhist state this principle can be seen at work, in particular, in the widespread growth of the *stūpa*-cult, and in the use of folk practices and ideas in the service of Buddhist teaching and devotion.

That this is a fairly accurate outline of what Buddhism was understood to be in the Ashokan period is confirmed by the fact that this is precisely the shape in which it was exported from India to Sri Lanka during Ashoka's reign.

The story is told in the Pāli chronicles of Sri Lanka, namely, 'The Island Chronicle' (*Dīpavaṃsa*), and 'The Great Chronicle' (*Mahāvaṃsa*) and in a work by Buddhaghosa called the *Samanta-Pāsādikā*,[1] written in the latter half of the fifth century AD. As we have already seen, the chronicles were not compiled until about the fifth and sixth centuries respectively, of the Christian era, or roughly the tenth and eleventh centuries of the Buddhist era. This was eight or nine centuries after the events which were described. Nevertheless Buddhaghosa and the chroniclers made use of the traditions which had come down to them, and which had been transmitted with that meticulous care in reproducing exactly what is repeated which characterizes Indian oral tradition. A modern Sinhalese Buddhist, Dr. G. P. Malalasekere, has put it in this way: 'Even today [in Sri Lanka] great respect is shown to the man who carries all his learning in his head; for "who knows whether books may not get lost or destroyed and become not easy to lay hands on?" And the person who trusts to books for reference is contemptuously referred to as "he who has a big book at home, but does not know a thing". Anyone visiting a village monastery in Sri Lanka at the present time will find the *ola* leaf books carefully wrapped up in costly silk cloths and reverently packed in beautifully carved bookcases, that the faithful devotees may offer to them flowers and incense and thus pay honor to the Buddha's word. The monk is expected to carry all his learning in his head.'[2]

The account which the chronicles give us of Buddhism as it existed in the third century BC, and as it was taken to Sri Lanka, agrees very well with what has already appeared from the evidence of Ashoka's stone inscriptions, and with the profile of Buddhism in the canonical writings. The story of the coming of Buddhism to the island is told in a number of clear, successive stages.

THE ESTABLISHMENT OF BUDDHIST KINGSHIP AND *SANGHA*

The first was the establishment of very cordial relations between Devanam-piya Tissa, who had just succeeded to the throne of Sri Lanka, and Ashoka. This came about, according to the chronicler, in the following way. At the accession of Devanam-piya Tissa a great quantity of precious stones of all kinds was discovered in the island and its surrounding waters: sapphire, beryl, ruby, pearls, and many other 'priceless treasures' were found. Tissa's immediate response was to send a magnificent gift of these jewels to the emperor of India, 'to my friend, Dhamma Ashoka', for he 'and nobody else is worthy to have these priceless treasures', said Tissa. We are told by the chronicler that 'the two monarchs, Devanam-piya Tissa and Dhamma Ashoka had already been friends a long time though they had never seen each other.[3] Four officials of Tissa's court were appointed as envoys, and with the support of a body of retainers, they carried the precious stones to Pataliputra, Ashoka's capital. Ashoka received both the jewels and the envoys with enthusiasm; upon the latter were bestowed appropriate titles of honour.

What is more significant, however, is the further response which was made by Ashoka in assembling and sending to Tissa all that was necessary for an Indian royal consecration. The list of the requisites of royalty given in the chronicle reads as follows: 'a fan, a diadem, a sword, a parasol, shoes, a turban, ear-ornaments, chains, a pitcher, yellow sandalwood, a set of garments that had no need of cleansing, a costly napkin, unguent brought by the *nagas*, red-coloured earth, water from the lake Anotatta and also water from the Ganges, a spiral shell winding in auspicious wise, a maiden in the flower of her youth, utensils as golden platters, a costly litter, yellow and emblic myrobalans and precious ambrosial healing herbs, sixty times one hundred wagon loads of mountain-rice brought thither by parrots, nay, all that was needful for consecrating a king, marvelous in splendor....'[4] With these things Ashoka sent Tissa envoys 'with the gift of the true doctrine, saying, "I have taken refuge in the Buddha, the *Dhamma*, and the *Sangha*. I have declared myself a lay-disciple in the discipline of the Shakyan. Seek then even thou, O best of men, converting thy mind with believing heart refuge in these best of gems!" and saying moreover [to the envoys]: "Consecrate my friend yet again as king." '[5]

On their arrival back in Sri Lanka the gifts were delivered, and the consecration of Tissa was carried out in accordance with Ashoka's instructions. The second stage in this story of the coming of Buddhism to Sri Lanka, after the reconsecration of the king in the style of Ashoka and the delivery of the message of advice to him to become a Buddhist lay-disciple like Ashoka, was the introduction of the *Sangha* into the island. This, according to the chronicle, was the work of the great Buddhist leader in India, Moggaliputta, who sent an elder (*thera*) and four *bhikkhus* to Sri Lanka to 'establish the discipline of the Conqueror',[6] that is, of the Buddha, in the island. The elder was Mahinda, Ashoka's son by his first wife, Devi. Mahinda had been a member of the *Sangha* for twelve years by the time he was sent to Sri Lanka, having been admitted to full membership of the Order at the age of twenty. On his arrival in Sri Lanka he made an occasion for meeting king Tissa when the latter was out hunting. Although Tissa had been reconsecrated according to Ashoka's instructions, he had not yet become a Buddhist lay-disciple, even formally. Having engaged the king in conversation, in order to find out what kind of mind he had, and having discovered the king to be a keen-witted man, Mahinda delivered to him one of the Buddha's discourses known as 'The Discourse on the Simile of the Elephant's Footprint'.[7] This covers a range of topics: it tells of the Buddha 'a perfected one, a fully self-awakened one, endowed with right knowledge and conduct, a well-farer, knower of the [three] worlds, the matchless charioteer of men who are to be tamed, the Awakened One, the Bhagavan'.[8] It tells also of the *Dhamma* which he proclaims, and of the new standards of morality which are adopted by one who hears the *Dhamma* and is convinced of its truths; the sobriety and simplicity of life, the attitude of nonviolence, the control of mind and senses which such a person develops, and how he loses all restlessness and worry, lives calmly, without doubts or perplexity. At the end of the discourse, its original hearer, a brahman is recorded as saying, 'It is wonderful, good Gotama.... It is as if good Gotama, one might set upright what had been upset, or might disclose what had been covered, or might point out the way to one who had gone astray, or might bring an oil-lamp into the darkness so that those with vision might see ... even so is *Dhamma* made clear in many a figure by the good Gotama.'[9] He then declares his resolve, in the usual three-fold formula, to resort to the Buddha, the *Dhamma* and the *Sangha* for as long as life lasts, asking the Buddha to accept him as a lay-disciple. The recital of the discourse by Mahinda is said to have had the same effect upon King Tissa, who at the end of it, together with his companions, similarly declared his intentions to resort to the Buddha, his *Dhamma*, and his *Sangha*.[10] The next day Mahinda was invited to expound the Buddha's teaching to the women of the royal household. Of the three discourses which he is said to have used on this occasion, one dealt with the various sad fates which had befallen those who dwelt in the world of ghosts as a result of their previous evil lives (the *Petavatthu*),[11] another by way of contrast described the happy state of those who dwelt in heavenly palaces because of their previous moral goodness (the *Vimānavatthu*),[12] and a third set out the four noble truths of Buddhist morality.[13] After they had listened to Mahinda, the women of the royal household became 'stream-enterers', that is to say, those who have embarked on the Buddhist life and have taken the initial step towards crossing to 'the further shore'. Many of the local townspeople, too, having heard of the arrival of Mahinda and his companions, and of the great impression they had made, came together in a crowd and asked for Mahinda to come out and address them. He did so, using on this occasion the *Deva-dūta-suttanta*, or 'Discourse on the Heavenly Messengers', another homily cast in the form of popular legend, making use of the folk-beliefs in Yama, the god of death. His messengers, according to this *Sutta*, are old age, disease, and the fact of death, and they are meant to remind men of the transitoriness of human pleasure, and the wisdom of living a morally good life. As a result, many of these townspeople also, we are told, became 'stream-enterers'. During the following days even larger crowds assembled to be addressed by Mahinda, with correspondingly wider public adherence to the Buddhist morality and way of life.

As a suitable place for Mahinda and his companions to spend their nights, a place neither too noisy nor on the other hand too far removed from the city and difficult of access, the king presented them with a piece of parkland, the Mahāmegha. It was here a little later that the *vihāra* or 'residence' for the *bhikkhus* was built which was eventually to be known as the 'Great *Vihāra*' of the city of Anuradhapura, and the headquarters of the Theravada school of Sri Lanka. An important feature of the proper establishment of such a residence for *bhikkhus* was the tracing out of its boundaries.[14] This was done in a ceremony performed by the king, who ploughed a great circular furrow round the area. Boundary marks were then set up along the circle which had been ploughed, and so the territorial 'parish' of the *bhikkhus'* residence was permanently delineated. When that had been done a dwelling-house and a refectory were built, and a place was reserved for the planting of a cutting from the bodhi-tree which was to be brought from India. A place within the park had been already allocated for the eventual building of a *stūpa*.

PROVISION FOR A BUDDHIST POPULACE

The decision to build a *stūpa* was partly in acknowledgement of the now wide adherence of the people of Anuradhapura to the Buddhist system, and partly in order, so it is said, to provide for the *bhikkhus* themselves an appropriate focus for their devotion. We are told that at the end of the rainy season Mahinda raised the matter with the king: 'We have had no sight of the Buddha for a long time, O Lord of men. We live as men without a master. We have no way of paying our respect to the Buddha.' The king was puzzled by this: 'I thought you told me that the Buddha had entered *nibbāna*.' 'Yes,' they replied, 'but vision of the relics is vision of the Conqueror.'[15] (This is perhaps a crude translation, but it helps to suggest the double sense of vision which seems to be implied in the text.) The king replied that they knew already of his intentions to build a *stūpa*, and added, 'I will build the *stūpa*; you must find out about the relics.'

It is evident from the style of the Pāli chronicles that already popular ideas of miracles and marvels had made themselves at home in the Buddhist tradition. As S. Paranavitana has put it: 'Mahinda and his companions transport themselves by air from Vedisagiri to Mihintale, gods are at hand to make smooth the path of the religious teachers, and impress the multitude with the efficiency of their doctrines. Earthquakes which do no harm to anyone vouch for the veracity of the prophecies.... At sermons preached on important occasions, the *Devas* in the congregation outnumber the humans. Elephants, without anyone's bidding, indicate to the king the exact spot on which sacred shrines are to be built.'[16] It should be noted that the marvels which are related are not in any special sense religious phenomena, that is, connected with god or gods. If the *devas* are mentioned, so also are earthquakes and elephants, and feats of intercontinental air travel, so we must regard the appearance of the gods as simply part of a general background derived from the popular world-view of the time. Paranavitana points out that 'in spite of this legendary overlay, the main event, i.e., that Buddhism was accepted by the people and the ruler of Sri Lanka' is attested by epigraphical evidence.[17]

The manner in which sacred relics were brought from India to Sri Lanka is similarly described in the chronicles in terms of superhuman marvels: an air-trip to the Himalayas to visit Sakka, the Lord of the gods; a parasol that bowed down of its own volition in the presence of the relics, and an elephant which did the same; a relic-urn which moved through space of its own accord, and more quaking of the earth in connection with these events. What most concerns us, however, is the fact that very early in this complex process by which ancient Sri Lanka became a Buddhist state there was the building of a *stūpa*, and that this was apparently regarded as a necessity. A similar necessity for the proper functioning of the system (that is, presumably, the system known to function in Ashokan India) was the importation from India of a bodhi- or bo-tree. But the most important aspect of the establishing of the Buddhist system (i.e., the *Buddha-sāsana* or discipline) was the coming into existence of an indigenously produced *Sangha*. A remark attributed to Mahinda[18] makes this clear. When Tissa asked him whether the *Buddha-sāsana* was now well established in the island, Mahinda replied that it was, but that it had not yet become firmly rooted. 'When will it become firmly rooted?' asked the king. Mahinda's reply was: 'When a son born in Sri Lanka of Sri Lankan parents becomes a *bhikkhu* in Sri Lanka, studies the *Vinaya* in Sri Lanka, and recites it in Sri Lanka, then the roots of the *Sāsana* are deep set.' The first two of these requirements had already been met; a son born in Sri Lanka of Sri Lankan parents had become a *bhikkhu*, Maha-Arittha by name, and had studied the *Vinaya* in Sri Lanka. Arrangements were then made for a recital or teaching session of *Vinaya* to take place in the presence of the king. This clearly portrays the intimate relation which was conceived to exist between the life of the *Sangha*, which was ruled by the *Vinaya*, and the life of the state, which was ruled over by the king. It emphasizes, too, the national, indeed, in a sense, even nationalist, character of the *Buddha-sāsana*; its full realization involved the existence also of a Buddhist national state.

The *stūpa* having been built by the king for the relics which had been brought from India, and the bodhi-tree, brought from India by Ashoka's daughter Sanghamitra, having been planted, the essential ingredients for the Buddhist state after the Ashokan pattern were all present: a king who was a Buddhist disciple; an indigenous *Sangha*; and provision made in the form of a *stūpa* and a bo-tree for popular devotion to be expressed by the mass of the people, a large number of whom were now Buddhists adherents or lay-disciples.

The extent to which this outline of events is authentic historically, cannot be seriously doubted. It is certainly very like the pattern of the Ashokan Buddhist state, as we have seen it through the evidence of the inscriptions of Ashoka. If it be argued that this is a projection back into third century BC Sri Lanka of the Buddhist pattern of the chroniclers' own time, that is, the fifth and sixth centuries AD, then it is all the more noteworthy, that in sixth-century Buddhist Sri Lanka the pattern so closely adhered to what it had been in Ashoka's India eight centuries before. However, the Pāli chronicles of the fifth century AD, which tell how Sri Lanka became a Buddhist state in the third century BC, tell also of the other missions of Ashoka at that time—into the Himalayan region for example. This was not a region in which the Sinhalese had any particular interest, yet the Sinhalese chroniclers recorded the tradition which had come to them. It was pointed out by T. W. Rhys Davids that the historicity of this mission to the Himalayas had been clearly confirmed by archaeological evidence found at Sanchi.[19] This suggests that what the chroniclers recorded was based on sound historical tradition, so far as the essentials are concerned, although, as we have seen, allowance has to be made for the extent to which the popular world-view of the time has affected the details of the story, by way of exaggerations and miraculous embellishment.

MODERN REJECTION OF THE IDEA OF THE EARLY BUDDHIST STATE

A modern Sinhalese Buddhist, Dr. Walpola Rahula, finds himself somewhat embarrassed by the story of Buddhism having been 'established' in Sri Lanka in the way in which it is related in the chronicles. 'The idea of the "establishment" of Buddhism in a given geographical unit with its implications is', he says, 'quite foreign to the teaching of the Buddha ... nowhere had he given injunctions or instructions regarding a ritual or a particular method of "establishing" the *Sāsana* in a country. Buddhism is purely a personal religion.'[20] Apart from the fact that it is difficult to understand how a system of philosophy which denies the validity of the concept of an individual person can be called 'a personal religion', a more important issue is raised when, in continuation of this line of thought, Dr. Rahula says: 'The notion of establishing the *Sāsana* or Buddhism as an institution in a particular country or place was perhaps first conceived by Ashoka himself', and adds that 'Ashoka was the first missionary king to send out missions for the conversion of other countries.'[21] Since Ashoka was also, according to Dr. Rahula, an 'organizer and psychologist', he thought up a suitable ceremonial which could be used to demonstrate to the ordinary people that the new 'religion' was now established among them.[22]

Dr. Rahula is by implication making two claims: first, that Buddhism had by Ashoka's time, already been reduced from being a comprehensive, humanistic theory of existence, with an accompanying social and political philosophy, to being a spiritual cult, a purely 'personal religion', with no societal dimension at all; second, that Ashoka radically changed the character of Buddhism, in that he was the first person to conceive the idea of the Buddhist state, an idea which, in Rahula's view, is 'quite foreign to the teaching of the Buddha', and that it was this radically-changed Buddhism which Sri Lanka received. A great Sri Lanka Buddhist of the fourth century did not think so; Buddhaghosa records that the Buddhism of the city of Anuradhapura was as that of India at the time of the Buddha.[23] Since the first part of this book was devoted to showing that the idea of a Buddhist society coterminous with the political state is implied in the discourses of the Buddha, there is no need to make any further comment on either of Dr. Rahula's contentions. The significance of his view of Buddhism as 'purely a personal religion' is that it indicates the extent to which some modern Buddhists, in their desire to expound Buddhism in terms the West will understand, have tended to assimilate Buddhism to the other 'isms' which are lumped together under the general title of 'religions' and of these it is particularly Protestantism (known in Sri Lanka continuously since the coming of the Dutch in the middle of the seventeenth century) which seems to provide Rahula's model of what a religion should be. For, among the variety of Western religion, it is Protestantism (as seen in its characteristic form in the USA) which has been proud of its individualism over against all collectivism, of its dislike of constitutional links between church and state, of its encouragement of free enterprise over against ideas of corporate social responsibility, and its insistence that in the end all that matters is the destiny of the individual's indestructible soul, that is, either eternal salvation or eternal damnation. This certainly 'is purely a personal religion', and it is in these terms that some Buddhists in Sri Lanka, exposed at fairly close quarters to Protestant influences, have sought to interpret Buddhism. Buddhist history, in Sri Lanka and elsewhere, cannot fail to be a source of confusion and embarrassment to those who wish to see Buddhism in such purely 'personal' terms.

SUBSEQUENT HISTORY OF THE BUDDHIST STATE IN SRI LANKA

By the end of Mahinda's life, some forty-eight years after his arrival in the island, the pattern of the Ashokan Buddhist state had been faithfully reproduced in all its essentials: Buddhist king, *Sangha* and people; this was the pattern of society implied in the discourses of the Buddha, realized in the reign of Ashoka, and still accepted as the classical norm when the Sri Lanka chronicles were compiled eight or nine centuries later.

This pattern persisted throughout much of the succeeding centuries, with interruptions during periods of invasion and foreign rule by South Indian kings. But whenever and wherever a Sinhalese king ruled in Sri Lanka there was usually some kind of approximation to the classical pattern of the Buddhist state. The tradition was maintained through the centuries with varying degrees of stress and strain until the many dynasties of the Sinhalese kings came to an end in modern times, with the annexation and political control of the whole island by the British in 1815. Throughout the entire period from the time of Tissa, when Sri Lanka became a Buddhist state, until 1815, it was accepted that in the state of Sri Lanka only a Buddhist could by right be ruler of the country. Dr. Rahula cites epigraphic evidence from the tenth century AD to the effect that 'the king of Sri Lanka had not only to be a Buddhist but also a Bodhisattva'.[24] We may note the occurrence of this belief in Burma, too. Rahula quotes a Sinhalese work which is even more explicit on the subject of the inalienable right of the Buddha over the island of Sri Lanka: 'This Island of Lanka[25] belongs to the Buddha himself; it is like a treasury filled with the Three Gems[26] ... Even if a non-Buddhist ruled Sri Lanka by force awhile, it is a particular power of the Buddha that his line will not be established.'[27] This concept of territorial proprietorship, which as Rahula shows, continues down to the nineteenth century, is striking evidence of the political dimension which was an accepted feature of Buddhism in its classical form. There is a clear parallel here with the concept of *dar-ul-Islam*, the territory which belongs to Allah, in the tradition of Islam, which also, as we noted in chapter 2, was in its original form a civilization before it was reduced to a religion. In the Buddhist case there is the additional point that, certainly by the tenth century, it was explicitly held that the *Sangha* conferred kingship, 'selecting princes for the throne, and supporting their favourites, even to the extent of violating the succession'.[28]

To attempt to compress, or even to comment on, the long history of the Buddhist state in Sri Lanka over a period of more than two thousand years, in the space at our disposal here, would be ludicrous. What can be done, with some profit perhaps, is to select a few characteristic 'moments' in that history. Some will be moments of prosperity, peace and honor; others will be moments of adversity, distress and shame. Both kinds are well represented in Sri Lanka's history.

The first half of the first century BC[29] in Sri Lanka was occupied by the reigns of three kings: *Duttha-gamini* (101–77 BC), *Saddha-tissa* (77–59 BC) and *Lanja-tissa* (59–50 BC). Each of these reigns presents a different facet of Buddhist civilization in Sri Lanka.

RECIPROCITY BETWEEN KING AND *SANGHA*

Duttha-gamini's reign commenced at a time of crisis for the state. The north of the island was occupied by Tamil invaders from South India. The Sinhalese Buddhist dynasty had withdrawn from Anuradhapura to a town called Mahagama in the region known as Rohana, in the south of Sri Lanka. After forty-four years of Tamil occupation of the northern part of the island, the young prince Duttha-gamini succeeded to the throne of the Sinhalese kingdom. He was deeply committed to the ideal of a restored Buddhist polity throughout Sri Lanka.

Even before his father's death, Duttha-gamini had begun to make preparations to march against the Tamil king, Elara; he had raised a large force from among the Sinhalese in the southern part of the island, and at the head of this force he now set out for Anuradhapura. Reaching the bank of the Great Ganga river of Sri Lanka, which formed the frontier between the Tamil-occupied north and the rest of the island, he said: 'I will go to the land on the further side of the Ganga in order that the *sāsana* (of the Buddha) may be made bright.'[30] As a token of this intention and because the sight of them would be auspicious and give his men security, he took also five hundred *bhikkhus* with him. The chronicler emphasizes that Duttha-gamini's campaign, which quickly began to be very successful, was not prompted by motives of personal aggrandizement or power, but had as its aim the restoration of Buddhist polity to the whole island: 'Not for the pleasure of having dominion do I make this effort, but always with the intention of establishing firmly the *sāsana* of the Buddha.'[31]

Having defeated the Tamil king, and achieved what was necessary for the whole island to be once again a Buddhist state, Duttha-gamini reflected on the cost in human lives which this had necessitated and was overcome with remorse: 'he, looking back upon his glorious victory, great though it was, knew no joy, remembering that thereby was wrought the destruction of millions of beings.'[32] His reign from then onwards was marked by the kind of activity which showed his devotion to the Buddhist tradition. He undertook the building of a new *stūpa*, and with it a great new college (*vihāra*) for the *Sangha* which took three years to complete; he had a palatial nine-storied meeting hall built, in which the *Sangha* could hold the twice-monthly *uposattha*-ceremony[33] and which incorporated also a library and places for study and the discussion of problems. The pillars which supported this vast building can still be seen at Anuradhapura. But the most meritorious of his works, in the view of the chronicler, was the construction of the Great *Stūpa*.[34] Whereas the story of the building of the new college, the Maricavatti, is told by the chronicler in twenty-six verses, and that of the building of the great meeting hall in forty-eight verses, the story of the preparations for, and the building of, the Great *Stūpa*, the obtaining of relics, the making of the relic chamber and the enshrining of the relics, takes altogether three hundred and forty verses. The same scale of valuation seems to be reflected in the book of the king's meritorious deeds, which, we are told, was read out when the king was on his deathbed,[35] for the record of the amounts expended on these three works is given as being in the proportion 19:30:1,020. This great memorial shrine was, in the words of Malalasekere, 'the most stupendous and the most venerated of those at Anuradhapura'.[36] Not only was it the largest and most splendid *stūpa* to have been built in Sri Lanka, but it is said to have been the largest anywhere in the Buddhist world at that time.[37] A great deal of prominence is given by the chronicler to the fact that this undertaking of Duttha-gamini was carried out without any use of forced labor (the normal method of getting public work done in the ancient world) but rather by the employment of workmen who were paid fair wages. Various kinds of welfare services which Duttha-gamini provided for the people are also mentioned, including eighteen centers at which medical treatment and medicines were made available.[38] It is significant that in the Sri Lanka tradition Duttha-gamini is connected with the Buddha, not only as his disciple but also as his kinsman. According to the Great Chronicle tradition he was a direct descendant of Gotama's paternal uncle, Amitodana.[39] Moreover it is foretold that from the Tushita heaven into which Duttha-gamini entered at his death, as the proper reward for his piety, he will eventually be reborn on earth in the days of the next Buddha, Metteyya. The two will, in fact, be Sons of the same mother and father: 'The great king Duttha-gamini, he who is worthy of the name of king, will be the first disciple of the sublime Metteyya; the king's father will be his [Metteyya's] father, and the king's mother his [Metteyya's] mother. The younger brother Saddha-tissa will be his second disciple....'[40]

It was Saddha-tissa, the younger brother mentioned here, who succeeded Duttha-gamini at his death. He, too, is remembered in the Buddhist tradition of Sri Lanka as a king who 'accomplished many works of merit'.[41] His reign of eighteen years was one of peace; he inherited the stable situation which his elder brother had brought about, and the most notable aspect of his reign from a public point of view appears to have been the steady program of *vihāra*-building which he carried out. The close and cordial relationship which existed between the king and the *Sangha* during his reign is illustrated by a story found in a fourteenth century work.[42] In this compilation in Sinhalese of episodes from Indian and Sri Lanka Buddhist history we are told that during Saddha-tissa's reign the famous elder, named Buddharakkhita, delivered a discourse which lasted through the whole night. The king, having arrived late, unannounced and unexpected, and not wishing to cause a disturbance, remained standing outside the hall. The Sri Lankan style of public hall, with its open sides, makes it easy to hear from such a position, and there he remained until the discourse ended, at dawn. When the speaker learnt that the king had been so long outside he said, 'You are king, sire, and not accustomed to such discomfort. How was it possible for you to remain standing outside throughout the night?' The king replied that he would willingly stand listening to such a discourse not one night, but many nights in succession. The two of them thereupon embarked on a discussion of the *Dhamma*, and so impressed was the king that he offered to resign his throne in favour of the other. The elder returned the compliment, with the significant words: 'Do thou, O King, rule the country on behalf of the *Dhamma*.'[43]

Whatever the authenticity of this story, its importance for our present concern lies in the evidence which it provides of a continuing tradition in Sri Lanka, from at least the time of the chroniclers of the fifth century to this Sinhalese source in the fourteenth century, a tradition that the kings of Sri Lanka are the agents of the Buddhist *Dhamma*, and that the great kings are those who maintain close and sensitive relationships with the *Sangha*.

Another incident from Saddha-tissa's reign shows that the role of the king in relation to the *Sangha* was not only that of the acceptance of moral guidance and the putting into effect of the requirements of the *Dhamma*, but also of reminding the members of the *Sangha* of the standards of conduct required of them as guardians and exponents of the *Dhamma*. According to the great commentator Buddhaghosa, writing in the fifth century, the easy conditions which the *Sangha* enjoyed during Saddha-tissa's reign, as a result of both his and Duttha-gamini's liberality, and the prosperity of the times, appear to have brought about a slackening of discipline among the *bhikkhus* of Anuradhapura. By way of reprimand, Saddha-tissa discontinued his alms to them, and gave the alms to the *bhikkhus* of Cetiyapabbata only. Thereupon the lay people asked what was the reason for this. The function of the lay people in cases of disagreement between king and *Sangha* on more than one occasion in Sri Lanka Buddhist history appears to have been to lend their support to whichever side could show itself to be in the right. On this occasion, by way of reply, the king the next day resumed his almsgiving to the *bhikkhus* of Anuradhapura, and now that the people's attention had been drawn to the matter, he was able to justify his temporary suspension of alms 'by pointing out to the people the unsatisfactory manner in which the *bhikkhus* behaved in accepting the food',[44] that is, in a greedy and disorderly manner.[45]

Duttha-gamini's attitude towards the *Sangha* had been one of extreme respect and veneration; it was that of a king who had made strenuous efforts and ventured much on behalf of the Buddhist tradition, and who reverenced above all those who were the guardians of that tradition. Saddha-tissa also had shown a high respect for the *Sangha*, as we have seen, but this was for the *Sangha* at its best, personified in the wisdom and eloquence of Buddharakkita. To the *Sangha* at considerably less than its best he was prepared to show his disapproval, to the extent of withdrawing his economic support of its unworthy members. Both these kings, in their attitudes to the *Sangha*, are representative of many others in the history of Sri Lanka since their time. There is, however, yet another type of relationship, and that is represented by Lanja-Tissa.

THE *SANGHA*, THE STATE AND THE PEOPLE

At the death of Saddha-tissa the chief ministers of state and the whole assembly of the *bhikkhus* of the Thuparama came together to discuss the question of the succession. For reasons which we are not told, they decided to consecrate Saddha-tissa's second son, Thulatthana, as king, rather than his first son, Lanja-tissa. It has been suggested that Thulatthana was known to be more likely to work in harmony with the *Sangha* in the maintenance of the Buddhist state, or, to put it in other words, that those responsible were 'choosing the better man'.[46] With the support of the *Sangha*, therefore, Thulatthana was consecrated king. When Lanja-tissa, who was in the south of Sri Lanka, heard of it he traveled to Anuradhapura and 'having seized'[47] (which probably means 'having killed') his brother Thulatthana, he took command of the state himself. For the next three years relations between Lanja-tissa and the *Sangha* were very strained. He showed them disrespect, we are told, and neglected them,[48] thinking to himself; 'They took no notice of seniority'.[49] The chronicler appears to consider that Lanja-tissa was in the wrong, however, since he goes on to tell us that after three years a reconciliation was effected, and Lanja-tissa made atonement, or, literally 'imposed a punishment on himself'[50] by devoting a large amount of money to build additional embellishments to the various shrines at Anuradhapura, spending 300,000 pieces of silver here, another 100,000 there, and so on, and distributing new sets of clothing to 60,000 bhikkhus. This 'atonement' suggests that he was regarded as the guilty party, and therefore, by implication, that the action of the chief ministers and the *Sangha* in naming and consecrating Thulatthana as king had been justified. This view of a fifth or sixth century Buddhist chronicler conflicts with those modern writers who, starting from the presupposition that *bhikkhus* are and always have been a-political, take the view that the members of the *Sangha* were in the wrong in their 'intervention in political matters',[51] as it is described by one; or their 'unfortunate intervention in politics in an attempt to place their favourite on the

The Buddhist State in Sri Lanka

throne in violation of the law of succession', as an earlier modern writer had put it.[52] It is hardly justifiable to suggest, as another does,[53] that this 'interest in the affairs of state' on the part of the Buddhist *Sangha* was a new thing in the first century BC, unless, of course, the Buddha is not to be reckoned a Buddhist. The fifth century chronicler has the advantage of writing from within what was as yet an unimpaired Buddhist civilization, rather than from a Buddhist civilization mutilated by foreign political domination, and infected by alien notions that Buddhism is, like Protestantism a 'religion', and that, therefore, it is improper for it to have a national, political and social dimension.

The chronicles from which most of our information concerning the Buddhist history of Sri Lanka is derived were the work of *bhikkhus*. The compilers were *bhikkhus* and the sources which they used had also been produced by *bhikkhus*. That members of the Buddhist Order should in one generation after another devote so much of their time to producing what are, in effect, dynastic histories, is in itself a significant fact. The major characters throughout these chronicles are the kings: first Ashoka and then, in the present case, the kings of Sri Lanka, and in the case of other chronicles the kings of Burma[54] and of Thailand.[55] The royal activities in which the chroniclers are most interested are those undertaken on behalf of the Buddhist Order in particular, and also on behalf of the people generally. In Wilhelm Geiger's words, the chroniclers tell us 'of the *vihāras* built by the king, of the repairs he had undertaken on the more ancient buildings, of his bounty to the needy, the poor and the sick, and above all to [the *Sangha*]'.[56] Those who maintain that political and economic affairs lie outside the range of interest of Buddhism have a difficult task in explaining the very great interest shown by generations of Buddhist chroniclers in affairs of state and the condition of the people.

Nowhere is this interest shown more clearly than in the continuation of the Great Chronicle, which although it is known as the 'Little' Chronicle (*Culavamsa*) in fact adds a further sixty-four chapters to the thirty-six contained in the Great Chronicle. These additional chapters continue the history of the Buddhist state in Sri Lanka from the end of King Mahasena's reign, in 362 AD, to the coming of the British and the end of the kingdom in Sri

217

Lanka in 1815. This is the work of several chroniclers, each of whom extended the story to his own time, in the thirteenth, the eighteenth, and the nineteenth centuries respectively.

The condition of the people suffered badly, for example, from the civil war which lasted for the greater part of the seventh century. In sixty-five years there were fourteen changes of king. These dynastic struggles, although fought 'with mainly mercenary troops in a limited area round the capital',[57] nevertheless had a disastrous effect on the welfare of the country. Commenting on the struggles of the second quarter of the century the chronicler tells us that 'each [of the two kings] drove out the other in turn. But the whole people, suffering under the wars of these two kings, fell into great misery and lost money and field produce.'[58] Another equally offending aspect of these kings' activities was their contemptuous and vandalistic attitude towards the symbols of the Buddhist *sāsana*. One of them seized everything of value that he could find in the three great *vihāras* of the Buddhist Order in the capital, and 'broke in pieces the golden images and took the gold for himself and plundered all the golden wreaths and other offerings'. At another shrine 'he took away the golden crowning ornament on the temple and smashed the umbrella on the *cetiya* (*stūpa*) which was studded with costly precious stones.'[59]

Another feature of the disturbed political situation was, as B. J. Perera points out, that kings thus engaged in more or less continuous local conflict could not give their attention to the proper administration of the country's affairs, and these suffered in consequence.[60] Moreover, needing all the support they could possibly get from the nobility or from dignitaries and high officials of the state, the feuding kings were not in any position to risk alienating them by taking too careful an interest in the administration. Thus, one of the proper functions of a good Buddhist king was neglected; the nobility increased their power, and epigraphic evidence bears eloquent testimony 'to the travails of the masses under the officialdom of these days'.[61] It is important to notice that the chroniclers are concerned not only with the *Sangha*, and the relationship of kings with the *Sangha*, but also with the general condition of the citizens of the state, and their treatment at the king's hands, both in matters relating to economic and general welfare, and in those things which concerned the maintenance and proper observance of the Buddhist tradition, the *sāsana*.

THE REIGN OF PARAKKAMA BAHU I

Of the Culavamsa as a whole, approximately a third is devoted to one king, Parakkama Bahu I, whose reign covered the period 1153–1186 AD. Just as in the first and second parts of the Mahāvaṃsa it is Devanam-piya Tissa and Duttha-gamini who stand out as the central figures, to be given epic treatment, in the continuation, the Culavamsa, it is undoubtedly Parakkama Bahu who receives this treatment. 'There is no name in the annals of Sinhalese history', writes Dr. Malalasekere, 'which commands the veneration of the people in such measure as that of this prince of the "mighty arm", Parakkama Bahu, since he united in his person the piety of Devanam-piya Tissa and the chivalry of Duttha-gamini.'[62]

A good deal of change had occurred in the Buddhist state of Sri Lanka, however, between their reigns and his. There had been changes in the nature of Buddhism, both within the *Sangha* itself; and in the popular practices which had come to be associated with Buddhism among the people as a whole, and there had been considerable social change, mostly in the direction of a decline in the general welfare, both of the nobility and of the poorer people. At the outset of his reign as king of Sri Lanka, from his new capital at Polonnaruva, Parakkama Bahu, we are told, thought thus: 'By those kings of old who turned aside from the trouble of furthering the laity and the Order ... has this people aforetime been grievously harassed. May it henceforth be happy and may the Order of the great Sage—long sullied by admixture with a hundred false doctrines, rent asunder by the schism of the three fraternities and flooded with numerous unscrupulous *bhikkhus* whose sole task is the filling of their bellies—that Order which though five thousand years have not yet passed is in a state of decay, once more attain stability. Of those people of noble birth who here and there have been ruined, I would, by placing them again in their rightful position, fain become the protector in accordance with tradition. Those in search of help I would fain support by letting, like a cloud overspreading the four quarters of

219

the earth, a rich rain of gifts pour continually down upon them.'[63] His intention is seen to be three-fold: first, to reform and purify the Order, which had been affected by what today would be called revisionist doctrines, and purge its ranks of imposters and idlers; second, to restore to their proper status the dignitaries of the land; and third, to make provision for the sick and the needy. The chronicle then describes how all this was carried out, and is confirmed by epigraphical evidence.[64]

After describing the achievements of this great reign in detail for some six chapters, or 987 verses, the chronicler brings his account of the reign to a close with the words, 'Thus Parakkama Bahu, the Ruler of men, by whom were performed divers and numerous kinds of meritorious works, who continually found the highest satisfaction in the teaching of the Master [the Buddha], who was endowed with extraordinary energy and discernment, carried on the government for thirty-three years.'[65]

A great deal of attention is devoted by the chronicler to describing Parakkama Bahu's policy and practice because it was an outstanding example of the Buddhist ideal, although by no means the only example. Other kings of Sri Lanka, before and after him, approximated to this same ideal. Generous provision for the *Sangha*, and support for them in the study, preservation and public teaching of the Buddhist tradition was a primary duty of the kings of Sri Lanka.

The building and equipping of shrines, in order to encourage the practices of meditation and the honoring of the Buddha was another equally characteristic feature. Vigorous measures for improving the material condition of the people were also an important part of the Buddhist ruler's proper exercise of his power. The ensuring of an adequate food supply for a growing population required large irrigation works, and these were frequently undertaken by the Sinhalese kings. Dhatusena, for example, is remembered for the large reservoir which he had built, covering an area of ten square miles, whose waters were conveyed to the dry areas where they were needed by a canal fifty-four miles long. Parakkama Bahu was the author of a scheme to provide island-wide irrigation. 'In the realm that is subject to me', he said, 'there are, apart from many strips of country where the harvest flourishes mainly by rain water, but few fields which are dependent on rivers with permanent flow, or on great reservoirs. Also, by many mountains, by thick jungle, and by widespread swamps my kingdom is much straitened. Truly in such a country not even a little water that comes from the rain must flow into the ocean without being made useful to man.' According to the chronicles he made good the damage which time and neglect had done to the irrigation works constructed by earlier kings, and in addition carried out new construction projects which far exceeded the scope of anything which had been done previously.[66]

Another characteristic feature of Sinhalese Buddhist civilization was the attention which was given to establishing and maintaining centers for the treatment of the sick. 'This was the most highly advanced branch of the social services provided for the people by the state', observes C. W. Nicholas. 'The Chronicles often record additional endowments to the national medical service by several kings, and these statements are fully corroborated by the inscriptions. High dignitaries of state also founded or endowed hospitals. There were, in addition to general hospitals, homes for cripples, the blind and the incurable. Lying-in homes for women were established in several localities. Sick animals were also cared for.'[67]

It is important to recognize the extent to which all this was associated with adherence to Buddhist values. The kings who were most active in promoting the welfare of their people were also most prominently concerned with the state of the *Sangha*, and with the encouragement of Buddhist morality throughout the kingdom through enhancement of Buddhist tradition, provision for teaching, and so on. The pattern of Sinhalese civilization agrees remarkably closely with that of Ashokan India, and both of them with the ideal structure of society which is adumbrated in the discourses of the Buddha.

The extent to which Buddhist tradition permeated the life of the people of Sri Lanka would have varied from place to place, and from one reign to another. In general it can be said that in Sri Lanka there was a gradual and steady growth throughout the centuries in the extent and the depth of permeation of popular religious cults and beliefs by Buddhist ideas and values, a process which is still at work today. The understanding of this process requires some analysis of the relations between Buddhism and popular religion, and to this subject we shall turn in the final chapter.

One further point which must be mentioned here, however, is the practice which had developed in Sri Lanka of donating land to monasteries. The land so donated provided the monastery with a regular source of food. The tenants of the land also provided services of various kinds for the monastery. This practice seems to have been established at least as early as the sixth century AD, for it is admitted in the Sri Lanka Chronicles that King Aggabodhi I (568–601) made grants of land and monastery-servants to one *Vihāra*, and granted villages to others.[68] This, as Paranavitana points out 'was an innovation which went against the ideals of early Buddhism'.[69] The *Sangha* came to accept such grants as safeguards, ensuring a continuing economic basis for its life in hard times, such as they had in fact experienced under hostile kings, when the continued existence of the *Sangha*, and with it of the *Buddhasasana*, seemed to be threatened. 'The members of the *Sangha*, however, in order to satisfy their conscience, were expected to refuse when an offer of land grant was made, but to be silent when it was said that the grant was made to the *stūpa* [the pagoda]'.[70]

By the time the capital city was shifted from Anuradhapura to Polonnaruva in the eleventh century AD, the 'biggest landowners were the monasteries, which owned far greater extents of fields, singly and in the aggregate, than any other private owners'.[71] The produce of the land belonged to the monasteries; some of the villagers who worked on the land received a share of this for their own use; others were tenants of cultivable land in return for the services they performed for the monastery.

There are numerous references to such grants of lands in the Sri Lanka chronicles; the practice of making grants is confirmed by the evidence of inscriptions, some dating from as early as the first century BC.[72] The practice was not confined to Sri Lanka, however; grants of land to Buddhist monasteries in India are well attested by inscriptional evidence. The reason given by the donor was almost always the enhancement of his own store of merit.[73] In Sri Lanka, since land belonging to monasteries was exempt from royal taxation, the permission of the king was required before a would-be donor was allowed to make the transaction. The form of petition which had to be submitted ran as follows 'I am desirous of making this present to the *vihāra* for my good, and I pray Your Majesty will permit me, as it is equally for your good.'[74] Acceptance of the gift by the *Sangha*, however, as we have seen, implied a tacit recognition of the economic vulnerability of the *Sangha* under the other, older arrangement whereby the *bhikkhus* depended on the generosity of lay people to supply their needs day by day. Under this arrangement, the king, as the leading layman, would usually be one of the most generous donors, and normally there was no real threat to the *Sangha's* livelihood. But experience had shown that in troubled times, when the peace of the state was seriously disturbed, the very existence of the *Sangha* could be in danger. Seen from that point of view, the receiving of grants of land by the *Sangha* was wise and provident, but in times of prosperity the possession of such resources of wealth could become a source of corruption and a shifting away from the original perspective. In particular this seems to have happened in the case of some of the great monastic centers which developed in India, and can be seen as one contributory cause of the decline of the *Sangha* and, therefore, eventually of the virtual disappearance of Buddhist civilization from India. There were, however, other, more important reasons for the relatively short period that Buddhist civilization lasted in the land of its origin; the factors which brought it to an end had already been operating for many centuries. The rise of great and wealthy monastic schools (Nalanda, for example) only emphasized the retreat from the local 'parish' monasteries which was already far advanced in most parts of India, so successfully had the opponents of Buddhism done their work.

11   The Fate of Buddhist Civilization in India

Buddhist civilization was short-lived in India. The reason for this was that its two principal characteristics were opposed by two perennially powerful factors in the Indian situation. These two characteristics were Buddhism's humanistic stance, and its political-ethical implications. The first of these ran counter to the overwhelmingly theistic trend of the time, which found expression in a multiplicity of devotional cults, and succeeded in converting the *Buddha-sāsana* into yet another of these. The second of Buddhism's major characteristics inevitably aroused the opposition of the priestly brahman class, who had their own theory of the state, one which honored brahmans and made them indispensable, a role which Buddhist teaching certainly did not ascribe to them. Brahmanical opposition prevented any serious expansion and development of the Buddhist state in India after the death of Ashoka. The possibility which would appear to have been open to Buddhism in those circumstances was to return to what it had been before Ashoka, the blueprint of a civilization, an ideology waiting to be embodied once again in a social and political reality. But the nature of the Indian situation was such that even this denouement was rendered impossible. Not only did Buddhism cease to be a civilization after Ashoka (apart from one or two temporary local or regional exceptions); it suffered also a transformation of its original humanistic character: it became a theistic religion.

We have already noted the rise in India, by the time of Ashoka, of a cult of Buddha as *bhagava* or lord, a development which was probably inevitable once Buddhism had been divested of political and public relevance. If any explanation for the remarkable intensity of the *bhakti* or devotional mood in ancient and medieval India is to be offered, the most plausible is that where men are totally cut off from participation in political processes, and from having any kind of responsibility, however small, for the course of mundane events, they are likely to find compensation in devoting themselves with intensified zeal to the affairs of a supramundane realm. This is a case which has been argued elsewhere by Guy Swanson, for example, in his book *The Birth of the Gods*. In Hindu India the mass of men were cut off from effective participation or the possibility of it; the difference between the Buddhist state and the brahmanical state is that, in the former, ordinary men, of any level of society are able to enter the *Sangha* and thus became members of a body which has a recognized status and a real advisory and even admonitory role in relation to the political ruler. In a Buddhist state and society every man is a potential member of the *Sangha*. In a brahmanical state, however, such options are not open to the majority of ordinary men, only to the small elite of brahmans who act as ministers and advisers. No man has the option of becoming a brahman; only he is a brahman who is born to such a station. It is noteworthy that India has been of all countries of the world the most religious, if this is judged by the number and variety of deities which are worshiped, the bizarre extravagances which are associated with the devotion offered to them, and the widespread public acceptance of such ideas and practices. It is noteworthy also that India has in the past been renowned for her caste system—a system which irrevocably allotted a man his place in the social structure, at the head of which (in its traditional form) was an hereditary priesthood and an absolute monarch. The only word for 'government' in Hindu India was *Raj*, that is, king. Manuals of statecraft have been numerous in the course of Indian history, and they have been the work of brahmans. Visvamitra says that whatever act, on being done, is approved by the Aryans versed in the canon is law, and what they blame is held to be its opposite.[1] Politics in classical India, as represented by the great work of Kautilya (the brahman minister of state) and as practiced by Indian kings and their hard-hearted advisers, writes U. N. Goshal, 'is based upon a creed of gross materialism, heartless cruelty and base superstition'.[2] It was partly for that reason, because of Indian experience of the antagonism between politics and ethics, that the early Buddhists sought to set forth anew relationships between the two, and worked for the establishment of a Buddhist state. But the political power of the brahman and the 'idiocy' (that is, the self-contained nature) of village life, which even now is still the life lived by 80 per cent of India's people, have supplemented and aided each other. It is difficult to resist the conclusion that the two together have not some close connection with the extreme and intense theistic devotion which also has characterized Indian life through the centuries.

THE RISE OF THEISTIC BUDDHISM OR MAHAYANA

We return to the point, therefore, that when its brahman enemies had brought to an end its one magnificent demonstration of how politics and ethics may be brought into harmony in the Buddhist state, it was virtually inevitable that in the Indian situation Buddhism should in large part be transmogrified into a theistic devotional cult. This change was expressed before very long in a material form, in the representation of the Buddha, the lord of the cult, in iconographical form, for the purposes of devotional ritual (see chapter 9, p. 195). The accompanying *ideological* consequence of the *bhakti* mood in India was the emergence of a conception of the Buddha as divine. It has been suggested that 'the raising of the Buddha to divine status in the Mahayana creed parallels the Roman deification of the Emperor in the same way that the aspiration to a creed promising salvation may be discerned in later Buddhism, Roman literature of the Imperial period, and in Christianity.'[3] Certainly the material expression of this was, at first, in terms which were borrowed from Greco-Roman culture. The earliest known *Buddha-rūpas*, or Buddha 'images', as they are called in the West, which come from Gandhara, to the north-west of India, were adaptations of the concepts and techniques of Greco-Roman sculptors, just as were the early representations of Christ in Christian art. 'It is not surprising', writes B. Rowland, 'in the earliest Gandhara Buddhas to find Shakyamuni with the head of a Greek Apollo and arrayed in the *pallium* or toga, carved in deep-ridged folds suggesting the Roman statues of the period of Augustus.'[4] Later on the specifically Indian form of *Buddha-rūpa* was produced, showing the Buddha seated, with crossed legs, in the characteristic *asana* or posture of the yogin. There were ancient antecedents in India for this kind of iconography; for yogic figures seated in this posture are found in the art of the Indus Valley civilization of the second millennium BC. In the still later stages of the development of the *Buddha-rūpa* in India conventional devices were introduced in order to represent the supernatural quality and powers which had by then become essential features of the Mahayana conception of the Buddha. Together with such representations of the eternal, divine Buddha, there developed also an iconographical tradition of Bodhisattva-figures. In Mahayana doctrine the Bodhisattva was a being who had advanced, through many existences, to the penultimate stage where he was now on the threshold of Buddha-hood, and who had acquired great spiritual power, by means of which he was able to help other, lesser beings in their progress towards the ultimate goal. He, or more properly they, for a feature of the Bodhisattva idea in Mahayana Buddhist tradition is that there are many of them, were thus credited with 'saving' power, and were called on, in faith, by their pious devotees. Functionally they were indistinguishable from the many gods of Hindu India, and indeed some of them owed the characteristics attributed to them in the elaborate mythology which was woven around each of them, to Indian and Iranian folk-lore.

It will be seen that the emergence of the Bodhisattva-yana, or Mahayana school, was part of the general tendency present in all Buddhist schools to allow an open frontier so far as external relations with folk-culture were concerned. In the Theravadin tradition this open frontier was allowed in the interests of the *Sangha's* expansion of its influence into cultural areas which were not yet permeated with Buddhist values. Such elements of folk culture which were thus brought within the realm of popular Buddhist practice were made subordinate to the Buddha and his *Dhamma*. The difference between the Theravada and the Mahayana schools was thus, to a large degree, in practice, a matter of different policies. More precisely, they differed on the question of how closely the *Sangha* should adhere to the original perspective, expressed in the Vinaya and the *Dhamma*, the Discipline and the Doctrine, which they had inherited. In the view of the matter which is being presented here it is suggested that the Theravadins were more effective in retaining the original perspective of a philosophy of human existence which had clear implications in the realm of government and social administration, while the Mahayana schools succeeded in transforming

227

Buddhism into a mystical philosophy, another of the numerous varieties of Indian Gnosticism, a system of belief in heavenly saviors and an ultimately unreal earth, of salvation by divine grace, through faith; in short, a theistic religion.

CONTRASTING FEATURES AND FORTUNES OF MAHAYANA AND THERAVADA

Of the many factors which aided the growth of the Mahayana schools in India, two are outstanding and of particular relevance here. One was the greater influx into the Buddhist *Sangha* of men of brahmanical birth and upbringing, as a consequence of the royal approval of Buddhism in the Ashokan state. The other was that in the aftermath of the Ashokan Buddhist state, and the resurgence of brahmanical state polity, it might well have seemed that there was little prospect of a revived Buddhist state of the Ashokan kind, and that the form of Buddhism for the future was, therefore, the Mahayana.

In the event, it has been the Theravada form, committed to the concept of a Buddhist national and international structure, which has proved the more durable of the two in South and South-East Asia. In the last resort it was because the Theravadin *Sangha* retained its belief in the value of a *socially-structured* Buddhism that it has survived. The Mahayana schools, pre-occupied as they were with metaphysical and mythological questions, were largely indifferent to matters of social structure. Even the social structure of the Buddhist community itself which was provided for in the *Vinaya*, was a matter of small moment to those whose attention was fully engaged in expounding the *voidness* of all concepts and constructs whatsoever. The notion of '*bhikkhu*-hood', of becoming a member of the institutional Order, is for the Mahayanist not essential; it is at the most only an aid, advisable for some, perhaps, but not necessary for all.[5] For those Mahayanists who do enter the Order, the *Vinaya* will be of some interest, and indeed some Mahayanists have achieved reputations as scholars of the *Vinaya*. But, in general, as S. Dutt has observed 'the preservation by different sects of the *Vinaya* rules in their respective canons does not mean that the rules in their actual bearing on *Sangha* life or, in other words, in the practical operative aspect, were taken by all sects in the same way as by the Theravadin.'[6] It is where the Theravada prevails today, in Sri Lanka, Burma, Thailand, Laos and Cambodia, that the *Sangha* and the *Vinaya*, as embodying its classical constitution, are regarded as basic and indispensable to the existence of Buddhism. It will be seen that the difference between the Theravada and the Mahayana is ultimately a difference about Buddhism itself— whether, as in the tradition of the Theravada countries, it is to be regarded as a way of life and a culture, nourishing a civilization by means of which certain distinctive values are given political, social and economic expression in the life of the people; or whether it is to be regarded as a purely metaphysical or theosophical system.

The rivalry between these two points of view was not unknown in Sri Lanka, and it was with such schism that King Parakkama Bahu was concerned. But in Sri Lanka it was the Theravadin tradition which prevailed and which has endured. In India, however, the outcome was different. One of the areas where the Mahayana had met with most success was in the north and north-west of India. From the evidence provided by the Chinese pilgrim, Hsuan Tsang, it appears that even by the seventh century AD the scene in much of this area was one of desolation and ruin so far as Buddhism was concerned. In Gandhara over a thousand monasteries and most of the *stūpas* were crumbling into ruins and there were few Buddhists left. Where *bhikkhus* were to be found, in Balor for example, they were ignorant men, not observing the rules of the Order, and careless of their moral conduct.[7] In Kashmir, where both Hinayana and Mahayana existed side by side, the pilgrim found that conditions were better and that there were more than a hundred *vihāras* in use, housing over 5,000 *bhikkhus*. The king favored Buddhism, supported the *Sangha*, and received the pilgrim with great respect. Hsuan Tsang found a number of centers of thriving Buddhist learning and discipline in Kashmir and spent altogether two years there. Elsewhere, however, in the Punjab, the scene was largely one of desolate monasteries and few monks. In contrast, there were many temples to the gods of Hindu religion. What had happened here seems to have been repeated in most of the other areas of India where once Buddhism had existed in its classical form, that is, where the

Buddha, the *Dhamma* and the *Sangha* had been recognized as its indispensable elements, providing its definitive form. When, in the development of Mahayana ideas and practices, one of these elements, the *Sangha*, was neglected or abandoned, Buddhism sooner or later ran into the shifting sands of Indian polytheism and was lost.

A question which may be raised at this point is why the Buddhist *Sangha* in India did not heed the warning which was provided by the fate of the *sāsana* in areas which had once been strongly Buddhist, particularly the north-west and the south, but where, by the seventh century it was in decline or ruin. The disappearance of Buddhism from India did not happen in a day; it was so long-drawn-out a process that it might be thought that someone could have perceived the reasons for what was happening, and halted or reversed the process.

The Theravada school in India would appear to have been the obvious agency. It cannot be assumed that the Theravadins failed to see the danger. The very fact that the Theravadin tradition was maintained is evidence that there were those who were convinced that in the interests of the *Dhamma* this was the form of Buddhism to which loyalty should be given. And once or twice in the later centuries of Buddhist history in India—that is, between the seventh and twelfth centuries—the classical pattern, the Buddhist state, ruled by a king sympathetic to the aims and attitudes of Buddhism, did emerge. But in India the Theravadins were, as we have seen, at a particularly severe disadvantage. Since the form of Buddhism which they espoused presupposed a Buddhist ordering of society, it was inevitable that their program and policy continued to be the special target for brahmanical attack. It has recently been argued by Lalmoni Joshi that just as brahman hostility undermined the Ashokan Buddhist state, so brahman hostility to Buddhism was more potent a cause of Buddhism's decline and final disappearance from India than the attacks of the Muslim Turks in the twelfth and thirteenth centuries. He argues that constant brahmanical hostility towards Buddhism succeeded in loosening Buddhism's hold on the Indian people even in areas where it had managed to retain some place, and that the anti-Buddhist propaganda in brahmanical literature was not a mere 'war of the pen' but was periodically accompanied by social boycott and royal edicts against those who violated the 'divinely ordained' scheme of Caturvarnya [the brahmanical four-class system] and forceful confiscation of landed property of Buddhist establishments by brahmanical kings.[8]

If this is so, we have at least two major reasons for the eventual final disappearance of Buddhism from India. One was the continuing hostility of the brahmans towards what they recognized had been and was a threat to their theory of the state and of society (a hostility which would be felt more keenly by the Theravadins, whose conception of Buddhism was in social-structural terms). The other was the self-weakening effect which was produced within Buddhism by the Mahayana school, which had more in common with brahmanical philosophy and was nourished by brahmanical learning. The essential social dimension of Buddhism was lost sight of in the excessively metaphysical preoccupation of the Mahayana school, and their contempt for what they held to be the unimaginativeness of the Theravadins who, in their view, were unnecessarily preoccupied with the regulations and the discipline of the *Sangha*, and with a form of practice in which the primary emphasis lay so unimaginatively on the simple pursuit of morality.

This is certainly the view of the matter which is suggested by the later history of Buddhism in Bengal. For some fifteen centuries altogether Bengal was a land in which the *Sāsana* was alive and respected.[9] It was a largely Buddhist area when the Chinese pilgrim, Fa-hsien, visited it in the fifth century AD. Two centuries or so later, the Chinese pilgrim, Hsuan Tsang, visited various regions of Bengal and he too described the many temples and monasteries he found, although he seems to have been aware also of the beginnings of decay in some places. It appears that by this time the non-Buddhist shrines, the *devālayas*, were more numerous than were the Buddhist, and that the trend was in that direction. Even when, a century or so later, Buddhism was clearly in decline in other parts of India, there was a period of new development in Bengal under the Pala kings from the eighth century onwards. At least three great Buddhist centers of learning are known to have existed in Bengal during that period: Vikramasila, on the bank of the Ganges in central Bengal, Somapur, in the same area, and Jagaddala, in the Bogra district

231

(now Bangladesh). From the description given by other Chinese pilgrims, and from archaeological discoveries, it appears that these were vast, elaborate complexes of magnificent buildings, each at the height of its prosperity providing places for well over a thousand monks, possibly many more. Some of the *bhikkhus* who at that time lived in the monasteries of Bengal adhered to the Mahayana, but there were many who were Theravadins.

However, certain aspects of the development of these great centers may also help to explain the subsequent disappearance of Buddhism from most of Bengal. One feature of the Buddhism which found its focus principally in these *mahāvidyālayas* has been described in caustic terms by the Indian historian, D. D. Kosambi. 'Clearly, this was nowhere near the Buddhism preached by the Founder in sixth-century BC Magadha. There still existed ascetic monks who traveled barefoot, slept in the open, begged their way on leavings of food, and preached to the villagers or forest savages in country idiom, but their status and numbers diminished steadily. The monk's prescribed garment of discarded rags pieced together had been replaced by elegant robes of fine cotton, excellent wool or imported silk dyed in the costliest saffron. One feels that the great Teacher would have been laughed out of the exquisite and magnificent establishments run in his name....'[10]

The tradition of learning at these centers was predominantly, though not exclusively, that of the Mahayana philosophers. Some of these Bengal centers of Buddhism fostered the later development of Madhyamika and Yogacara doctrine which moved in the direction of the Vajrayana or Tantra. In their excessive preoccupation with metaphysical problems, the Mahayanists seem to have lapsed into an attitude to matters of *Vinaya* discipline which can only be described as somewhat more than liberal. It is not surprising, therefore, that lay adherents, the people of the villages, finding that the matters with which the Mahayana philosophers were preoccupied were far beyond their comprehension, turned their attention more and more to ideas and practices which were at best only marginal so far as the central doctrines of the Buddha were concerned. They became absorbed in cults of female deities, introduced in the first instance as female Bodhisattvas. These cults were directed towards the goal of self-fulfillment and incorporated a variety of material derived from the folk-culture of Bengal. It was from these that there then developed, as Sushil Kumar De observes, 'all the coarsening features of decadent Tantra, in both its Hindu and Buddhist guises, and which 'with their mystic exaltation of the female principle in the universe, and their emphasis upon the religious value of sexual passion and sexual use of women formed an undesirable legacy of a great system'.[11] At a later stage these Buddhist folk-deities were to be absorbed into the popular Vaishnavism and Shaivism of Bengal under such names as Manasa, the snake goddess, and Chandi the forest-goddess, who came to be thought of as the spouse of the god Shiva. It was in Vaishnavism that certain elements of Buddhism lived on in Bengal, albeit considerably modified: for example, in the democratic and anti-caste mood of Vaishnavism, its strongly vegetarian emphasis, and its opposition to violence. Even the Buddha was afforded a place in Vaishnavism as *Buddha-dev*, one of the incarnations of Vishnu and one of the many deities in the Hindu pantheon; pictures representing him so are frequently found adorning the walls of Bengali houses today. But Vaishnavism in Bengal can hardly be regarded as a successor to Buddhism in certain other of its aspects. J. C. Ghosh says of it that 'Vaishnavism was one of the main influences responsible for the intellectual black-out, and the emasculation of national life, in pre-British Bengal. This was due to its over-emotional nature, to the almost exclusive attention it paid to the life of love (*prem*) and devotion (*bhakti*) in preference to the life of thought (*jñāna*) and action (*karma*). In its craving for union with a personal god it lived entirely absorbed in the emotion of love, and entirely preoccupied with how to intensify that emotion to the utmost. With its elaborately designed cult of love, and its frenzied mass singing (*kirttan*) and dancing, it induced those states of mystical ecstasy and trance (*bhav-dasa*) in which the intellect is blotted out and the powers of action are paralyzed.'[12]

THE CRUCIAL ROLE OF THE *SANGHA* AND ITS DISCIPLINE

In addition to the hostility of the brahmans, two further aspects of the later history of Buddhism in Bengal now suggest themselves as possible reasons for its decline and disappearance: (1) what Kosambi calls the 'corrupting influence of wealth' in the great monasteries, which eventually dominated the scene so that the smaller local monasteries withered away; and (2) the excessively intellectual preoccupation of the Mahayana monks which resulted in the neglect of the basic elements of the *Buddha-sāsana* at the level of the ordinary people and left the field entirely open to the invasion of popular Buddhism by luxuriant folk-cults.

It is important, however, to notice that it is not the attitude of tolerance towards popular cults and beliefs which, by itself can be held responsible for the decline of Buddhism. The crucial factor in the survival or disappearance of a Buddhist culture embodying distinctively Buddhist values, seems to have been the *Sangha*. It was argued in chapter 8 that the distinguishing characteristic of Buddhist civilization is the triangular relationship between *Sangha*, king and people. The optimum conditions for the maintenance of a flourishing Buddhist civilization are when all three are harmoniously related and functioning according to the classical pattern of the Ashokan state. However, there were times in Indian history when the cooperation of the king could not be counted on. In areas where Buddhism had formerly flourished, the *Sangha* might, with a change of dynasty, find itself deprived of royal support; the new dynasty might show a clear preference for some non-Buddhist ideology, such as Shaivism or Jainism. When this happened Buddhism did not thereupon disappear altogether from the region concerned. It might suffer an eclipse; it might, sometimes but by no means always, suffer persecution. But often it would be preserved in sufficient measure by a faithful *Sangha* to be able to revive again if and when conditions became more favorable.

Clearly, therefore, much depended on the faithfulness of the *Sangha*, that is, on their adherence to those norms and values which had been transmitted to them as their Buddhist heritage. In the development of the Mahayana there was a relaxing of hold upon these traditional norms and values; on the one hand there was an accommodation to brahmanical ideas, encouraged perhaps by what may have been the desire to placate or assuage brahmanical hostility towards the *Sangha*. In these circumstances adherence to traditional norms would suffer. The open frontier

234

with popular cults and beliefs would no longer be controlled by a strong, tradition-oriented *Sangha*, and the consequence would be a further tilting of the balance against Buddhist values. If the withdrawal of royal support in what had been an area of Buddhist civilization occurred in such circumstances as these, the likelihood of the *Sangha's* maintaining the Buddhist tradition until royal support was regained would be much slighter.

THE ECONOMIC BASIS OF THE *SANGHA'S* EXISTENCE

However, there is a further aspect of the matter to be considered. Even in circumstances when the *Sangha* adhered to the traditional norms, it could scarcely survive as an institution if it were deprived of the support both of the king and of the people simultaneously. If in addition to deprivation of royal patronage, the *Sangha* should suffer for some reason loss of lay support it would then be almost impossible for it to maintain itself for long. If the *Sangha* was properly maintaining its traditions of morality of life and service of the people, if it was providing a source of teaching and exemplary conduct which the lay people would esteem, the only reason why the lay people would be likely to fail to support the *Sangha* would be that of economic stringency. That is to say, if the surplus of resources of food and materials which a society needs to have at its disposal for the feeding and clothing and housing of its *bhikkhus* were to be cut off, in some relatively permanent way, it would become virtually impossible to maintain the *Sangha* in that society any longer. This was very probably the case at the time of the devastating raids and territorial conquests made by the Turko-Afghan Muslims across north India in the twelfth and thirteenth centuries. These invasions seriously disrupted the agricultural economy. 'Muslim historians have recorded only the plunder of jewels, gold and silver, but they are almost silent about the forcible seizure of crops standing in the field or lying in the granary of the peasant', writes Bhakat Prasad Mazumdar.[13] Military campaigns were usually waged in the fine weather of the Indian cool season, after the harvest. It is obvious that expeditions in which sometimes as many as twenty thousand foot soldiers were engaged were not provided at the outset with food to carry with them for the entire campaign. It was, therefore, the custom whenever possible, in the waging of campaigns in India to time them to begin when the countryside was rich with harvest. At such a season the commander 'can obtain fodder [for his troops and horses] and at the same time inflict an injury on the other party, by destroying the crops standing in the fields.'[14] It was generally recognized that it was the cultivators who had to bear the brunt of the movement of armies, in the form of the loss of their food supplies. In the last quarter of the thirteenth century this is what was happening in East Bengal which had been until then a strongly Buddhist area. The Muslim conqueror of the Tippera and Dacca districts, Tughral Khan, 'forcibly acquired a considerable wealth' in these parts in the year 1275 AD, a modern Pakistani historian records.[15] It can be assumed that the life of the countryside suffered accordingly, so that the economic surplus out of which the *bhikkhus* had been supported would exist no longer. It is significant that Tughral Khan immediately made a very handsome gift of money to a dervish for the building of a Khangah near Dacca; effective steps were taken to colonize the whole area with Muslims, while non-Muslims began to migrate out of the district.[16]

Thus, an area in which, until then, the *Sangha* had continued to maintain the norms of Buddhism, now became incapable of providing the basic economic support which the continued existence of the *Sangha* required. The *bhikkhus* would be forced either to put off their robes and cease to be *bhikkhus*, or to migrate to the neighbouring territories of Burma and Tibet, while the monasteries of East Bengal fell into decay and were overgrown, to disappear, often without trace.

12 The Survival of Buddhist Civilization in Sri Lanka

In the classical three-fold structure of the Buddhist state, where king and *Sangha* and people each had their proper and necessary part to play, the crucial member of the trio was the *Sangha*. But the classical structure could be damaged when any one of the three ceased to be able to function in the normal manner. We have seen that in India the loss of a Buddhist laity able to support the *Sangha* could lead to the *Sangha's* disappearance. We have now to consider how in Sri Lanka the loss of Buddhist kingship in the modern period has also had lasting effects of an adverse kind. The role of the king in the classical pattern of the Buddhist state is to protect the *Sangha* and promote the *Dhamma*, both by his support of the *bhikkhus* and by wise legislation designed to promote a society with a public ethos of the kind in which Buddhist morality can be pursued by the maximum number of the people. When there is no longer a Buddhist king these functions go by default; if alien cultural and ethical values are introduced there may be a falling away from Buddhist values on the part of the people, and eventually perhaps on the part of the *Sangha* also This is what can be seen to have happened in Sri Lanka since the beginning of the sixteenth century. The story has been told often enough before, in a variety of ways.[1] What follows is a brief recapitulation of the main events in order to show how they illustrate the delicate nature and workings of Buddhist civilization.

The kind of misfortune which befell Buddhism in Bengal at the end of the thirteenth century: namely, a violent and determined invasion by the bearers of an alien culture, occurred in Sri Lanka some three centuries later. There were, however, a number of external attacks from south India after the death of King Parakkama Bahu I in 1186 which weakened the kingdom and aggravated the political and administrative decay which had set in by the close of the twelfth century. Added to this there were internal dissensions. The irrigation system established by Parakkama Bahu gradually fell into disrepair and the land in the dry zone of north central Sri Lanka, deprived of its water supply, became desolate. The former economic prosperity of the region, where the royal capitals had been, now gave way to crop failure, famine and disease. During the following centuries malaria seems to have made its appearance in Sri Lanka, to sap the vitality of the people still further.[2] There was a general shift of population away from the dry northern and south-eastern plain to the wet, western lowlands. The great monasteries and pagodas of northern Sri Lanka were deserted and fell into ruins and were almost forgotten until their rediscovery in the twentieth century.

A new center of government was established at Dambadeniya, thirty miles inland from the west coast. The elders of the *Sangha* gathered there, and together with the king, they made an attempt to revive and purify the life of the *Sangha*, and establish a proper discipline once again after the dislocation and general decline of the preceding years. The vitality of the *Sangha* recovered, and by the middle of the fourteenth century its reputation in the Theravadin countries of South-East Asia was sufficiently high for the Thai king to invite the head of the Sri Lankan *Sangha* to come and reorganize the *Sangha* in Thailand. On a number of occasions during the fourteenth century members of the Burmese, Thai and Cambodian *Sanghas* visited Sri Lanka to study canonical texts and monastic discipline and organization, and then to return to their own countries to put into effect what they had learned.

By the end of the fifteenth century, however, a decline had once again begun in Sri Lanka. The country was divided politically, so that a deputation from Pegu, in Burma, which arrived in Sri Lanka in 1476, found it impossible for some time to reach the capital because of rebel forces which stood in the way. By 1477 the island was divided between three kingdoms, Jaffna in the north, Kandy in the central highlands, and Kotte in the western lowlands. The ruler of the last of these, the king of Kotte, claimed to be lord of the whole island, but his claim had little foundation in fact. Many of the coastal towns were in the hands of Muslim traders and merchants. The political division of the rest of the island, and the disintegrating effect of this on the Buddhist civilization of Sri Lanka at the end of the fifteenth century has been described by G. P. Malalasekere. Apart from the coastal towns the rest of the island was 'governed by chieftains holding mimic courts at various centers. These petty tyrants, even more degenerate in their character than they were humiliated in station, no longer manifested the patriotism and the zeal for the public welfare which had so significantly characterized the former sovereigns of Sri Lanka. They had ceased to occupy their attention with the advancement of religion or with the development of institutions calculated to benefit the people.'[3] The island's food supply had been seriously affected by internal disturbances, and the shortage was such that food had now to be imported from south India. The divided and depressed state of the country was inevitably reflected in the condition of the *Sangha* which was, once again, at a low ebb. We noticed earlier how prominent is the concern of the chroniclers of Sri Lanka with the relationship between king and *Sangha*; they sensed the vital importance of this relationship, and it is clear that 'the decline of the one reflected the lapse of the other'.[4]

It was in this condition that Sri Lanka was confronted by the first of the invaders from Europe, the Portuguese, whose ships dropped anchor off the west coast in 1505. From then onwards Sri Lanka was not to be free of European domination for four-and-a-half centuries. In Sri Lanka, as in the other lands the Portuguese invaded, the sequence of events was conquest and conversion. Like modern urban gangsters, they moved in to give the king of Kotte their 'protection'. Subsequently, a young prince of Kotte, entrusted to Portuguese priests for education, was converted to Christianity. At his death he bequeathed the whole island to the Portuguese, an act of generosity which was both unnecessary and unrealistic. The part of the island which was his to bequeath was already well under their control, and as for the rest, his claim was fictitious. Extensive confiscation of Buddhist *Sangha* buildings and land greatly enriched the Christian religious orders in the island. The *bhikkhus*, displaced in the lowlands, moved up country to Kandy, and the *Sangha* virtually disappeared from the western coastal plain. Portuguese priests took over not only the property of the *Sangha* but also its place in the rural society of the lowlands. They presented a form of Christianity which was tolerant of local cults and beliefs, and the transition so far as the

239

village people were concerned, from folk religion within a Buddhist framework to folk religion within a Catholic framework, was not too uncomfortable for those who did not resist. It is clear that the Portuguese, through their own sufferings during the early days of their settlement in the island, 'came closer to the people of the country than either the Dutch or the British'[5] who succeeded them. Many of their priests, moreover, were from the indigenous population of south India, and it was partly the zeal and devotion of these humble men which won adherents to Catholicism in Sri Lanka, and maintained the Catholic community during the time of persecution under the Dutch.

The kingdom of Kandy, in the central highlands, thus became the residuary upholder of Buddhism in Sri Lanka. There the traditional pattern of king, *Sangha* and people was preserved. During the middle decades of the eighteenth century a considerable revival of the *Sangha* was brought about, largely through the initiative of the Kandyan kings, Siri Vijaya (1739–47), and his successor, Kitti Siri (1747–82).

THE EIGHTEENTH-CENTURY REVIVAL OF BUDDHISM UNDER IMMIGRANT RULERS

It is interesting that both these kings were foreigners. The previous king, Narinda Singha, had married a princess from Madhura, in south India, and with her to Sri Lanka had come her brother, Siri Vijaya. At the death of Naninda there was some dispute over the succession, and one party at court favored the claim of a son of Narinda's by a concubine. But this candidate withdrew voluntarily and Siri Vijaya, who was strongly favored by others at court, succeeded as king. The case is interesting for the light it throws on the acceptance by the Kandyan chiefs only seventy-six years later of another foreign 'claimant' to the throne—the British governor, Robert Brownrigg, whom they expected to slip into place and maintain the traditions of a Buddhist state as other foreigners had done (see p. 242). King Siri Vijaya also took as his queen a princess from south India (from Madhura) and she too was accompanied to Sri Lanka by her brother, Kitti Siri, and their father. Again, therefore, at the death of Siri Vijaya, a south Indian prince became king of Kandy. Not only did he become king, but like his brother-in-law he became an enthusiastic upholder of the Buddhist state. During Siri Vijaya's reign young men began to come forward, as they had not done for some time, to take the robe as novices (*samaneras*) in the Buddhist *Sangha*. Arrangements were made by the king and his household for all such novices to be properly instructed in the tenets of Buddhism. Funds were made available for the production of Buddhist manuals of instruction. The king encouraged the holding of public festivals, and occasions for the public teaching of *Dhamma*. He had Buddha statues erected in many places, new *cetiyas* built, and old shrines restored. The one important measure which needed to be taken for the revival of a Buddhist state was the reconstitution of the *Sangha*. The higher ordination, or *upasampadā*: that is, ordination as *bhikkhu*, was no longer possible in Sri Lanka, as there is a requisite number of *bhikkhus* to form a chapter and carry out such ordination and they could not be found. Aided by the Dutch, who provided him with a ship, Siri Vijaya sent envoys to Pegu (lower Burma) and Ayudhya (capital of the Thai kingdom) to request *bhikkhus* from those kingdoms to come to Sri Lanka to carry out the *upasampadā*. But both expeditions suffered shipwreck; in the first case only one, and in the second a mere handful of survivors returned to Sri Lanka to tell what had happened.[6]

Success was achieved, however, during the reign of Kitti Siri. A man of great virtue, according to the Pāli chronicle, and devoted to the Buddha, the *Dhamma* and the *Sangha*, he had already made a resolve to restore and protect the *Sangha* in Sri Lanka.[7] Accordingly he sent messengers, with gifts, and a letter in the Pāli language, to the Thai capital, Ayudhya. There the envoys were received with honor, and the Thai king made arrangements at once for a chapter of *bhikkhus* to go to Sri Lanka. The whole party, 'with books on the doctrine and the monastic discipline [which were lacking in Sri Lanka] a golden image of the Buddha, and a superb golden book, a magnificent royal letter, gifts of various kinds, and dignitaries of the King of Ayudhya [as envoys]' came safely to Sri Lanka.[8] In July 1756 a great ceremony of ordination was held in Kandy and many novices, some of whom had waited long for this occasion, were made *bhikkhus*. The newly ordained were instructed by the members of the *Sangha* who had come from Ayudhya, and the king himself drew up a code of conduct for their guidance, in accordance with the precepts of the Vinaya. A revival of Pāli learning followed, and a renewal of literature activity. It was recognized that the concern of the *Sangha* with the ills which afflict mankind covered ills of mind and of body. So, in addition to giving themselves to the study of Dhamma and its practice for the purification of men's minds, the *bhikkhus* took up the study of medicine too; this was another result of the revival of learning.

THE IMPACT OF THE BRITISH INVASION OF SRI LANKA

By the end of the eighteenth century British naval interests in the coastal waters of India had led to the capture by Britain, from the Dutch, of the large harbor and port of Trincomalee, on the northeast coast of Sri Lanka. This happened in 1782, and thus encouraged, in 1796 the British seized the port of Colombo, also from the Dutch. Dutch power in the island thus came to an end, and the maritime provinces passed into the hands of Britain, to be declared a Crown Colony in 1802. The surviving kingdom of Kandy, in central Sri Lanka, was now surrounded by a new band of foreign adventurers.

The circumstances in which, in 1815, the Kandyan kingdom, at whose head was a young man of nineteen, became a British colony, entail a story of treachery which does no credit to the Sinhalese traitor, Pilame Talawe, who was the prime mover, or to Frederick North, the British governor who encouraged him in his murderous intentions. That was in 1798, two years after the British had seized Colombo from the Dutch (with the aid of Swiss mercenaries whom they bought over from Dutch service). North was confided in by the would-be assassin, and in his eagerness to make the most of the opportunity to set up a military protectorate at Kandy, comments Sir James Tennent, 'Mr North not only forbore to denounce the treason of the minister, but lent himself to intrigues inconsistent with the dignity and honor of his high office.'[9] It was, however, ten years after North had departed from Sri Lanka that the train of events he had set in motion finally brought about a situation in which North's successor, Robert Brownrigg, was able to order the British troops to march into Kandy to restore order and take the young king prisoner. On 2

March 1815, the king was solemnly deposed and his entire realm vested in the British crown. The Convention of Kandy, a form of agreement which the British drew up, set out the conditions under which the new regime would operate; it stated that a 'tyrannous' king had been deposed for having waged 'war' against Britain, and that 'for the time being' the control of the kingdom would be in the hands of the British governor. This agreement, which was signed on behalf of the king of England on the one side and the chieftains, of Kandy on the other, included a clause (Article 5), which read as follows: 'The religion of Boodhoo [the Buddha] professed by the chiefs and inhabitants of these provinces is declared inviolable; and its rites, ministers and places of worship are to be maintained and protected.'

The Sinhalese version of this document, however, makes it clear that it was Sinhalese Buddhism, in its *popular* as well as its *monastic* aspect which was meant, since reference is made both to the 'religion of the Buddha and to the *Agama* [religion] of the *Devas* [local gods], and protection is promised to the *Vihāras* [Buddhist temples] and the *Devālayas* [temples of local gods]'[10]

This is important, because it indicates that it was not only the 'pure' Theravada which the British government undertook to protect, but the whole range of popular Sinhalese religion. One important, indeed essential, element of Buddhism they had, however, removed when they deposed the king of Kandy. For without a king the traditional structure of the Buddhist state was seriously distorted; it meant that there was no longer a Buddhist civilization in Sri Lanka. Buddhism had, in fact, been reduced to a religion, and that is what the British called it.

What had been taken away when the king was deposed was the guardianship of the Buddhist ethic in its public and social dimension. There was no longer a Buddhist who possessed political authority which he could use to promote the kind of society which would foster the values and practices of Buddhism. What is more, with the setting up of their rule over the whole of Sri Lanka, and the commercial enterprises which they soon introduced, the British very seriously affected the nature of Sinhalese society over the next century and a half introducing alien values and attitudes, and doing so in such a way as to give high prestige to these alien values compared with the traditional values of Buddhist Sri Lanka.

The campaign on the part of Christian missionaries to have the connection between Buddhism and the British government severed had made use of three major arguments: that Buddhism was a system of idolatry; that 'interference' in the religion of the country by the British would be interpreted by the people of Sri Lanka as implying approval of that religion; and that the only thing which kept Buddhism alive was the support of the State.[11] Each of these three arguments was the expression of a half-truth. Sinhalese Buddhism, it is true, including as it does the cults of local and Indian gods and spirits, certainly appears, at the popular village level, as the kind of paganism which was most frequently described by nineteenth-century missionaries as 'idolatrous'. That the appearance which Sinhalese Buddhism thus presents is due to the tolerance of the beliefs of unsophisticated people by a highly sophisticated and rational system of analysis is a point which the cultured Western despisers of this particular 'idolatry' have missed. Again, it was not so much 'interference' as non-interference in the religion of their country which the Buddhists of Sri Lanka felt they had a right to expect from their alien overlords; the complaint now, as then, is not that the British failed to 'approve' of Sinhalese Buddhism, but that they positively disrupted it by severing an important connection, a connection which had traditionally existed between the religion of the people and the ruler of the people. However naive their religious system might be, it was the right to maintain it intact which was being disputed. In a similar fashion Christians in a Western country might feel themselves alienated from a government which took positive measures to undermine their religious beliefs and practices on the grounds that their religion was superstitious or idolatrous. Finally, Spence-Hardy and his missionary colleagues, in their contention that it was only Government support which kept Buddhism in Sri Lanka alive were comforting themselves with what was at most only a half-truth. It is true that the Buddhist state requires for its full and proper functioning the cooperation of a ruler whose policy and legislation is in keeping with the *Dhamma*. But, as events have shown, it is untrue to say that the Buddhist culture and civilization will inevitably disappear as soon as the country is deprived of such a ruler. The crucial element in the classical Buddhist structure is the *Sangha*. In Sri Lanka the *Sangha* survived, albeit for a time much handicapped and weakened, and it is to this fact that the survival of Buddhism in its traditional form in Sri Lanka must be credited.

The fact remains that the promise which the British government had made in 1815, in Article 5 of the Convention of Kandy, was not kept. In England, William Wilberforce, an evangelical Member of Parliament, stated his objection to the clause more openly: it would, he feared, prevent missionary attempts to convert the Buddhist of Sri Lanka to Christianity; he objected, moreover, to the religion of the Buddha being described as 'inviolable'.[12] Nevertheless, as K. M. de Silva points out, 'the Kandyans believed that the relationship between Buddhism and the British Government defined in 1815 was to be permanent.'[13] For them, with their long tradition of Buddhism as something more than a religion—the tradition of a Buddhist state—it was perfectly natural that the authority in whom (so they had been led to believe) they had vested political power over what had always been a Buddhist state should maintain it as such. It was necessary, for the proper working of a Buddhist state, that there should be an authority corresponding to that of a king, which would function as a Buddhist king would, to promote the welfare and maintain the institutions of a Buddhist population. This was perceived by Tennent, who wrote: 'it is not protection which they look to us for.... It is not our management they want.... But what they really want under the semblance of interference and appearance of control is really our identification with their religion and the prestige of the Government name as associated with their appointments and patronage.'[14] What the Kandyan chiefs were expecting would simply be a repetition of what had happened before; the Nayakkar dynasty, whose kings had ruled Kandy since 1739, had also been of foreign, that is, of south Indian origin, as we have noted earlier. But he who ruled a Buddhist state, whether he was south Indian or English, would, the Kandyans supposed, rule it according to the hallowed tradition of Buddhist Sri Lanka.[15]

That they were naive is understandable. The Kandyan kingdom had been largely cut off from the affairs of the wider world, and its people were disposed to think in terms of their

Buddhist tradition and its values. They did not understand at first what it was that had come to them with the arrival of British troops and a British governor in Kandy. They could not be expected to understand the complex commercial rivalries of the European nations, of their navies and armies in South-Asia as well as in Western Europe, and how this was now involving their simple and remote kingdom in the hills. When, in 1817, they began to get an inkling of how different the new situation really was from anything which had been experienced before, they made their protest, in a rebellion against those whom they now recognized as alien overlords. The rebellion was crushed, and with British power already considerably stronger than in 1815, it became possible for the British Government in Sri Lanka to make a new Proclamation, on 21 November 1818, which showed a considerably less deferential attitude both to the chiefs and to Buddhism.

HOW BUDDHISM IN SRI LANKA BECAME A 'RELIGION'

From 1818 onwards the speed of Westernization of Sri Lanka was accelerated. Educational developments were directed away from traditional learning within the context of Buddhist culture, and led either in the direction of secularism or Christianity (evangelical, Catholic, or Church of England). The young Sinhalese found it necessary to avail themselves of these new forms of education if they were to be appointed to government posts and continue to have any part at all in the running of their country. Monastic education declined correspondingly in importance and in quality.

To some extent, however, this was a stimulus to Buddhism. It could be seen that all depended now on the *Sangha*. The role of the *bhikkhus* as the voice of Buddhism, critical of un-Buddhist acts on the part of alien rulers, was now greatly enhanced. It was this reaction to the enslavement of the traditional way of life to Western values during the British colonial period which first drew *bhikkhus* into direct political activity in Sri Lanka.[16] In spite of the disabilities which the *Sangha* suffered, such as the alienation of monastery lands and property, and the by-passing of the monastic educational system, it managed to survive the one hundred and thirty years of British rule after the destruction of the kingdom of

Kandy. During the latter half of this period it benefited from the encouragement and help which had now begun to come from Western sympathizers, notably the American Colonel H. S. Olcott, and from Madame Blavatsky and Mrs. Annie Besant who came from England. Ludowyk has pointed to an important modification in the Buddhist response to Christian missionary activity: 'it had perforce to express itself in forms decided for it by Christian activity... the battle joined had to be fought with weapons similar to those used by the Christian missionary; hence such things as Buddhist Sunday Schools and even Buddhist carols'.[17] In this way Buddhism in Sri Lanka gradually became even more of a 'religion', as the modern West understands the term.

But this was largely in respect of the face which it turned to the West. So far as the wholly Sinhalese, village situation was concerned the frontier with local deities and cults remained open, and the relative importance of this within Sinhalese Buddhism as a whole may well have increased as the public status of the *Sangha* declined. The extent to which folk-beliefs and practices have been allowed to coexist in close association with Buddhism in Sri Lanka has for long puzzled the more superficial Western observers. The juxtaposition of Buddhist devotion and popular Sinhalese cults has given rise to Western judgments in terms of 'syncretism' or 'corruption'. This is illustrated in the procedure followed by the Sinhalese Buddhist when he visits a *vihāra*. He does very much as his Buddhist forebears would have done in ancient Anuradhapura.[18] He goes first to the *stūpa* (or *dagoba*), and circumambulates it, keeping it on his right. He pays his respect to the Buddha, whom the *stūpa* represents, by offering flowers and also perhaps lights (in the form of a coconut oil lamp) and incense. After that it is usual to venerate the bodhi-tree. Finally, he visits the *Buddha-rūpa*, usually kept in a shrine-room or temple, and venerates that in the same manner. But in the same compound, or temple-enclosure, there may be, in addition to the three items to which Buddhist ceremonial respect has been offered, another temple, devoted to specifically Sinhalese deities, local or national, or possibly to deities of Hindu India. After, but only after, respect has been offered at the Buddhist places, he visits the *devālaya*, in order to seek some particular immediate mundane boon: to pray for the birth of a child, or for a relative's recovery from illness, or for success in some business venture.

Another of the features of Sinhalese Buddhist culture which has often confused and perplexed the outside observer is its public pageantry, when, for example, the Tooth Relic is taken out of the Temple at Kandy and carried in procession round the city for all the people to venerate. This, too, has given rise to questions from non-Buddhists about the justification for such practices, or objections that this is alien to what is found in the Pāli Canon, and is not Buddhism, or not 'pure' Buddhism. It is only recently that the inner cohesion of Sinhalese Buddhism has begun to be understood in the West, largely through the writings of social scientists. It will therefore be useful at this point to provide a brief survey of some of their work.

MODERN SINHALESE BUDDHISM FROM THE VIEWPOINT OF SOCIAL SCIENCE

Until just over a decade ago, Western accounts of Sinhalese Buddhist religion, whether descriptive or analytical, were hard to come by. Copleston[19] devoted less than a sixth of his *Buddhism, Primitive and Present in Magadha and Sri Lanka*, to contemporary Sinhalese Buddhism. Most of the book consists of descriptive writing of a largely impressionistic kind, and clearly indicates the viewpoint of the writer, that of a Christian missionary-bishop. T. W. Rhys Davids's article in the *Encyclopedia of Religion and Ethics* on Sri Lankan Buddhism provides the kind of scholarly treatment of the history, doctrines, and monastic structure of Theravada Buddhism that one would expect from this great Pāli scholar, but has disappointingly little about the popular practice of Buddhism which he, as a resident of Sri Lanka, might have given us. Sir Charles Eliot[20] devoted four pages to some aspects of the contemporary practice and structure of Sinhalese Buddhism and to the relationship between the life of the monasteries and that of the lay people. He speaks of three religions within Sinhalese Buddhism: 'local animism, Hinduism, and Buddhism are all inextricably mixed together'.[21] He notes that the practice of Buddhism in Sri Lanka entailed a 'pageantry' and an 'ornate ritualism' which 'is not authorized in any known canonical text'.[22] Copleston speaks of 'the two Buddhisms' in Sri Lanka. On the one hand there is the moribund tradition of the lay people and the villages; on the other there is that of the Pāli texts and the monasteries and of the educated elite of Colombo, which in his day was alive with the spirit of revival. Between these two, he considered, there was an extreme divergence.[23] For while the Buddhism of the educated classes claimed to be compatible with modern scientific thought, it was tolerant of much superstition and polytheism.[24] Sri Lankan Buddhism was, he said, 'inconsistent, just where inconsistency does the most harm'.

This apparent dichotomy within Sinhalese Buddhism had, however, already been noted by the seventeenth-century Englishman, Robert Knox, who spent eighteen years in Sri Lanka. Among other examples of what Ludowyk has called Knox's 'power of observation and his ability to see the essentials'[25] was his now frequently-quoted dictum that the Sinhalese have 'Budu for the soul, and the gods for this world'. By 'the gods' is meant the whole complex of rituals and beliefs associated with local and national deities. Knox perceived that there was an important difference in function and status between the two cults.

There is much in Sinhalese practice to support the notion of two religions, Buddhist and non-Buddhist, coexisting side by side, or even, to some extent, syncretistically. This can be seen, for example, in the practice of pilgrimage, and in the hospitality given to non-Buddhist cults within the precincts of Buddhist temples. While there are places of pilgrimage which are of a primarily Buddhist character, the sacred city of Anuradhapura, for example, there are others which are associated primarily with the guardian deities of Sri Lanka, such as Kataragama, a famous shrine in the jungle of the dry-zone of the extreme south-east of the island. Nur Yalman records that 'thousands of pilgrims from Sri Lanka and South India, Buddhists as well as Hindus (and even Muslims and Christians) flock to this deserted locality and bring it alive for a few weeks every year.'[26] There are other shrines which combine both Buddhist and non-Buddhist elements, such as Sri Pada (Adam's Peak): this is revered from a Buddhist point of view on account of the foot-print of the Lord Buddha which is found on its summit, and it is held sacred, too, as the abode of the Sinhalese god, Saman. Leonard Woolf in his novel of Sinhalese life, *The*

Village in the Jungle, gives an account of a pilgrimage of village people to the shrine of the Hindu god 'Kandeswami', in which he notes their acceptance of the fact that 'though the god is a Tamil god, and the temple a Hindu temple, the *kapuralas* (that is, the ministrants) are all Buddhists and Sinhalese'.[27]

We have noted that within the precincts of temples devoted to the Buddha there will often be found subsidiary shrines called *devālayas*, devoted to Hindu and Sinhalese gods. These, and other similar features of Sinhalese practice, have led Western observers in the past to regard the situation as one of the 'corruption' of Buddhism by 'animism', or else to speak of Buddhism in Sri Lanka (as in Burma and Thailand) as merely a thin veneer covering the 'real religion' of animism, or yet again to regard it as an example of thorough-going religious syncretism.

Some rather different accounts of the cultural structure of the Theravada countries of South Asia have become available recently in the writings of social scientists who have worked in that area in the past decade or so. The most notable names in connection with Sri Lanka are those of Ryan, Obeyesekere, Ames, Yalman and Evers.

In 1958 Bryce Ryan, a sociologist, provided a valuable descriptive account of the main features of the two elements in Sinhalese culture, Buddhist and non-Buddhist.[28] In chapter 6 of *Sinhalese Village*, 'From Buddhism to the wonderful world', he describes the features of Sinhalese belief and practice which are related more directly to the Buddha and his teaching; in 'The wonderful world: gods and demons', chapter 7, Ryan deals with the non-Buddhist features, viz., the cults of Hindu, local Sinhalese, and planetary deities, the placation of demons, and various magical practices. The important point to be kept in mind is that there is a large overlap in the clientele of the Buddhist shrine and that of the gods, an overlap which includes the majority of the lay people. 'Pure Buddhism', comments Ryan, 'is a philosopher's abstraction. Sinhalese Buddhism is pure; Buddhists are not. The Sinhalese are Buddhists, but in the same breath we may as rightly say that the Sinhalese are believers in numerous gods, sub-gods and demons, and that non-Buddhist supernaturalism in the form of planetary influences, wood-sprites, sorcery, and ghosts is ubiquitous.'[29]

In Ryan's view, a real distinction exists, not merely at the level of anthropological analysis, but in the consciousness of the villager himself, between Buddhist and non-Buddhist beliefs and practices. So far as the Buddhist aspect is concerned, both for monks and laymen, attention is focused chiefly on the acquiring of merit.

The attainment of *nirvāna* is held to be far beyond the reach of ordinary man in this age; gaining merit is a more practicable immediate goal, and is at the same time consistent with acceptance of the idea of *nirvāna* as the ultimate goal. Merit is acquired principally by various forms of worship and by the practice of almsgiving or generosity. Over against this, and distinct from it, Ryan sees the variety of belief in supernatural powers and the accompanying various practices of astrology, spirit-propitiation, exorcism, and so on. These 'powers', in his view, are not hierarchically graded, except that 'the Buddha stands above all others, and toward Him there is unique reverence and worshipfulness.'[30] Demons are regarded as agents of illness and other various human disorders. Belief in demon-caused disease, he notes, tends now to be confined to those illnesses of a more mysterious kind, not readily amenable to treatment by Western medicine. Astrology, he considers, is given the place of a natural science rather than a metaphysical belief-system.

However, Ryan indicates that the two spheres are not entirely distinct. The chanting of *pirith* by Buddhist monks as a 'generalized antibiotic' against evil influences, and pilgrimages to sacred shrines have both to be placed somewhere between these two spheres. 'If the *pirith* ceremony takes us one step into the borderland between philosophic Buddhism and practical supernaturalism, the pilgrimage to sacred shrines is at least midway between these theoretically distinct spheres.'[31] Elsewhere he speaks of *pirith* and pilgrimage as representing a merging of Buddhism and the cult of the gods. 'In the former the power of the Buddha is given supernatural quality, and in the latter the merger is a wedding of convenience between Lord Buddha and the gods.'[32]

Obeyesekere sees the relationship between them in terms of hierarchy. In the first place there is the hierarchy of supernatural powers, with presidential status ascribed to the Buddha. 'The positions of all other supernatural beings derive, directly or indirectly from, or are measured against, this initial presidential status of the Buddha.'[33] Below the Buddha are the guardian deities of Sri Lanka, and below these are gods of local authority or power, who are thought of as subservient to the national deities, and as their attendant ministers. Below these comes the host of demons who are able to punish people with disease, and below them the spirits of dead men, ghosts who are often spiteful and harmful. Corresponding to the hierarchical structure of the pantheon is the gradation of symbolic gestures used in connection with the various rituals. This is a marked feature of Sinhalese practice, and has been well summarized by Obeyesekere as follows:

> The Buddha as head of the pantheon, is worshiped with the hands on the head or forehead. In rituals in Buddhist temples, vegetarian foods and fruit juices are placed on his altar, and he is honored with incense and flowers. The gods are worshiped with the hands farther below or with the fists clenched and placed against the chest. Since gods are considered noble beings (and even potential Buddhas), they too are offered vegetarian foods, auspicious flowers, and incense. This respectful obeisance is not given the demons at all—they are offered neither auspicious flowers nor incense, but are typically invoked with certain flowers considered inauspicious and with resin, an inferior incense.... Hence the kind of offering symbolizes status in the pantheon.'[34]

Obeyesekere presents this account of the pantheon in the context of his argument that Sinhalese Buddhism, the popular religion of Sri Lanka, is to be understood as a 'little tradition', subordinate to the 'great tradition', which is the Theravada Buddhism of South-East Asia as a whole.

Robert Redfield's concept of great and little traditions is here used by Obeyesekere and applied to the Sri Lanka situation because, in his view, it makes possible a more realistic analysis than is to be found in those accounts of South-East Asian Buddhism which employ the notion of different cultural 'layers' or 'strata', one on top of the other. It also avoids the necessity to deal with the folk religion of these countries in terms of 'animism'—'a convenient label under which one could subsume beliefs or customs he did not fully comprehend, or was impatient with'.

The important point here is that Sinhalese Buddhism is to be viewed in its entirety as 'a single religious tradition', that is, an integrated system, and not a juxtaposition of radically different or competing elements, Buddhist and non-Buddhist; nor even a situation of peaceful coexistence of disparate elements. Just as there is a single pantheon of the Buddha, gods, demons and lesser supernatural beings, so also the whole range of Sinhalese Buddhist belief and practice displays a single, consistent structure, or constitutes, as Obeyesekere calls it, a 'moral community'. In his view, moreover, Sinhalese Buddhism is locally institutionalized in each village, so that the religion of the village can also be seen, 'for methodological purposes as a unitary structure', that is, a smaller moral community. This Obeyesekere works out in detail, arguing that the local village ritual, differing slightly from one village to another, 'validates the social structure of the village, defines its limits, and demarcates the village as a moral community over which the (local) gods have protective jurisdiction and authority'.[35] The rituals and values which are common to the Sinhalese, the rituals associated with the national deities of the island, contribute the wider moral community of Sinhalese Buddhism; and, finally, the rituals and values associated with the Buddha constitute the 'great' moral community of Theravada Buddhism. The little tradition of Sinhalese Buddhism is thus linked quite consistently (*pace* Copleston) with the great tradition of South-East Asian Theravada Buddhism by a common set of meanings, derived from the great tradition: *karma*, merit, *dana* (giving, or generosity), *sila* (morality), '*arahant*-ship' and *nirvāna*. 'The common salvation-idiom,' says Obeyesekere, 'is the ideological channel which facilitates movement from one tradition to the other', that is, from 'great' to 'little', or the reverse. But in the different countries of Buddhist South-East Asia the salvation-idiom is phrased in different languages, so to speak; that is, in terms of the different local peasant cultures. This, he says, agrees with Robert Slater's conclusions regarding Burmese Buddhism, in his book, *Paradox and Nirvāna*,[36] that it is

Buddhism and not animism 'that constitutes the governing ethos of the people'.

Whereas Obeyesekere lays great emphasis on the continuity of hierarchical structure from local village religion to pan-South-East Asian Buddhism, Ames and Evers are concerned to emphasize the degree of conceptual difference within the Sinhalese situation. Ames argues that although the Sinhalese may in practice fuse Buddhist, and what he calls 'magical-animist' practices, they never confuse them.[37] There is a clear distinction, he says, in the mind of the villager between the sacred ritual of Buddhism and the profane ritual of magical-animism. Ames sees the policy of Buddhist *bkikkhus* in allowing the practice of local cults alongside the cult of veneration of the Buddha, as mainly one of accommodation. He quotes the words of one of the *bhikkhus*: 'People are going to propitiate the deities anyway, no matter what we say. Besides, Buddha never said they should not; he never said it was demerit. Therefore, if we keep shrines in our temple compounds, whatever their reason for coming, people will at least come—and learn to venerate Buddha while invoking the deities.'[38]

This Ames regards as a case of dangling carrots before the horse, or, in this case, the peasant, and points out that Buddhism is not the only religious system to do this. He finds a parallel in the 'sacramentals' of Catholicism, as distinct from the sacraments. When local or national deity shrines are placed within the precinct of the Buddhist temple, this is in order 'to bring magic under the control of the monks, and the spirits under the suzerainty of the Buddha'. It is not, he emphasizes, syncretism. There is still a radical division between the concerns of a man when he is venerating the Buddha and when he is engaging in the rituals of magical animism. Veneration of the Buddha and the acquiring of merit thereby is concerned with the trans-temporal world; the spirit cults are concerned very much with this world and its immediate day-to-day needs. The dichotomy is not between the great tradition and little tradition, as separate unitary systems, though connected by a progression of values; at every level the dichotomy is between other-worldly (*lokuttara*) and this-worldly (*lokiya*) values and aims.

Ames suggests that these two Pāli terms, *lokuttara* and *lokiya*, as they are used by the Sinhalese, have meanings very close to Durkheim's concepts of 'the sacred' and 'the profane'. His explanation of the existence of these two levels in Sinhalese Buddhist practice is that it is due to the nature of Buddhist doctrine. There is only one way to salvation, in the Buddhist view; it is very difficult and the goal is far distant. 'For the ordinary Buddhist, salvation is considered very difficult because it demands arduous meditation; it is very distant because the necessary practice takes thousands and thousands of rebirths.'[39] Ames, unlike some earlier Western observers of Buddhism, avoids falling into the error of saying simply that its practice entails a complete turning of one's back on this world and renouncing all interest in it and its affairs. 'Because of the evaluative supremacy of the world-negating *nirvānaya* ideal, relations with the world are always strained. But because of the concern with rebirth and comfort, relations with the world are also necessary and important.'[40]

On the basis of his analysis of Sinhalese practice in terms of sacred and profane concerns, Ames proceeds to identify four religious subsystems which he claims have developed within Sinhalese Buddhism as a consequence of the remote nature of the Buddhist goal, i.e. *nirvāna*. The first sub-system is that which is wholly concerned with the sacred, namely, the Buddhist religious belief-system, with its own special practices and institutions. The second and third subsystems are the temple-estate, and the nation-state. These are, at best, only quasi-sacred. The fourth sub-system is that of the spirit cults, which the Sinhalese regard as entirely profane (*lokiya*). This four-fold analysis Ames develops in detail in the course of a review and interpretation of the whole spectrum of Sinhalese religious and non-religious practices. Buddhist practice, whether it be meditation, or merit-making by means of worship, generosity of action, and so on, is directed solely towards an other-worldly end. No immediate mundane benefits are expected. Ames emphasizes particularly the non-reciprocal intention in Buddhist giving, whether to monks or to one's neighbors. One does not give in order to receive any reciprocal boon. In the magical cults, however, this is precisely what one does expect: to receive an immediate boon in return for offerings made. The spirit-cults, unlike Buddhist practice, cater for needs which are 'specific, concrete and mundane'.[41]

Just as Ames rejects the great tradition/little tradition dichotomy, so also he rejects the earlier notion that there are three 'religions' existing side by side (as Eliot suggested) namely, the religion of the Buddha, Hinduism and the deity-cults, and the cults of hobgoblins and spirits. In his view there is one system which has reference to the sacred; it embraces both monk and layman, without radical separation between them, in a pyramidal structure of different types of practitioners and graded activities and statuses, from the lowliest kind of merit-making at the bottom of the pyramid to the highest kind of meditation-practice at the top. This is Sinhalese religion. In contrast, there is another system of belief and practice, which has reference to the profane, that is, to the spirit-cults. This is Sinhalese magic. It will be seen that Ames's dichotomy owes something to the kind of distinction between religion and magic made by Malinowski, as Ames himself acknowledges.

The two systems interact, in ways which can be fairly clearly traced. Ames does this, representing the interaction in diagrammatic form.[42] Between these two systems, polarized in terms of the religion/magic distinction, come the two intermediate sub-systems of the temple-estate and the state. All owe their special characteristics to the nature of Buddhist religion. For example, the state, in the Sinhalese tradition of the pre-British period, was what it was because 'the King was dedicated to upholding the faith and protecting (Buddhist) religious institutions ... this was the political aspect of religion'. The spirit-cults, similarly, hold their position in the culture of Sri Lanka, not by their own right so much as by right of the need which Buddhist religion creates in day-to-day life, by virtue of the remoteness of its salvation-ideal. Ames points out that where the salvation-ideal is modified, in the direction of becoming less remote, the status of the spirit-cults is also modified as a consequence: that is, the need for this kind of cult depreciates. 'It is precisely the modern Buddhist enthusiast who believes that salvation is attainable within this or the next few lives who also claims that magic is superfluous.'[43]

Hans-Dieter Evers agrees with Ames's analysis in general, and from the point of view of his own studies of the Buddhist *Sangha* provides supporting evidence of the clear-cut theoretical distinction between the two realms, sacred and profane, Buddhist and non-Buddhist. The distinction is clearest, he finds, in the case of the respective roles of Buddhist and non-Buddhist cult-specialists—that is, the *bhikkhus* and the magicians or exorcists. It is with these that Evers is primarily concerned. At the level of the non-specialist lay people the two realms overlap. But it is significant, Evers points out, that among the lay people there are no sectarian divisions along Buddhist/non-Buddhist lines. The same constituency of laymen participates in both kinds of rituals. 'Doctrinal differences have, as a matter of fact, not led to social differentiation and the formation of sects.'[44] Since the same group of laymen may hold both sets of beliefs, this suggests that these are not different, competing sets of religious doctrines, but rather that one set is religious (having reference to the sacred), and the other is non-religious, mundane or secular (having reference to the profane). Evers sees Buddhism as constituting the religion of the Sinhalese, but he sees it as an 'incomplete religion', that is, it leaves certain kinds of mundane needs uncatered-for, which have to be met by secular agencies. There is, however, in this concept of an 'incomplete religion' some confusion of definitions. If Ames's Durkheimian analysis is adhered to, it will be seen that a religion is 'complete' when it meets men's needs with reference to the sacred. The meeting of mundane needs is not primarily or properly the business of religion, even though religion by the values it fosters, may have an effect on the way secular agencies meet secular needs.

Yalman's concern is almost wholly focused on the non-Buddhist rituals, within which he finds, as an important and interesting feature, a binary structure. That is to say, the basic purpose of the rituals appears to be to bring about a desired end which will be the reverse of some present, undesirable situation. There is thus a structure of opposed categories: sickness and health, enmity and friendship, and so on. He finds that this characterizes Buddhist belief and practice also, so that there is a parallelism of structure between the two systems, Buddhist and non-Buddhist. Yalman's primary concern to some extent bypasses the important question of the total structure of Sinhalese culture, as Ames observes. However, in so far as Yalman appears to accept a general distinction between Buddhist and non-Buddhist rituals his analysis does not conflict with Ames's. Ryan's account also implies a distinction of a kind between 'Buddhist' and 'the wonderful world' of gods and demons; the latter, says Ryan, is 'no more than casually associated with the Lord Buddha and that which is of the gods'.[45]

Broadly, therefore, two kinds of analysis of the Sinhalese religious-cultural situation are possible. There is that of Obeyesekere, who sees a hierarchy of closely-structured moral communities of belief and practice in which Buddhist and non-Buddhist elements in varying degrees, form integrated systems, and which can be compared with one another in terms of 'little tradition' and 'great tradition'. On the other hand, there is that of Ames, who identifies two distinct realms of belief and practice, sacred and profane, each of which has its own complete, self-contained structure. Nevertheless, the two realms affect each other: the kind of emphasis which is being made at any given time within the Buddhistic monastic-lay system will have its effect upon the nature and the status of the secularly-oriented-ritual system.

These two views of Sinhalese religion and culture have some important implications for the interpretation of contemporary ideological and social change in Sri Lanka. If Obeyesekere's analysis is accepted, the consequences of the modernization and industrialization of Sri Lanka are likely to be that damage will be done to the structure of these holistic cultural systems or moral communities, in so far as they are increasingly infiltrated by alien ideas and, more important, techniques for dealing with everyday human cares and ills. The effect of modernization will be construed as being one of secularization, in the sense in which Bryan Wilson, for example, uses it, meaning thereby a loss in the social importance of religious beliefs and rituals.

If Ames's analysis is accepted, a rather different view of the same process becomes possible. The distinction between sacred and profane areas of concern enables us to see modernization as a process which may affect one of these more immediately and more drastically than the other; it is not the whole structure of

Sinhalese Buddhism which is likely to be affected, but only that system which has secular needs as its field of interest. Illness, for instance, will, in the process of modernization, be regarded less and less as the work of demons, who need to be placated or exorcized; the appropriate remedy will be seen increasingly in terms of scientific medical knowledge.

However, complications are likely to arise in the course of modernization. For the astrological and spirit-cults are resorted to for reasons other than illness; they may be used, for example, by those who seek a change of luck, or to remedy a personal grievance, or to gain some personal advantage. This may explain why these cults show little sign of becoming obsolete in modern Sri Lanka. The author, when in Sri Lanka in 1970, was told by informants that the number of people resorting to the *devālaya* shrines in the Colombo area had shown no decrease, but rather the reverse. This is not difficult to understand; in conditions of rapid modernization like those in the Colombo area, awareness of personal stresses and strains may become more acute, as it appears to have done in Japan since the end of the Second World War.[46] Sri Lanka suffers also from an internal conflict of cultures, Buddhist and Western. The gap left by the removal from what had been a Buddhist state of one of its most vital functionaries, the Buddhist king, and the introduction of alien institutions and values may have been a prime cause of social and cultural tension of a complex order, a classic case of anomie, which is reflected in the increasing tendency of Sinhalese people to resort to the *devālayas* for the remedying of immediate and urgent personal disabilities and ills. More research of a comparative nature is needed on this question.[47]

THE UNACKNOWLEDGED IMPORTANCE OF POLITICAL AND
ECONOMIC FACTORS

What seems to emerge from this review of Buddhist civilization in India and Sri Lanka is that it was not openness to the local cults which weakened Buddhism; this was, if anything, a means of integrating Buddhist and non-Buddhist, Buddhist and not-yet-Buddhist practices, aims and ideals. What weakened Buddhism in both India and Sri Lanka was its sensitivity and vulnerability to political assault and change, and also to economic depression or change, whenever discontinuance of an agricultural surplus left the *Sangha* unprovided for and unable to survive. The difference between the economy of the wet-rice-growing river plains and that of the hills is an important factor in the geographical distribution of Buddhist culture and civilization within any major region, whether in India, Sri Lanka or South-East Asia. The difference between the two types of economy and their associated cultures has been admirably dealt with by Edmund Leach, although too few students of Buddhism pay attention to the kind of distinctions to which Leach has drawn attention in connection with Burma.[48] Certainly, the large part played by the economic factor does not appear to be recognized, or at least admitted, by many modern *bhikkhus*. The author found this to be the case in discussion of population growth and control in Sri Lanka and Thailand.[49] That, however, is one of the issues whose discussion cannot adequately be attempted within the scope of the present book. A brief look at some of these issues may, however, be allowed in the concluding pages.

Epilogue: Beyond the Present Horizons

We have now seen in general outline the characteristic development of a Buddhist civilization in certain parts of India, followed by its decline and virtual disappearance. We have observed the same kind of development, in its essential features, in Sri Lanka, but here the decline was later and was arrested in time to preserve Buddhist civilization in principle, although its classical structure in Sri Lanka has since been damaged by European invasion and conquest.

BEYOND INDIA AND SRI LANKA

No attempt has been made, since it would be impossible within the space available, to deal with the development of Buddhist civilization in those countries outside India where the Mahayana has been the predominant form in which Buddhism spread: that is, in China, Japan, Korea, Tibet and Vietnam. Moreover, in the characteristic form of Buddhist civilization with which we have been concerned here, the *Sangha* is one of the principal and indispensable elements. Since the Mahayana accords less importance to the *Sangha*, the structure of the Buddhist civilization which would have to be traced in the Mahayana countries would be of a somewhat different kind. Moreover, Buddhist civilization as we have characterized it places a high value on the adherence to Buddhism of the political ruler, in order to make possible the kind of political and economic structure which will facilitate the pursuit of Buddhist morality by the maximum number of the citizens of the state, since in this more humanistic form of Buddhism primary importance attaches to human moral effort. Where the adherence of the ruler could not be secured, it was rather more as a theistic religion of supernatural salvation that Buddhism made its way. The outstanding example of this is to be found in China throughout much of the history of Buddhism in that land, although it is to the later rather than the earlier period that this properly applies.

However, it is worth noting that in certain of the countries where the Mahayana form has prevailed, notably Japan and Tibet, the introduction of Buddhism was jointly the concern of the

261

political ruler, who wished his country to adopt Buddhist culture and civilization, and of the *Sangha*, who had already entered the country or were brought in to cooperate with the ruler in setting up a Buddhist state. It is clear that in these cases, therefore, the essential characteristics of Buddhist civilization were recognized, and duly realized.

In Japan, for example, Buddhism was introduced at a time when 'a central authority was being established and the classes and tribes of the numerous islands were being welded into a nation', and when 'communication with the Korean peninsula provided a continual stimulus to change and movement'.[1] The first Buddhists to enter the country, from Korea, were artisans and scholars who came as the bearers of the various arts of civilization.[2] In 538 AD a delegation was sent to Japan by the Prince of Kudara, a principality in the south of Korea, and this was accompanied by Buddhist *bhikkhus*, with Buddhist literature and articles for ceremonial use. The ruling class in Japan was divided over the new ideology: some favored it and some did not. The division reflected a struggle for political supremacy among conflicting interests. The triumph of those who favored Buddhism came with the accession of Prince Shotoka to the regency of the country in 593. His reign, says Anasaki, was 'the most epoch-making period in Japanese history, and it was marked by the striking advance of Buddhist influence and continental civilization. He became the founder of Japanese civilization....'[3] The public proclamation of Buddhism as the state religion of Japan was accompanied by the founding of a Buddhist institution, or group of institutions—a temple, where provision was made both for ceremonies for study of Buddhist philosophy and sciences by the *bhikkhus*, and for their residence; an asylum for orphans and old people; a hospital; and a dispensary.[4]

The political ruler acting as Buddhist head of state, concerned to establish a Buddhist style of public life, with appropriate institutions for the public welfare, in conjunction with the *Sangha* and on behalf of the people—this agrees closely with the pattern of Buddhist civilization established in India by Ashoka eight centuries earlier.

Similarly, it was a Tibetan king, Sron-btsan-sgam-po, who, about a century later, sought to introduce Buddhism into his country. A knowledge of its characteristics as a religious culture and civilization had come to him through his marriage alliances with Nepal and China. Success was eventually achieved when a Buddhist teacher from northwestern India, who understood the need for the 'open frontier' between Buddhist philosophy and popular ideas in the making of a Buddhist state, was invited to assist in the task. At a later period of Tibetan history, in the eleventh century, when Buddhism needed to be restored, it was a member of the Tibetan royal family who urged the great Atisha to leave Bengal and go and live in Tibet for the sake of the rebuilding of Buddhist civilization in that country.[5]

The even more important case of Buddhist civilization, which there is not the space to deal with adequately here, is that of South-East Asia. Particularly significant are the Theravada Buddhist countries of mainland South-East Asia: Burma, Thailand, Laos and Cambodia. The fact that a recognizable civilization of the kind with which we have been concerned survives in these countries today is due in large part to two factors. First, there was the work of the *Sangha* in gaining the adherence of the early rulers of the Burmese and Thai kingdoms to Theravada Buddhism. Second, there was the influence of the continuing tradition of Sinhalese Buddhism, which at various times in the history of Sri Lanka's relations with these South-East Asian countries had a stimulating effect on their development as Buddhist states. Such was the case in the late eleventh century when the Burmese kingdom of Pagan came to the help of the kingdom of Sri Lanka in resisting invasion by the Cholas of South India, with the result that Pagan benefited by the contact her *bhikkhus* had with the Pali Tipiṭaka tradition in Sri Lanka. Again, as a result of Parakkama Bahu's reform of Buddhism in Sri Lanka in the following century, *bhikkhus* from the Mon kingdoms of what is now south Burma and central Thailand, from the Burmese kingdom of Pagan, and from the Malay kingdom of Ligor (the modern Nakorn Si Thamarat in South Thailand) all greatly benefited, in learning and in understanding of the methods of Buddhist analysis and mind training, as well as in the experience of monastic and social organization which they gained as a result of the visits to Sri Lanka which so many of them made during the twelfth and thirteenth centuries.

South-East Asian kings played an important part in the growth and flowering of Buddhist civilization in the countries of the mainland during these centuries, especially Anawrahta, king of Pagan in the eleventh century, and Rama Kamhaeng, king of the newly-established Thai kingdom of Sukhothai in the thirteenth century. As a result of the policies pursued by kings and *Sangha* during these formative centuries, the Burmese and Thai, and eventually also the Laos and Cambodian people of the river-valley states, became supporters of the *Sangha* and willing participants in the benefits which Buddhist civilization brought them. Not all of the peoples of the mainland countries were brought within the aegis of Theravada Buddhism, however; the hill people remained largely untouched, with certain special exceptions, such as the people of the Shan States of eastern Burma and north-west Thailand. But in the main, it was the valley people who became Buddhists, and whose rice-fields provided the surplus which maintained and still maintains the *Sangha* in those areas, enabling it to function in what is still, in Thailand especially, its classic and traditional role within a Buddhist civilization. The part played by wise and farseeing kings such as Mongkut and Chulalongkorn in nineteenth-century Thailand in preserving Buddhist civilization and guiding its development in the conditions of the modern world, or the part played by a rash and unwise king such as Thibaw, the last Buddhist king of Burma, who precipitated his country's final conquest by the British in 1885, and thus brought about a disruption of the Buddhist state, are part of a larger story which must be told elsewhere.[6]

BEYOND 'RELIGION'

Buddhism, like any other living tradition, has developed and changed in the course of its history. As we survey the ground which has been covered here, it is possible to distinguish several major 'types' of Buddhism. There is the Buddhism of the pre-Ashokan period, of which the fullest, though not the only evidence, comes to us through the Pāli Canon. The emphasis in this early period is predominantly humanistic; the *Buddha-sāsana* is a system of mind training, for the restructuring of human consciousness, and thus, ultimately, of human society. At this stage Buddhism may be characterized broadly as a humanistic ethic seeking full embodiment in a political and social community, an ideology seeking to become a civilization.

The next stage is Ashokan Buddhism. At this stage Buddhism has realized its potential as a civilization; the cooperation of the *Sangha*, the political ruler and the people has been secured, and a Buddhist state has, in principle, come into existence. This does not mean that all the people have accepted Buddhist values and are acting upon them, or that they all understand the Buddhist doctrines of man, the world and human destiny. But the conditions have been established in which a gradual and steady approximation to these values, becomes possible for the whole people. What is more, Buddhist values are given recognition in the structure and the laws of the state. The national state is not, however, the ultimate goal; the vision is of a reconstituted humanity which goes beyond the national to the international community. The Buddhist ruler does what is in his power to commend Buddhist civilization to fellow-rulers, as Ashoka did to his friend and contemporary, King Devanam-piya Tissa of Sri Lanka. In such efforts to extend Buddhist civilization the members of the *Sangha* cooperate with the ruler or, in many cases, prepare the way for such royal enterprise by their own efforts in making known the *Dhamma*, as the *Sangha* did in north India before the time of Ashoka, and as the Mon *bhikkhus* of South-East Asia did, before the accession of King Anawrahta in Burma, and King Rama Kamhaeng in Thailand. There is no question, however, of either the national Buddhist state, or some international community of Buddhist states which might eventually come into existence, being the ultimate goal in view. The *Dhamma*, as it comes to us in the Pāli texts of Ashokan Buddhism, adumbrates a reconstituted humanity, in the social and political sense, but the vision is of more than that. It is recognized that the social structure has important consequences for men's understanding of the human situation and affects their attempts to cope with it and to improve the human condition. This is recognized in Pāli Buddhism to an extent which has not always been properly appreciated by Western writers about Buddhism. But a reconstituted social structure is not the ultimate goal, or the final answer. Alvin Gouldner has criticized his fellow-sociologist,

Talcott Parsons, for making the social system the answer to man's mortality, which he says, Parsons regards as the 'tragic essence' of the human condition. 'Over and against man's animal mortality, Parsons designs a "social system" that, with its battery of defenses and equilibrating devices, need never run down. What Parsons has done is to assign to the self-maintaining social system an immortality transcending and compensatory for man's perishability.' What this theoretical effort of Parsons assumes, adds Gouldner, is the immortality of the social system and, particularly, the American social system.[7] The same kind of objection might conceivably be raised against a theory of Buddhist civilization in which the Buddhist state was held to be the ultimate goal, the reality which comprehended, without remainder of any sort, the whole of the Buddha's teaching. This would be a mistake, for there is clearly recognizable, too, in Pāli Buddhism the sense of the sacred, as that which transcends all historical and empirical entities. 'There is, O bhikkhus, that which is not-born, not-become, not-made, and not-conditioned. If this not-born, not-become, not-made, and not-conditioned were not, then there would be apparent no release from that which is born, become, made and conditioned.'[8] Another name in Pāli Buddhism for this absolute which transcends the empirical world is *nibbāna*.

It is clear that it is this transcendent reality which is 'the sacred' in Pāli Buddhism. Whatever is venerated for its 'sacred' character is in Buddhism that which has a very close or special relationship to *nibbāna*—the *Dhamma* which proclaims it, the *bhikkhus* who are the bearers of the *Dhamma* and may in some cases be close to *nibbāna*, and the *stūpa* which symbolically represents it.

In speaking of Buddhist 'values', therefore, we are speaking of values which are derived from the affirmation of this transcendent sacred reality; Buddhist norms of action are norms which lead men towards *nibbāna*. To affirm the sacredness of *nibbāna* as the source of Buddhist values does not, however, contradict the characterization of Pāli Buddhism as humanistic. It is partly in order to distinguish Pāli Buddhism from the Mahayana and from Hinduism that we have characterized it in this way, that is, have emphasized its contradistinction from belief systems which are theistic. And it is to distinguish the Buddha's attitude, as it is portrayed in the Pāli Canon, from the brahmans and theists of his day, that he may be characterized as 'secular', that is, in contradiction to these 'religious' figures.

But there is a positive reason, too, for describing as humanistic a system of belief and values which center upon the affirmation of the reality of *nibbāna*. For this reality, according to the Pāli Buddhist view, is discoverable by man without divine aid; it was so 'discovered' by, or, more properly, it was a man who was 'awakened' (*buddha*) to this reality and who then proclaimed it to others, that they also might become 'awakened' to it. This is not to say that 'awakenment' or enlightenment is immediately available to any and every man. The necessary prerequisite is moral purification, purification of body and consciousness. For humanity in general this is the primary requirement which will inevitably absorb most of its effort and concern. But the implication is that humanity has it within its own power to achieve this; the doctrine is in that sense humanistic. It is humanistic also in that it sees human nature as the highest of the various levels of existence, in the sense that it is only from existence at the level of human nature that *nibbāna* is reached. Even the *devas* or celestial beings must come to birth in the human realm in order to be within range, as it were, of *nibbāna*. It is no contradiction therefore, to say that Pāli Buddhism has its concept of the transcendent 'sacred', and at the same time that it is a humanistic belief-system. Belief in the sacred does not necessarily imply theistic belief; nor are humanism and a sense of the sacred incompatible.

In the actual situations which Buddhist civilization entailed in India and Sri Lanka there was often a mixing, or at least juxtaposing, of values. The values held by the member of the *Sangha* who was far advanced in the Buddhist way would have been notably different from those of the villager in Ashoka's India, the villager who had barely as yet come under the influence of the *Dhamma*. Hence it was that with the establishing of Buddhism as a civilization there also went a dilution of the quality of the values held throughout the Buddhist state, compared with their much higher quality when the Buddhist community contained scarcely any 'laymen', but only *upāsakas*, or followers. Now, in Ashokan Buddhism, the *puthujjana* or 'ordinary man' was a constituent member of the Buddhist civilization; for him *Dhamma* had to be commended; he had to be encouraged and exhorted to live according to this *Dhamma* which had become the guiding principle of the state.

It was this aspect of Buddhist civilization in Ashokan India, the inclusion of large numbers of 'the masses' within the Buddhist state, in conjunction with the tolerant attitude of the *Sangha* towards the view of life and of the world from which the ordinary man started, which in time produced an important modification. This was the 'popularization' of Buddhist beliefs, in terms of spirits and celestial beings, and it was popularized Buddhism which formed one of the principal components of the third stage of Buddhist development, the post-Ashokan theistic Buddhism which is called Mahayana, or Bodhisattvayana. As we have seen, it is the role of the *Sangha* which is crucial in this kind of situation. The *Sangha*, as the bearer *par excellence* of *Buddhist* values, can successfully deal with such popularized Buddhism, so long as it is allowed to retain its proper status in the Buddhist system as the respected embodiment of wisdom and exemplar of morality. Where the *Sangha's* status is diminished, or its existence is a matter of indifference, effective permeation of popular culture by Buddhist values ceases to be possible. In India this is what happened eventually, but not before Buddhist civilization in its Ashokan form, in which the *Sangha's* crucial role was recognized, had been planted in Sri Lanka. There the proper role of the *Sangha* was retained and safeguarded. This book has attempted to look as carefully as possible within the space available at the difference in the factors present in India and Sri Lanka, and to suggest some answers to the question why it was that in India, where Buddhism began, the *Sangha's* place was undermined, and with it the whole of Buddhist civilization, while in Sri Lanka the *Sangha's* essential place was preserved, and Buddhist civilization with it. The factors which have been identified as important are three; they are: political—seen in the attitude of rulers, hostile or friendly towards the *Sangha*; social—that is, the existence or absence of social classes, such as the brahmans, who are antagonistic to the *Sangha*; and economic—that is, the continuing ability of the economy of a country to support the *Sangha*.

Although we have not dealt with South-East Asia, the principles are the same there, too. The *Sangha* survived because it retained the support of political rulers, at least until the British conquest of Burma disrupted Buddhist civilization in that country; and without such disruption until the present day in Thailand. It survived because it was not opposed by any seriously powerful social class or group acting as a rival for the allegiance of the people, and offering a rival ideology of the state, as happened in India. It survived, too, because in the Theravada regions of South-East Asia, that is, the rice-growing river-valleys and plains, agriculture can produce enough and to spare for the present population of the region; there has, therefore, until now, always been a surplus out of which the *Sangha* can be supported.

We have seen from the history of Indian Buddhism that the economic basis of the *Sangha's* life can be of two kinds. There is the situation in which it is supported by large-scale munificence on the part of royal patrons or very wealthy merchants. And there is the other, older system, that of local support by village people, contributing out of their agricultural surplus to the feeding of the *bhikkhus* and to the upkeep of the monasteries. In the latter case the organization, as in modern Burma, is very simple, like that of the primitive *Sangha*. Mendelson describes it as 'made up, in the main, of small discrete units ultimately responsible to themselves alone: monks living alone or in small groups with perhaps a small entourage of novices and schoolchildren, supported by the village on whose outskirts their monastery was built'.[9] When the economic basis of the *Sangha's* life is of this kind it is less exposed to the risks of a change of dynasty or the death of wealthy patrons; its basis is wider and, normally, more secure.

On the other hand, when the *Sangha* is a large landowner there is, we have seen, the danger to its life in the alienation from the needs and concerns of the ordinary people which can easily take place, as well as the attraction which the *Sangha* then holds for unworthy entrants. Nor is the land-owning *Sangha* entirely secure from the possibility of economic shortage, for this can come about whether the *Sangha* owns the land or not, by failure of crops, or destruction of crops by invading troops, or merely by defection on the part of the laymen on whom the *Sangha* depends for the cultivation of its land. On balance, the largest guarantee of

269

security and well being for the *Sangha* appears to be found in the system of the 'many small discrete units', supported in each case by the local people.

BEYOND BUDDHISM

Whether or not the increase in population in the Theravada countries is now running at such a rate that, before long, it will exceed the optimum size which allows an agricultural surplus to exist, sufficiently great to support both the non-agriculturally productive sectors of the national economy and the *Sangha* as well, is an open question. It is conceivable that the economies of Burma and Thailand could be so adversely affected by the present rate of population increase that a situation could be reached in which it would be difficult to maintain the *Sangha* at its present size and, therefore, its present level of effectiveness. What we have outlined here of the history of Buddhist civilization in India and Sri Lanka suggests that such an eventuality could seriously threaten the continued existence of Buddhist civilization in South-East Asia.[10]

The Sinhalese Buddhist writer, Dr. Walpola Rahula, takes the view that Buddhism lost something when it was adopted by Ashoka as a 'state religion'. The framework of reference which this book has attempted to set forth requires a different way of describing that development, and its consequences. Rahula holds that what was formerly a 'religion' gradually developed into 'an ecclesiastical organization with its numerous duties, religious, political and social'. Once this has happened to a religion, he continues, it has to change with the times, or perish.[11] In the view of the matter which has been presented here, one has to say, in contrast to Rahula's interpretation of the matter, that when an ideology for the restructuring of human nature and society becomes a religious cult, it gradually loses some of its original spirit of rationality and political relevance, and its professional representatives or bearers degenerate into a merely religious organization; that it is impossible for a psycho-social philosophy, once it becomes a religious cult, to maintain its effectiveness. The time then comes when it has to change, and reform, or perish; it has to purge itself of what were once popular, cultic, polytheistic religious ideas and practices. These may still retain their hold among rural people, but their days are numbered in a modernizing world. (Other forms of superstition may flourish in urban societies, but not these.)

The Buddhist *Sangha* seems now, however, to have accepted the role of being the professional bearers of a religious cult, one of the several religious alternatives open to men to choose from. Rahula's views are by no means unrepresentative. In the case of Theravada Buddhism, a great deal of the early Ashokan perspective, in which Buddhism was seen as a civilization, has certainly been preserved in one sense, through the preservation by the Theravadins of the Pāli texts and their teaching. But Theravada Buddhism as it actually exists today, in Sri Lanka and South-East Asia, is by no means identical with the Buddhism of the Ashokan period. Much has been acquired along the way since then in the form of devotional practices, institutional organization, and commentaries on the doctrine. In some Asian countries Buddhism retains a good deal of its original concern with the public dimension of life as distinct from the private world of soul-salvation, its character as an ideology capable of integrating a religiously and even culturally pluralistic society. It is in Western countries, on the whole, that there is the strongest insistence on regarding it as a religion competing with other religions; this is a view of it which is shared by some of its adherents, and the adherents of other faiths with which, in Western countries, it coexists.

Some of those citizens of Western countries who have come to call themselves 'Buddhists' affirm that what they have embraced is a religion, on the grounds that man has an innate need for religion and that nothing else but a religion can meet this need. This is a need which they feel, and which they believe has for them been met in Buddhism. There must, they say, be devotional practice, worship, mythology, faith; without these man cannot live, or cannot live at his full stature. 'Buddhism is still a religion, not a philosophy or a system of ethics, by neither of which alone can men live.... We may wish to prune religion of all myth but it should not be overlooked that myths represent man's attempt to express the ineffable and his attitude toward it. A spiritual vacuum must be avoided.'[12]

Certainly Buddhism has become a religion, and began to move in that direction within five hundred years from the time of the Buddha's death. But the intention here has been to demonstrate that, in origin, it was the ethos and the philosophy of a civilization. The Buddha was an 'analyst', not a propounder of dogmatic truth, and early Buddhism was characterized essentially by its rationalism (see chapter 7). The human 'need' to which the Buddha addressed himself was not that of man's need for religion, but man's need to overcome his condition of self-centeredness, and to identify with a greater, completely comprehensive reality. If man has any innate spiritual 'need', it would appear to be this, rather than religion. Religion provides one of the possible ways in which men identify with some all-embracing reality, but there are others. The assertion that religion is a basic human need can be countered by the fact that large numbers of men today live without resort to religion. Whether such men live adequately, or according to the deepest needs of their nature, is controversial. An equally tenable view is that men who live by religion are, partially at least, opting out of this world in favour of another, and therefore are not living fully in this world. Identification with that reality in relation to which the individual self is forgotten, the most comprehensive reality of which man is aware, which 'sanctions' man's existence,[13] can for some men lead to humanistic rather than religious activities. The man without a religion is not a man without values; the values by which he lives are differently derived. Acceptance or rejection of a particular religious position is governed to a large extent by the values which a man embraces, whether they are values he has always held (that is, inherited, or traditionally-received values), or whether he has recently come to hold them. Some people, holding certain sets of values, will take the view that they (and the rest of mankind) have an innate need for devotional practices, for mythology, for belief in a 'world' other than this one; this may itself be the value judgment from which they start. Others, with different sets of values, may not hold this view. Buddhism, especially in Westernized urban situations, has come to be very largely a system of belief and practice which appeals to certain of those who hold the former view, but does not appeal to those who do not feel any need for religion, and do not consider that this is a universal human need. For them, Buddhism is largely irrelevant, as irrelevant as any other religion, although they may acknowledge that it fills a need, and is true, for those who adhere to it.

The fact that Buddhism has, especially as it is understood in the West, arrived at the position where it has this specialized 'religious' character, is an illustration of the perennial religion-making tendency which appears to operate as actively in modern as in ancient societies. It is a continually recurring tendency, but this fact is not necessarily an indication of a universal human need, any more than the perennial recurrence of cholera epidemics in the hot season in India is an indication of men's need to have cholera. To point out that this religion-making tendency exists, and that it can and does transform into a religious cult, with its attendant mythology, a movement which started out as something quite different, is a proper part of the task of the historian of religion.

FROM THE ANCIENT INDIAN REPUBLICS TO THE MODERN REPUBLIC OF INDIA

Buddhism began as a theory of human existence with implications for human social structure, a philosophy not dependent in any way on theistic belief or theistic sanctions, nor having any divine revelation as its starting-point, and yet tolerant of the theistic beliefs current in the contemporary society, and capable of providing a way of transition from irrational to rational attitudes. In these respects at least, one can observe certain similarities between it and the secular constitution of the modern Republic of India. The fact is not without significance that the founders of the Republic adopted, as its emblem, a famous piece of sculpture known as the Sarnath Lion Capital of the emperor Ashoka, together with the other symbol of the Buddhist state, the Wheel of *Dharma* (*Dharmacakra*). It must be emphasized, however, that the Buddhist affinities, such as they are, of the modern Republic of India, are with the Ashokan state, not with Buddhism as it has now come to be practiced, as one 'religion' among others.

The Buddha, it will be recalled, is represented in the Pāli texts as favoring a republican form of government. But in the political circumstances of the Buddha's time monarchy seemed to be the only viable system, and the compromise which early Buddhism effected was one by which a republican community (the new *Sangha*), the prototype of a restructured human society, functioned as an advisory body to the monarch. In this way, in Ashokan India, the individualistic brahmanical conception of monarchy was modified in the direction of a limited degree of republicanism. So far as the religious beliefs and cults of the day were concerned the Ashokan state adopted the role of the tolerant patron of them all.

The Republic of India, unlike Britain, for example, and some of the other states in modern Asia, does not officially favour any one particular religion. Nor is its head of state required, either by tradition or by the Constitution, to be an adherent of a certain religion. On the other hand, it promises 'to secure to all its citizens ... liberty of thought, expression, belief, faith and worship'.[14] The political structure is one of elected representative government, the basis of the franchise being one man (or woman), one vote. This in itself is a remarkable testimony to the trust which the makers of the constitution placed in the people of India, since 85 per cent of them are non-literate. The trust appears to have been justified, as a political scientist outside India observed even as early as 1960.[15] The Constitution also sets out explicitly that, as a sovereign democratic republic, India intends to secure for all her citizens social and economic justice and equality of status and opportunity. It is perhaps significant that Jawaharlal Nehru, whose part in the shaping of the Constitution was very considerable, was himself strongly influenced by Buddhist ideas, and that the chairman of the body set up to prepare a 'Draft Constitution' (published in 1948) was Dr. Ambedkar, who himself later became a Buddhist, together with a large number of the community of the Mahars, to which he belonged. The caste structure, one of the salient features of traditional, post-Buddhist Hinduism is not merely not recognized in India's Constitution; it is by implication rejected. Jawaharlal Nehru as Prime Minister of India until 1964 vigorously pursued this line of policy; as W. H. Morris-Jones has put it, so frequently did he inveigh against communal and caste divisions that the composers of newspaper headlines were 'hard pressed to make the theme arresting'.[16] The final point in this brief comparison is that the Constitution of India guarantees the rights, of the individual, but carefully balances this with an equal emphasis on the unity of the nation, and the security of the state itself. In making this double emphasis the Indian Constitution guards against 'the tendency to engender an atomistic view towards society' which in the USA, for example, has resulted from emphasis on individual rights over against the common welfare.[17]

Criticism of the doctrine of caste, tolerant neutrality where all other religious beliefs and practices are concerned (so long as they are consistent with public safety and well-being), concern for social and economic justice, the promotion of rational attitudes and policies wherever possible and an avoidance of measures which would encourage atomistic individualism—these features of modern India's Constitution do not in themselves constitute Buddhism, but to some observers they may suggest that the same kind of problems which were engaging serious attention in the Buddha's day have in modern times been recognized afresh, and are being dealt with in a similar spirit. There is no question, of course, of 'Buddhism' and the ideology of the Republic of India being equated. In the case of the former the *Dhamma* is set out at great length and in great detail; the ideology of the latter has no such explicit exposition. In one sense there was no need in the latter case to set out the ideology, for this had been done already by one of India's greatest sons, the Buddha. It may well be that unconscious echoes of the *Dhamma* are to be heard in the Constitution of the Republic. As in the case of the Ashokan stage, what was envisaged in the way of social reconstruction did not immediately become a reality. The Constitution has to be implemented. But this is the direction in which India has chosen to move and in which she has already begun to advance. Between the republics of ancient India and the Ashokan Buddhist state there is a recognizable historical link, in the *Sangha*. Between the Ashokan state and the modern Republic of India there is again a recognizable affinity; even though the intervening period in this case is much longer, and the genealogy is more complex, what is aimed at in the Constitution of the twentieth-century Republic shares this same family likeness. The important point of difference between the Ashokan state and the modern Indian

275

Republic is that in the former, the *Sangha* was present as an essential element in the socio-political situation. In the latter it is not present, except 'in an extremely minor role, in certain parts of India, where it has in modern times begun to be reintroduced.

Abbreviations

List of Works Cited in the Notes

Acknowledgements

Appendix

Notes

Abbreviations

A.	*Aṅguttara Nikāya* (Pāli text)
ABORI	Annals of the Bhandarka Oriental Research Institute
Arthasastra	*Kautilya's Arthasastra*, transl. by R. Shamasastry, 8th edn., 1967
BSOAS	Bulletin of the School of Oriental and African Studies
D.	*Dīgha Nikāya* (Pāli text)
Dial.	Dialogues of the Buddha, Pt. I, Pt. II and Pt. III (see bibliography under Davids, T. W. Rhys)
Diod.	*Bibliotheca Historica of Diodorus Siculus*, in J. W. M'Crindle *The Invasion of India by Alexander the Great*, 1893, pp. 269——301
DPPN	Dictionary of Pāli Proper Names, 2 vols, by G. P. Malalasekere
Gradual	*The Book of the Gradual Sayings*, Vol. I, Vol. II and Vol.
Sayings	V by F. L. Woodward, 1932, 1933 and 1936; Vol. III and Vol. IV transl. by E. M. Hare, 1934 and 1935
HCIP	Bharatiya Vidya Bhavan's *History and Culture of the Indian People*, Vols. 1–10
IGI	*Imperial Gazetteer of India*, 9 vols., ed. by W. W. Hunter, 1881
Jat.	*Jātaka* (Pāli text)
JRAS	*Journal of the Royal Asiatic Society*
M.	*Majjhima Nikāya* (Pāli text)
Mv.	*Mahāvaṃsa* (Pāli text)
S.	*Saṃyutta Nikāya* (Pāli text)
Skt.	Sanskrit
Sn.	*Sutta Nipata* (Pāli text)
SBE	*Sacred Books of the East*
Vin.	*Vinaya Piṭaka* (Pāli text)

List of Works Cited in the Notes

ADHYA, G. L. *Early Indian Economics*, 1966

ADIKARAM, E. W. *Early History of Buddhism in Sri Lanka*, 1946

AMES, M.
  (i) 'Buddha and the Dancing Goblins: A Theory of Magic and Religion' in *American Anthropologist*, Vol. 66, Part I, 1964
  (ii) 'Sinhalese Magical Animism and Theravada Buddhism' in *Religion in South Asia*, ed. by E. B. Harper, 1964

ANESAKI, M. *History of Japanese Religion*, 1930, reprinted 1963

BAREAU, A. *Les Religions de l'Inde*, 1966

BARUA, B. *A History of pre-Buddhistic Indian Philosophy*, 1921

BASU, D. D. *Introduction to the Constitution of India*, 2nd edn., 1962

BEAUJEU-GARNIER, J. *Geography of Population*, transl. by S. H. Beaver, 1966

BHATTACHARYA, T. *The Cult of Brahma*, 2nd edn., 1969

BLOCH, J. *Les Inscriptions d'Asoka*, 1950

BOSE, Atindranath, *Social and Rural Economy of Northern India*, 1961

BROWN, D. Mackenzie *The White Umbrella: Indian Political Thought from Manu to Gandhi*, 1968

BROWN, J.C. and DEY, A. K. *India's Mineral Wealth*, 3rd edn., 1955

CHATTOPADHYAYA, D. *Indian Atheism*, 1969

COPLESTON, R. S. *Buddhism Primitive and Present in Magadha and in Sri Lanka*, 2nd end., 1908

COWELL, E. B. (ed.) *Jātaka Tales, Vols.* I-II, 1895; Vols. III-IV, 1901; Vol. V-VI, 1905

CUNNINGHAM, A. *Geography of Ancient India*, 1871

DASGUPTA, S. N. *History of Indian Philosophy*, Vol. I, 1922

DAVIDS, T. W. Rhys *Buddhist India*, 8th edn., 1959

Dialogues of the Buddha, Pt. I, 1899; Pt. II, 1910; Pt. III, 1921. repr. 1956, 1965 and 1966

DE, K. *Vaisnava Faith and Movement*, 1961

DE SILVA, K. M. *Social Policy and Missionary Organisation in Sri Lanka*, 1840-55, 1965

DE WIJESEKERE, O. H. 'Theravada Buddhist Tradition under Modern Culture', in *Proceedings of the 11th International Congress of the International Association for the History of Religions*, Vol. I, 1968

DREKMEIER, C. *Kingship and Community in Early India*, 1962

DURKHEIM, E. *The Division of Labour in Society*, English transl. by George Simpson, 7th impression, 1969

DUTT, S. *Buddhist Monks and Monasteries of India*, 1962

ELIOT, C. *Hinduism and Buddhism*, 3 vols., 1921

EVERS, Hans-Deiter 'Magic and Religion in Sinhalese Society' in *American Anthropologist*, Vol. 67 (i)

FROMM, E. *The Fear of Freedom*, 1942

GANGULI, B. N. (ed.) *Readings in Indian Economic History*, 1964

GATES, R. R., *Human Ancestry from a genetical point of view*, 1948

GEIGER, W. *Mahāvaṃsa, or the Great Chronicle of Sri Lanka translated into English*, 1912, reprinted 1964

Culavamsa, being the more recent part of the Mahāvaṃsa, Pt. I and Pt. II, 1928, reprinted 1953

GHOSH, J. C. *Bengali Literature*, 1948

GHOSHAL, U. N. *A History of Indian Political Ideas*, 1959

A History of Indian Public Life, Vol. II: The Maurya and pre-Maurya period, 1966

GOKHALE, B. G. *Ashoka Maurya*, 1966

GOULDNER, A. W. *The Coming Crisis in Western Sociology*, 1970

HARDY, R. S. *The British Government and the Idolatry of Sri Lanka*, 1839

HSUAN TSANG *Buddhist Records of the Western World*, 4 vols., transl. from the Chinese by Samuel Beal, reprinted 1957

JAYATILLEKE, K. N. *The Principles of International Law in Buddhist Doctrine*, 1967 (private circulation only)

Early Buddhist Theory of Knowledge, 1963

JOSHI, L. *Studies in the Buddhistic Culture of India*, 1967

KEITH, A. B. *A History of Sanskrit Literature*, 1928

KERN, H. *Der Buddhismus und seine Gesckichte in India*, 1882-4

KOSAMBI, D. D.

(i) *An Introduction to the Study of Indian History*

(ii) *The Culture and Civilisation of Ancient India*, 1965

LAMOTTE, E. *Histoire du Bouddhisme Indien: des origines à l'ère Saka*, 1958

LAW, B. C. *Indological Studies*, Vol. III, 1954

LEACH, E. R. *Political Systems of Highland Burma*, 1954

Aspects of Caste in South India, Sri Lanka and North-West Pakistan, 1960

LING, T. *History of Religion East and West*, 1968

LUDOWYK, E. G. *The Story of Sri Lanka*, 1962

The Modern History of Sri Lanka, 1966

MAHĀVAṂSA (Pāli text) edited by Wilhelm Geiger, 1908, reprinted 1958

MAJUMDAR, B. P. *Socio-Economic History of Northern India*, 1960

MALALASEKERE, G. P. *Dictionary of Pāli Proper Names*, 2 vols., 1937, reprinted 1960

The Pāli Literature of Sri Lanka, 1928, reprinted 1958

MCCRINDLE, J. W. *Ancient India as described by Megasthenes and Arrian*, 1877

MENDELSON, E. M. 'Buddhism and the Burmese Establishment' in *Archives de Sociologie des Religions*, Vol. 17, 1964

MOOKHERJEE, R. K. *Ancient Indian Education, Brahmanical and Buddhist*, 4th edn., 1969

MORRIS-JONES, W. H. *The Government and Politics of India*, 3rd (revised) edn., 1971

MORRISON, B. M. *Political Centers and Cultural Regions in Early Bengal*, 1970

MURTI, T. R. V. *The Central Philosophy of Buddhism*, 1955

NĀRADA, Thera *The Buddha and his Teaching*, 1964

NICHOLAS, C. W. and PARANAVITANA, S. *A Concise History of Sri Lanka*, 1961

NOTTINGHAM, E. 'Buddhist Ethics and Economic Development' in *World Buddhism Vesak Annual*, 1967

NYANATILOKA, *Buddhist Dictionary*, 1956

OBEYESEKERE, G.

(i) 'The Great Tradition and the Little in the Perspective of Sinhalese Buddhism', in *Journal of Asian Studies*, Vol. 22 (2), 1963

(ii) 'The Buddhist Pantheon in Sri Lanka and its Extensions', in *Anthropological Studies in Theravada Buddhism*, ed. by Manning Nash, 1966

O'MALLEY, L. S. S. *Bengal District Gazetteers: Birbhum*, 1910

PANDEY, M. S. *The Historical Geography and Topography of Bihar*, 1963

PIERIS, G. C. *Sri Lanka Today and Yesterday*, 2nd edn., 1963

PIERIS, P. E. *Sri Lanka and the Portuguese, 1505-1658*, 1920

Sinhale and the Patriots, 1950

PIERIS, R. *Sinhalese Social Organisation: The Kandyan Period*, 1956

RAHULA, W. *History of Buddhism in Sri Lanka: the Anuradhapura Period*, 2nd edn., 1966

RYAN, B. *Sinhalese Village*, 1958

SENART, E. *Essai sur la legende du Buddha*, 1875

SHAFI, M. *Land Utilization in Eastern Uttar Pradesh*, 1960

SHARMA, J. P. *Republics in Ancient India, c.1500 BC to500 BC*, 1968

SINGH, M. M. *Life in North-Eastern India in Pre-Mauryan Times*, 1967

SMITH, D. E. *India as a Secular State*, 1963

SPANN, R. N. (ed.), *Constitutionalism in Asia*, 1963

SWANSON, G. *The Birth of the Gods*, 1960

TAGORE, Sir R. *The Religion of Man*, 1931

TENNENT, Sir J. E. *Sri Lanka*, 2 vols., 1859

THAPAR, R. *Asoka and the Decline of the Mauryas*, 1961

THOMAS, B. J. *The Life of Ike Buddha*, 3rd edn., 1949

WAGLE, N. *Society at the Time of the Buddha*, 1966

WARDER, A. K. *Indian Buddhism*, 1956

WEBER, M. *The Religion of India*, 1958

The Sociology of Religion, 1963

WILSON, H. H. 'Buddha and Buddhism', *JRAS*, Vol. XVI, 1856

WIRTH, L. *On Cities and Social Life*, Chicago, 1964

WOOLF, L. *The Village in the Jungle*, 1913, reprinted 1961

YALMAN, N. 'Dual Organization in Central Sri Lanka' in *Anthropological Studies in Theravada Buddhism*, ed. by Manning Nash, 1966

Acknowledgements

I should like to express my indebtedness to the following friends for their helpful discussion and criticism of various parts of this work: to Professor R. C. Pandeya, and members of the staff and research scholars of the Buddhist Studies Department, University of Delhi, for allowing me the opportunity of conducting a seminar on the subject-matter of chapter eight; to Professor D. L. Jayasuriya, head of the Department of Sociology in the University of Colombo, for the opportunity of rehearsing some of the theme of this book at an earlier stage of its development at a seminar of the Urban Studies Unit; to Dr. Debiprasad Chattopadhyaya and his wife, Dr. Alaka Chattopadhyaya, for the gracious hospitality they extended to me, in their home in Calcutta, and, together with Dr. Devavrata Bose, for the stimulating comments they made and the suggestions they offered. I am grateful also to the editorial board of *Religion* (Oriel Press, Newcastle) for permission to reproduce, in slightly revised form, a contribution published originally in that journal, to the editor of *Vesak Sirisara* (Colombo), and to the editor of *The Aryan Path* (Bombay).

T.O.L.

Appendix

The table below is referenced in Chapter 9 Note 32 (see p. 302)

	MAJOR ROCK EDICTS			PILLAR EDICTS	
	Third	Fourth	Eleventh	Seventh	Second
1	Obedience to parents	Obedience to parents	Obedience to parents	Obedience to parents	
2	Good behavior to friends and relatives	Deference to relatives	Generosity to friends and relatives	[see 14 below]	[see 14 below]
3	Generosity (*dāna*) to brahmans and *shramanas*	Deference to brahmans and *shramanas*	Generosity (*dāna*) to brahmans and *shramanas*	Regard for brahmans and *shramanas*	
4		Obedience to elders		Deference to elders	
5				Obedience to teachers	
6			Good behavior to servants, etc.	Regard for servants, etc.	

| | MAJOR ROCK EDICTS | | | PILLAR EDICTS | |
	Third	Fourth	Eleventh	Seventh	Second
7				Regard for the poor and wretched	
8	Not to kill living beings (*anarambho*)	Abstention from killing (*anarambho*)	Abstention from killing (*anarambho*)	Abstention from killing (*anarambho*)	
9		Non-injury to living beings (*avihimsā*)		Non-injury to living beings (*avihimsā*)	
10	To spend little				
11	To have minimum possessions				
12					Few faults and many good deeds
13				Mercy	Mercy
14				Charity (*dāna*)	Charity (*dāna*)
15				Truthfulness	Truthfulness
16				Purity	Purity

	Third	Fourth	Eleventh	Seventh	Second
		MAJOR ROCK EDICTS		PILLAR EDICTS	
17				Gentleness	
18				Virtue	

Notes

Notes on Chapter 1

[1] The Pāli word *bhikkhu* is often translated into English as 'monk', but this word, with its European connotations of a life apart from other men, is misleading.

[2] Census of India, 1931, Vol. XI, Rangoon, 1933.

[3] *Rayngankansasanapracampi 2508* (Annual Report of Religious Affairs for 1965), Ministry of Education, Bangkok, p. 397.

[4] E. B. Tylor, Primitive Culture, 4th ed., 1903, Vol. I, p. 424.

[5] E. Durkheim, *The Elementary Forms of the Religious Life*, Chapter1, Section 2.

[6] Melford E. Spiro, in Anthropological Approaches to the Study of Religion, ed. by Michael Banton, 1966, pp. 88 f.

[7] D. II, p. 156.

[8] *Udana*, VIII, 3.

Notes on Chapter 2

[1] E. Nottingham, 1967.

[2] E. Nottingham, p. 38.

[3] *Voice of Buddhism*, Vol. 8, No. 3, Kuala Lumpur, September 1971, pp. 50–57.

[4] For some expansion of this point, see Trevor Ling, 'Buddhist Values and the Burmese Economy', in Patterns of Buddhism, ed. by Ninian Smart, 1973. See also pp. 209 and 247 in this book.

[5] *The Middle Way* (Journal of the Buddhist Society of London) in 1971 listed some thirty such groups, but the list is by no means exhaustive.

[6] The new suburb of Malaysia's capital, Kuala Lumpur.

[7] In the journal of the Buddhist Missionary Society of Kuala Lumpur, Voice of Buddhism (September 1971, p. 50) we read that 'in the years that followed the formation of the Buddhist Missionary Society in 1962, Buddhism [in Malaysia] underwent a major transformation. From a stagnant religion it has become a living force in this country.'

[8] It should be noted that, in the view of some Indian historians, there was no Aryan entry into India; the movement was in the other direction: in this view, that is, a language and a culture

moved out of India and spread into other parts of Asia and Europe.

[9] See T. O. Ling, *A History of Religion East and West*, sections 1.3 and 1.5.

[10] A. B. Keith, 1928, p. 443.

[11] *The Laws of Manu*, trans. by G. Buhler, *SBE*, Vol. XXV, Oxford 1886.

[12] *Muhammedanism*, London, 1911, p. 75.

[13] *Jesus and the Zealots*, 1967, p. 26.

[14] *Jesus and the Zealots*, p. 24.

[15] *Jesus and the Zealots*, p. 25.

[16] S. G. F. Brandon, *History, Time and Deity*, 1965, pp. 189 ff.

[17] L. Wirth, 1964, pp. 3 f.

[18] D. B. Smith, 1963, pp. 6 f.

Notes on Chapter 3

[1] The traditional date for the birth of Gotama is, according to the Buddhists of Sri Lanka and South-East Asia, 623 BC, and for the death, 543 BC. Thus, the 2,500th anniversary of the decease was celebrated in 1956/7. According to modern scholarship, however, the dates should be 60 years later, that is, 563 and 483 BC respectively.

[2] D. D. Kosambi, 1956, 137.

[3] B. C. Law, 1932, xx.

[4] It is important to distinguish between the 'Middle Country' of ancient India, which was called *Madhyadesa*, and the modern state of *Madhya-Pradesh*; the two are geographically different areas.

[5] M. Shafi, 1960, p. 8.

[6] *IGI*, Vol. I, p. 293.

[7] *IGI*, Vol. I, p. 293.

[8] This picture of India in the Buddha's time as a land of abundant food is one which some readers may find surprising, since it is commonly believed in the West that India has an 'age-old problem of poverty and hunger', to quote one recent example of this sort of ignorance. The widespread hunger of the Indian peasants, who invaded the city of Calcutta in the Bengal famine of 1943, is a relatively modern phenomenon. In 1943

the reason lay partly in distribution problems but the long-term reason was the low productivity of Indian agriculture by the end of the British period. Under British rule a landlord system developed which led to insecurity of tenure by tenant-cultivators, in the division and re-division of plots of land, to the point where farming became uneconomical. Cultivators fell into the hands of excessively usurious money lenders. In these circumstances they had little opportunity of increasing the productivity of the land. Moreover, the rate of population increase might have been less serious in its effects had India been able to develop industrially as the Western countries themselves had done and as Japan, free from foreign rule, was able to do. India's industrial development was limited to a few enterprises which were compatible with British economic interests—railways, coal mining to supply the fuel, a small iron industry mainly for the same purpose, jute and cotton milling, the development of which was limited by the interests of Dundee and Lancashire rivals, some sugar refining, glassware and matches. The Industrial Revolution which was needed to relieve India's growing population of its equally fast-growing poverty was not allowed to begin until independent India embarked on the first of her five-year plans in 1951. See P. S. Lokanathan 'The Indian Economic System', in *Economic Systems of the Commonwealth* ed. by Calvin B. Hoover (1962), for a short summary.

For a severe criticism of British economic policy in India by one who was an avowed admirer of British political and legal institutions see Romesh Dutt, *Economic History of India*, 2 vols, (2nd ed. 1906). For a longer account of the more recent situation, see Nasir Ahmud Khan, *Problems of Growth of an Underdeveloped Economy—India* (1961).

In the India of old there was food in plenty; a significant pointer is the widespread traditional use of fasting as a moral discipline; this is more likely to arise in a situation where people are well fed and need such a discipline than in one where they are already undernourished.

[9] *Diod.* II. 36; quoted in A. Bose, 1961, p. 122.
[10] J. W. McCrindle, 1877, p. 55.

[11] D. D. Kosambi, 1956, p. 128.
[12] e.g. *Jat.* 547, 499, 518, etc.
[13] R. R. Gates, 1948, p. 339.
[14] D. D. Kosambi, 1956, pp. 106 f.
[15] M. M. Singh, 1967, p. 201.
[16] J. Beaujeu-Garnier, 1966, p. 55.
[17] J. Beaujeu-Garnier, 1966, p. 126.
[18] M. M. Singh, 1967, pp. 247 f.
[19] M. M. Singh, p. 240.
[20] A. Bose, 1961, p. 226.
[21] *Arthasastra*, II, 1, 48.
[22] A. Bose, 1961, p. 226.
[23] *sarvamatthi*: This rather imaginative etymology is derived from the Pāli form of the name of the city, *Savatthi*.
[24] A. Cunningham, 1871, pp. 407–14.
[25] *IGI*, Vol. VIII, p. 112.
[26] E. B. Cowell (ed.), *Jātaka Tales*, Vol. II, 1895, p. 223.
[27] See pp. 152 ff.
[28] Such as, for example, the ruins of Kaushambi (modern Kosam) 25m. SW of Allahabad.
[29] A. Bose, 1961, p. 204.
[30] Bose, p. 204.
[31] *DDPN*, Vol. II, p. 276.
[32] M. S. Pandey, 1963, p. 144
[33] See p. 121.
[34] *DDPN*, Vol. I, pp. 765 f.

Notes on Chapter 4
[1] U. N. Ghoshal, 1966, p. 189.
[2] Ghoshal, p. 186.
[3] Ghoshal, p. 188.
[4] Ghoshal, pp. 192 f.
[5] For a comprehensive account of both the theory and the practice of government in the period under review see Ghoshal, 1959 and 1966.
[6] See Rhys Davids, *Dial.*, Pt. III, 1966, pp. 87 ff.
[7] Ghoshal, 1959, p. 65.
[8] Ghoshal, 1966, p. 532.

[9] Manu is the father of the human race in Indian mythology; he is regarded also as the first and greatest king and prime lawgiver. P. V. Kane, in his *History of Dharmasastra* (Poona, 4 vols., 1930–46) Vol. I, pp. xxv f, comes to the conclusion that the *Code of Manu* belongs to the period from the second century BC to second century C.E. in its present form, with possibly an earlier original.

[10] *The Law Book of Manu, SBE,* Vol. XXV, p. 217.

[11] Pratap Chandra Ray, The *Mahabharata,* Calcutta, 1883–96.

[12] A manual of statecraft and political philosophy composed by a brahman minister of state, probably of the early Mauryan empire. See p. 177.

[13] *A.* II. 74–6, trans. as *Gradual Sayings,* Vol. II, pp. 84 f.

[14] See D. Mackenzie Brown 1968, p. 39; and *The Law of Manu, SBE,* Vol. XXV, pp. 40–1.

[15] *The Law of Manu, SBE,* Vol. VII, p. 44.

[16] See Ghoshal, 1959, pp. 92 f and 131 f.

[17] *Arthasastra,* I, 4 and 5.

[18] *Mahabharata* XII, 56, 39–40.

[19] U. N. Ghoshal, 1966, p. 119.

[20] J. C. Brown and A. K. Dey, 1955, p. 178.

[21] Brown and Dey, pp. 178 f.

[22] There are, of course, six possibilities, which may be set out as follows. If A represents monarchy, B urbanism and C individualism, the six possible causal sequences are:

1 A ... B ... C
2 A ... C ... B
3 B ... C ... A
4 B ... A ... C
5 C ... B ... A
6 C ... A ... B

The three which have been mentioned in the text (6, 1 and 3) seem the strongest.

[23] Durkheim, 1969, Bk. II, chapter 2.

[24] Durkheim, Bk. II, p. 262.

[25] Durkheim, Bk. II, p. 403.

[26] Durkheim, Bk. II, p. 403.

[27] Wirth, 1964, p. 70.

[28] Wirth, pp. 71 f.
[29] E. Fromm, 1942, p. 23.
[30] Fromm, p. 23.
[31] C. Drekmeier, 1962, p. 55.
[32] It should be emphasized that 'urbanism' in this case means the single-city urbanism of the monarchies of ancient India.

Notes on Chapter 5

[1] As represented, e.g., in the Gupta period (fourth to sixth centuries AD) and throughout medieval Indian history down to the end of the Vijayanagar kingdom in S. India in the early sixteenth century.

[2] S. N. Dasgupta, 1922, p. 42.

[3] There has been considerable discussion as to whether the Upanishads are the work of brahmans, or of the *kshatriyas*, i.e., the nobleman class, some at least of whom were critical of the brahmanical sacrificial system, and proposed these ideas, found as the Upanishads, as an alternative. On the whole it seems that the Upanishads fairly early gained acceptance by the brahmans and that they may be regarded as broadly within the category of brahmanical literature.

[4] Dasgupta, 1922, p. 22.

[5] Dasgupta, 1922, p. 22.

[6] *Dial*., Pt. I, p. 163.

[7] *Dial*., Pt. I, p. 180.

[8] *Dial*., Pt. I, p. 164.

[9] *Dial*., Pt. I, p. 182.

[10] *Brahma Jala Sutta*, 21. See *Dial*. Pt. I, pp. 16 ff.

[11] *Vin. Texts*, *SBE*, Vol. XX, p. 152.

[12] *Sutta Nipata*, 927.

[13] That is, the RgVeda, SamaVeda, and YajurVeda *samhitas*.

[14] M. Bloomfield, writing at the end of the nineteenth century records, however, that influential scholars of Southern India at that time still denied the genuineness of the Atharva as a Vedic text. (See *SBE*, Vol. XLII, pp. xxviii ff.)

[15] *HCIP*, Vol. II, p. 464.

[16] *HCIP*, Vol. III, pp. 370 f.

[17] See Bhattacharya, 1969.

[18] *Dial.*, Pt. I, p. 31.

[19] *Middle Length Sayings*, Vol. I, p. 211.

[20] *Middle Length Sayings*, Vol. I, p. 212.

[21] *Theragatha* and *Therigatha*.

[22] *Vin.* II, 115.

[23] T. O. Ling, *Buddhism and the Mythology of Evil*, 1962, p. 80.

[24] A. K. Warder, 1956, p. 47.

[25] Warder, p. 47.

[26] S. Dutt, 1962, p. 47.

[27] Dutt, p. 47.

[28] Warder, 1956, p. 47.

[29] L. S. S. O'Malley, 1910, p. 3.

[30] Warder, 1956, p. 48.

[31] T. W. Rhys Davids, *Dial.*, Pt. I, 1956, pp. 69 f.

[32] Warder, 1970, p. 40.

[33] B. Barua, 1921, p. 305.

[34] *DPPN*, Vol. II, p. 398.

[35] *Dial.*, Pt. I, pp. 65–95.

[36] *Dial.*, Pt. I, p. 70.

[37] On the Jains, see: H. von Glasenapp, *Der Jainismus*, 1925; S. T. Stevenson, *The Heart of Jainism*, 1915.

[38] *Dial.*, Pt. I, p. 171.

[39] *Dial.*, Pt. I, pp. 73 f.

[40] *Dial.*, Pt. I, p. 75; see also pp. 37–41.

Notes on Chapter 6

[1] *Buddhism: its Essence and Development*, 3rd edn., 1957, p. 34.

[2] See, H. H. Wilson, 1856, pp. 248 ff.; E. Senart, 1875; H. Kern, 1882–4.

[3] T. R. V. Murti, 1955, p. 287.

[4] A. Bareau, 1966, p. 17.

[5] T. W. Rhys Davids, 1959, p. 20.

[6] *D.* I. 92. See *Dial.*, Pt. I, p. 114.

[7] *Dial.*, Pt. I, p. 113.

[8] *Vin.* II. 183; *D.* I. 90; *Jat.*, I. 88.

[9] E. B. Cowell, *Jātaka Tales*, 1901, Vol. V–VI, p. 92.

[10] *D.* III. 117. See *Dial.*, Pt. III, p. 111.

[11] E. B. Cowell, *Jātaka Tales* (No. 522), Vol. V–VI, 1905, pp. 64 ff.

[12] See N. Wagle, 1966, p. 28.

[13] See R. K. Mookerjee, 1969, p. 374.

[14] *HCIP*, Vol. II, p. 366.

[15] See *M.* I. 163–5. *Middle Length Sayings*, Vol. I, pp. 207–9.

[16] D. Chattopadhyaya, 1969, pp. 95 f.

[17] *ABORI*, 1968, p. 444.

[18] *M.* I. 163.

[19] E.J. Thomas, 1949, p. 51.

[20] *M.* I. 168. *Middle Length Sayings*, Vol. I, p. 212.

[21] For the story of Yasa, and subsequent events, see *Vin.*, Vol. I, pp. 15–20.

[22] *DPPN.*, Vol. I, pp. 794–8.

[23] *DPPN.*, Vol. I, p. 798.

[24] See *Samantapāsādikā* I. 9.

[25] *Dial.*, Pt. II, p. 79.

[26] *Dial.*, Pt. II, p. 92.

[27] *Dial.*, Pt. II, p. 103.

[28] *Dial.*, Pt. II, p. 125.

[29] *Dial.*, Pt. II, p. 161.

[30] *Dial.*, Pt. II, pp. 199 ff.

[31] *Maha Sudassana Jātaka* (No. 95). See E. B. Cowell, Vol. I, 1895, pp. 230 ff.

[32] *D.* I. 4.

[33] *Dial.*, Pt. I, p. 4 n. 3.

Notes on Chapter 7

[1] *Ariya-pariyesana Sutta. M.* I. 160 ff. See *Middle Length Sayings*, Vol. I, pp. 203 ff.

[2] *M.* I. 167. See *Middle Length Sayings*, Vol. I, p. 210 f.

[3] *M.* I. 27 f. See *Middle Length Sayings*, Vol. I, pp. 27–9.

[4] See *Dial.*, Pt. II, pp. 4 ff.

[5] *Dial.*, Pt. II, pp. 23 ff.

[6] In Indian thought the mind is included as the sixth sense. Like other senses, it is regarded as having its characteristic organ— the brain.

[7] D. L. Snellgrove, *Buddhist Himalaya*, 1957, p. 15.

[8] Nyanatiloka, 1956, p. 138.

[9] Nyanatiloka, p. 140.

[10] Buddhaghosa, *Visuddhimagga*, VII. 3.

[11] Buddhaghosa, *Visuddhimagga*, XXL. 3.

[12] For fuller details of the relationship of the three-fold to the eight-fold way see the author's article in S. G. F. Brandon, A Dictionary of Comparative Religion, pp. 257 f.

[13] G. S. P. Misra, 'Logical and Scientific Method in Early Buddhist Texts', *JRAS*, 1967–8, p. 54.

[14] 'Vibhajjavado ... aham ... naham ... ekamsavado': *M.* II. 469.

[15] Max Weber, 1963, p. 125.

[16] *Middle Length Sayings*, Vol. I, p. 251.

[17] Karl Marx, 'Theses on Feuerbach', in *K. Marx and F. Engels on Religion*, Foreign Languages Publishing House, Moscow, n.d., p. 72.

[18] Narada Thera, 1964, p. 408.

[19] See, for example, K. N. Jayatilleke, 1963, and G. S. P. Misra.

[20] Misra, p. 64. See Chapter 7, note 13.

[21] *BSOAS*, Vol. 18, 1956, p. 46.

[22] B. Malinowski, *Magic, Science and Religion and other essays*. Doubleday Anchor Books, 1954, p. 17.

[23] These were (1) the school whose tradition is embodied in the Pāli Canon of Sri Lanka—the *Sthaviravadins*, forerunners of the *Theravadins*; (2) the school which developed in northern India, known as the *Sarvastivadins*, whose literature is in mixed *Buddhist-Sanskrit*; and (3) one of the schools of the Mahayana, known as the *Yogacarins*, which also developed in India.

[24] The *Abhidhamma* is the essence of Buddhist teaching; it is the *Dhamma*, in the sense of the discourses of the Buddha, reduced to the bare bones. The 'bones' consist of abstracts, numerical analyses, lists of properties, conditions, etc., involved in mental processes, their relations, and inter-relations, and the new formations, in terms of restructured states of consciousness, which may result. These bones are sometimes very dry bones indeed, and the seven books which make up the *Abhidhamma Piṭaka* (the third section or collection in the three-fold *Tipiṭaka* of the Canon) make very

tedious reading. The non-Buddhist reader may wonder if such dry bones could ever have lived. What has to be remembered is the context of *Sangha* life and moral striving in which such subjects were studied, and still are studied, in the Buddhist countries of South-East Asia. See the articles *'Abhidhamma'* and *'Abhidhamma Piṭaka (Theravada)'* in *A Dictionary of Buddhism* by Trevor Ling, Scribners, 1972, for further details and bibliographical notes.

Notes on Chapter 8
[1] R. Tagore, 1931, p. 70.
[2] Still more misleading is the usage adopted, even in modern Buddhist countries (following European, often Portuguese, usage), of calling *bhikkhus* 'priests'.
[3] See *Oxford English Dictionary* under 'Monk'.
[4] Dutt, 1962, p. 36.
[5] *Khaggavisana Sutta*, Sections 35–75.
[6] For further information on the technical aspects of meditation see Buddhaghosa, *Visuddhimagga*; for a condensed account see E. Conze, *Buddhist Meditation*, 1956.
[7] *A*, I. 253.
[8] K. N. Jayatilleke, 1967, p. 498.
[9] *Vinaya Texts*, Vol. I, p. 305.
[10] Jayatilleke, 1967, p. 490.
[11] Dutt, 1962, p. 56.
[12] Dutt, 1962, p. 54.
[13] The religious-philosophical treatises which slightly preceded the *Upanishads* were known as *Aranyakas*, or 'Forest Writings'. The name for the third of the four *ashramas* or stages of life in the brahmanical scheme was that of the *vanaprastha* or 'forest-dweller'—that is one who dwelt in the forest as a hermit.
[14] For a fuller account of this stage of Buddhist development, see Dutt, 1962, pp. 45–65.
[15] *D*. II. 100. *Dial.*, Pt. II, p. 107.
[16] *D*. II. 100. *Dial.*, Pt. II, p. 108.
[17] Dutt, 1962, p. 86.
[18] Sharma, 1968, p. 241.

[19] For the view that the *Sangha* was organized simply in imitation of the tribal *Sangha*s, see Jayaswal, *Hindu Polity* (3rd edn., 1955) p. 86, and for the view that it was a deliberate attempt to perpetuate an obsolescent institution, see D. P. Chattopadyaya, *Lokoyata*, 1959.

[20] Jayatilleke, 1967, p. 518.

[21] G. De, *Democracy in Early Buddhist Sangha*, Calcutta, 1955, p. xv.

[22] *D*. II. 76 f.

[23] One of the two major classifications of the traditional canonical literature of Buddhism, the other being the collection of the Buddha's discourses known as the *Sutta-Piṭaka*. A third collection of material, the *Abhidhamma-Piṭaka* was added later. See Note 24 to chapter 7. The *Vinaya* ('Discipline') contained the *Patimokkha*, or list of offences to be avoided, various other regulations concerned with the life of the Order, and some narrative sections dealing with the early history of the order. (For an English transl. see *SBE*, Vols. 13, 17 and 20.)

[24] *Mahavagga*, X.

[25] *Cullavagga*, XII. 2, 8.

[26] in Pāli, *Sangha-bheda*.

[27] Dutt, 1962, p. 84.

[28] Criteria of Buddhist orthodoxy and unorthodoxy are to be found, e.g., in *Vin*. II. 10.

[29] *D*. II. 74 ff. See also chapter 6, pp. 122 ff., above.

[30] Sharma, 1968, p. 241.

[31] See, e.g., *Middle Length Sayings*, Vol. I, p. 293 ('uninstructed ordinary man'); *Gradual Sayings*, Vol. I, p. 25 ('uneducated manyfolk'); Vol. IV, p. 108 ('common average folk'), etc.

[32] *Sutta Nipata*, 859.

[33] *M*. I. 239.

[34] *S*. IV. 201.

[35] *S*. IV. 196.

[36] *A*. IV. 157.

[37] *A*. I. 27.

[38] *Sn*. 706.

[39] *Sn*. 816.

[40] *S*. IV. 206.

[41] *Sn*. 351.

[42] *A*. I. 147; *S*. II. 94 f.

[43] *A*. III. 54.

[44] *A*. I. 267; II. 129.

[45] *A*. IV. 206.

[46] *A*. II. 163.

[47] *M*. I. 1, 7.

[48] *A*. IV. 68.

[49] *A*. IV. 157. In addition to the references in the Pāli Canon given in this paragraph, see also, for similar references: *M*. III. 64, 227; *S*. 1. 148; *S*. II. 151; III. 46, 108, 162.

[50] Sharma, 1968, p. 242. See also L. Whibley, *Greek Oligarchies, their Character and Organisation*, London 1896, p. 187. Whibley's further point about the Greek oligarchies, that the multitude were to be 'excluded from citizen rights', does not apply to the Buddhist attitude to the common people.

[51] *Sigāla-vada Sutta*: *D*. III. 180–193. See *Dial*., Pt. III, pp. 173–184.

[52] i.e., Buddhaghosa.

[53] T. W. Rhys Davids, *Buddhism*, London, 1890, p. 148.

[54] See, e.g., the accounts given by J. G. Scott in *The Burman: His Life and Notions*, 3rd edn., 1909; H. Fielding Hall, *The Soul of A People*, 4th edn., 1902; Manning Nash, *The Golden Road to Modernity*, 1965.

[55] By this word in the *Sigāla-vada Sutta* was meant heaven, the *devaloka*, as an *immediate* goal. The long-term goal remained, of course, beyond rebirth in heaven, *nibbāna*.

[56] E. Durkheim, *Elementary Forms of the Religious Life*, Collier Books, New York, 1961, pp. 355 f. (The emphasis is mine.—T.L.)

[57] *A*. I. 211 f. See *Gradual Sayings*, Vol. I, pp. 190–2.

[58] See, e.g., the collection of discourses to Pasenadi contained in the *Kosala Saṃyutta* (S. 1. 68 ff). See *The Book of the Kindred Sayings* Vol. I, pp. 93–127.

[59] *DPPN*, II, 285 f.

[60] Whose work, *A History of Indian Political Ideas*, has been adjudged 'the most scholarly and comprehensive work on the

subject ever to have been written'. (A. L. Basham in *BSOAS*, London University, Vol. 25 (1962), p. 178.)

[61] Ghoshal, 1959, p. 69.

[62] E.g., *Jat.* 194, 334, 407, 501, 521, 527, 533, 534, 540, 544.

[63] *Jat*,V. 378.

[64] Jayatilleke, 1967, p. 530.

[65] See, e.g., *Jat.* V. 222 ff.

[66] E. B. Cowell, 1905, p. 115.

[67] *Gradual Sayings*, Vol. II, p. 85.

[68] *Jat.* 334.

[69] *Dial.*, Pt. I, pp. 175 f.

[70] *Dial.*, Pt. II, pp. 199–217.

[71] *Cakkavatti-Sihanada Sutta.*

[72] *Dial.*, Pt. III, p. 65.

[73] *Dial.*, Pt. III, p. 66.

[74] *Dial.*, Pt. III, p. 67.

[75] *Dial.*, Pt. III, pp. 69 f.

[76] Ghoshal, 1962, p. 73.

[77] See *Gradual Sayings*, Vol. III, p. 114 f.

[78] *A*. I. 76 f. See *Gradual Sayings*, Vol. I, p. 71.

[79] Ghoshal, 1962, p. 79.

[80] *balacakram hi nisraya dharmacakram pravartate.* Jayatilleke, 1967, p. 530.

Notes on Chapter 9

[1] *K. Marx and F. Engels On Religion*, Foreign Languages Publishing House, Moscow, n.d., p. 42.

[2] In the Marxist case this is contained largely in K. Marx: *Economic and Philosophic Manuscripts of 1844* transl. by M. Miligan, Moscow, 1959.

[3] See R. K. Mookerji, 'Chandragupta and the Maurya Empire', in *History and Culture of the Indian People*, Vol. II, chapter 4; and B. G. Gokhale, *Asoka Maurya*, New York, 1966, chapter 1.

[4] *HCIP*, Vol. II, pp. 31 ff.

[5] See P. H. L. Eggermont, *The Chronology of the Reign of Ashoka Moriya*, Leiden, 1956.

[6] See B. G. Gokhale, *Asoka Maurya*, 1966, chapter 2.

[7] Gokhale, 1966.

[8] Gokhale, 1966, p. 107.

[9] *Mahāvaṃsa*, V. 66.

[10] *Appamada-vagga*, found in the *Sutta-Nipata*.

[11] *Mahāvaṃsa*, V. 34–72, English transl. by W. Geiger, 1912 (1960), pp. 28–32.

[12] See L. S. Perera, 'The Pāli Chronicles of Sri Lanka' in *Historians of India, Pakistan and Sri Lanka*, ed. by C. H. Philips, 1961.

[13] See J. Bloch, *Les Inscriptions d'Asoka*, Paris, 1950, and E. Lamotte, *Histoire du Bouddhisme Indien*, Louvain, 1959, Addenda, pp. 789 ff. For an English transl. see R. Thapar, *Asoka and the Decline of the Mauryas*, Oxford, 1961, Appendix V, pp. 250–66; or Gokhale, 1966, Appendix, pp. 151–70.

[14] The question of what is meant by the gods mingling with men will be dealt with later—see pp. 189 f.

[15] R. Thapar, *Asoka and the Decline of the Mauryas*, 1961, p. 259. I have amended the punctuation after 'if they are earnest' in order to express the meaning of the original more clearly. See Bloch, 1950, pp. 147–8.

[16] Identified as the modern town of Kanakagiri.

[17] The three are: The Bairat Stone Inscription, the Barabar Hill Cave Inscription, and the Kandahar Inscription. See J. Bloch, 1950, pp. 154, 156, and E. Lamotte, 1959, p. 793 for the text of these.

[18] This title occurs 59 times in the 29 inscriptions. In one of them, the Seventh Pillar Edict, it is repeated 10 times.

[19] See R. K. Mookeiji in *HCIP*, Vol. II, p. 73.

[20] The title *Piyadassi*, which may be translated loosely as 'the Splendid', is frequently used as a name for Ashoka in the inscriptions.

[21] The Thirteenth Major Rock Edict, transl. by Thapar, 1961, p. 256 f. See Bloch, 1959, pp. 125–8, for text.

[22] Just as the *Chakravartin* is conventionally referred to as 'father' so Ashoka declared 'all men are my children' (Second Kalinga Rock Edict, Thapar, p. 258).

[23] Thapar, p. 266; Bloch, p. 172.

[24] Thapar, p. 261; Bloch, pp. 154 f.

[25] Thapar, p. 261; Bloch, p. 157. For the story of the modern discovery of this pillar, in the forests of the Nepal border, see S. Dutt, *The Buddha and Five After Centuries*, 1957, chapter 2.

[26] Eleventh Major Rock Edict: Thapar, p. 254 f; Bloch, p. 120.

[27] Third Major Rock Edict: Thapar, p. 251 Bloch, pp. 96—7.

[28] Fourth Major Rock Edict: Thapar, p. 251; Bloch, pp. 98–9.

[29] Thapar, p. 266; Bloch, p. 172.

[30] Thapar, p. 262; Bloch, p. 162.

[31] Thapar, p. 266; Bloch, p. 171.

[32] For convenience, an analysis of the expositions of *Dhamma* in the Ashokan inscriptions is given in the Appendx on p. 285; set out synoptically this enables the evidence, on which the summary given in the text of chapter 9 is based, to be seen at a glance.

[33] First Major Rock Inscription: Thapar, p. 250; Bloch, pp. 92–3.

[34] Kandahar Bilingual Rock Inscription: Thapar, p. 260.

[35] Fifth Pillar Edict: Thapar, p. 264; Bloch, pp. 165—6.

[36] Fourth Major Rock Edict: Thapar, p. 251; Bloch, pp. 98–9.

[37] Eighth Major Rock Edict: Thapar, p. 253; Bloch, pp. 112–13.

[38] Second Major Rock Edict: Thapar, p. 251; Bloch pp. 93–5.

[39] A *kos* is approx. 2 miles, and 8 *kos* = 1 *yojana*, or the normal distance for a day's march for soldiers in those days in India.

[40] Thapar, p. 265.

[41] *Dhamma mahamatra.*

[42] Fifth Major Rock Edict: Thapar, p. 252; Bloch, pp. 102–4.

[43] Thapar, p. 250; Bloch, pp. 90–1.

[44] Ninth Major Rock Edict: Thapar, pp. 253 f; Bloch, pp. 113–15.

[45] Minor Rock Edict 'from Suvarnagiri': Thapar, p. 259; Bloch, p. 146.

[46] Barabar Cave Inscriptions I and II, and Seventh Pillar Edict: Thapar, pp. 260 and 265; Bloch, pp. 156 and 170 f.

[47] As Ghoshal (1966), for instance, does.

[48] *D.* II. 118.

[49] See T. W. Rhys Davids, *Dial.*, Pt. I, pp. 272–3, and his *Buddhism*, 1890 (1962), pp. 174–7.

[50] *D.* II. 141. See *Dial.*, Pt. II, p. 154.

[51] *D.* II. 141. See *Dial.*, Pt. II, p. 154.

[52] Dutt, *The Buddha and Five After Centuries*, 1957, p. 169.

[53] Dutt, p. 167. See also B. Rowland, *The Art and Architecture of India*, 3rd edn., 1967, n. 1 to chapter 6, p. 279.

[54] The Pāli Chronicles credit him with building numerous *cetiyas*, or *stūpas*. See *Mv*. V. 175. See also Dutt, p. 171; and Rowland, p. 48.

[55] For modern examples of this, see Ling, *A History of Religion East and West*, 1968, pp. 371 ff.

[56] Philip S. Rawson, *Tantra*, Arts Council of Great Britain, 1971, p. 33.

[57] Thapar, 1961, p. 255.

[58] Dutt, 1957, p. 217.

[59] Kathāvatthu, pp. 176–7.

[60] Kathāvatthu, pp. 178–9.

[61] Kathāvatthu, p. 202.

[62] See, e.g., *Milinda's Questions*, Vol. I, transl. by I. B. Horner, 1963, IV. 6, in which 'the natural weakness of the Lord's physical frame' is repeatedly mentioned.

[63] For a summary of the debate, particularly between Hariprasad Sastri and H. C. Raychaudhuri, see Thapar, pp. 198–205.

[64] *Manu*, IX. 225.

[65] *Manu*, V. 89.

Notes on Chapter 10

[1] This is Buddhaghosa's commentary on the *Vinaya Piṭaka*. See G. P. Malalasekere, 1928, pp. 94 f.

[2] Malalasekere, 1928, pp. 45 f.

[3] *Mahāvaṃsa*, XI. 19, transl. by Geiger, 1912, p. 78.

[4] *Mahāvaṃsa*, XI. 28–32, transl. by Geiger, pp. 79 f.

[5] *Mahāvaṃsa*, XI. 33–36, transl. by Geiger, p. 80.

[6] Pāli: *jinasasanam patitthapetha*. Geiger's translation as 'found the religion of the Conqueror', reflects modern conceptions and is possibly misleading. The word *sāsana* means strictly 'a discipline', or 'teaching'.

[7] Strictly, 'the lesser discourse on ... etc.' (*Culahatthipadupama Suttanta*). In its context as a discourse of the Buddha it is found in the *Majjhima-Nikāya*, I. 175. See *Middle Length*

Sayings, Vol. I, transl. by I. B. Horner, London, 1954, pp. 220–30.

[8] *M.* I. 179.

[9] *M.* I. 184. *Middle Length Sayings*, Vol. I, p. 230.

[10] *Mahāvaṃsa*, XIV. 23, transl. by Geiger, 1912, p. 93.

[11] This is a separate book, found in the *Khuddaka-Nikāya*.

[12] Also a separate book of the *Khuddaka-Nikāya*.

[13] The *Sacca-Saṃyutta*, found in the *Saṃyutta-Nikāya*. For the four noble truths, see above, chapter 7, p. 111.

[14] According to Buddhist custom already established in India.

[15] *dhatusu ditthesu ditthohoti jino*: *Mv.* XVII. 3.

[16] C. W. Nicholas and S. Paranavitana, 1961, p. 49.

[17] Nicholas and Paranavitana, 1961, pp. 49 f.

[18] *Samantapāsādikā*.

[19] *Buddhist India*, 1959, pp. 299 ff.

[20] Rahula, 1966, p. 54.

[21] Rahula, 1966, p. 55.

[22] Rahula, 1966, p. 55.

[23] *Visuddhi Magga*, I. 91.

[24] Rahula, 1966, p. 62.

[25] The correct name of the island. The name 'Sri Lanka' is a European corruption.

[26] That is, the Buddha, the *Dhamma* and the *Sangha*.

[27] *Pujavaliya*, Colombo, 1926, p. 656. See Rahula, 1966, p. 63.

[28] See Rahula, 1966, pp. 69 f.

[29] The dating followed here is that of Wilhelm Geiger, based on the evidence of the chronicles, and set out in detail in his translation of the *Culavamsa*, Vol. II, pp. ix–xi. On the other hand, according to the chronology followed by Nicholas and Paranavitana, 1961, these three reigns cover the period 161–109 BC (p. 341).

[30] *paragangam gamissami jotetum sasanam aham Mv.* XXV. 2. Alternatively, the words might mean, that the *sāsana* (of the Buddha) might be made clear.

[31] *rajjasukhaya vayamo nayam mama, sadapi ca sambuddhasasanasseva thapanaya ayam mama. Mv.* XXV. 17.

[32] *Mahāvaṃsa*, transl. by Geiger, p. 177.

[33] The ceremony at which the Vinaya regulations which govern the life of the *Sangha* are recited, and any infringements are confessed and dealt with.

[34] The *Mahā Thūpa*—known also as the Ruvanveli Dagoba—'the Relic Chamber of the Golden Sands'.

[35] *Mv.* XXXII. 1–47.

[36] Malalasekere, 1928, pp. 35 f.

[37] Nicholas and Paranavitana, 1961, p. 67.

[38] *Mv.* XXXII. 38.

[39] See E. W. Adikaram, 1946, p. 65, n. 3.

[40] *Mv.* XXXII. 81–2.

[41] *Mv.* XXXIII. 13.

[42] *Saddharmalankaraya*, Colombo edition, n.d., p. 123.

[43] Malalasekere, 1928, p. 40.

[44] Adikaram, 1946, p. 71.

[45] See Buddhaghosa's commentary on the *Vibhanga*, *Sammohavino-dani*, 473.

[46] Adikaram, 1946, p. 73.

[47] *gahetva*: *Mv.* XXXIII. 19.

[48] Or 'caused them to decline': *parichapayi*. *Mv.* XXXIII. 20.

[49] *na janimsu yathavuddham.*

[50] *dandakammattham*. *Mv.* XXXIII. 21.

[51] Adikaram, 1946, p. 73.

[52] Malalasekere, 1928, p. 40.

[53] Rahula, 1966, p. 81.

[54] The *Susanavamsa*, composed in Burma in 1861 by a *bhikkku* named Pannasami.

[55] The *Jinakalamali-pakaranam* composed in Thailand, in the early sixteenth century by Ratanapanna, a Thera of Thailand.

[56] *The Culavamsa*, Part I, transl. by Wilhelm Geiger and C. M. Rickmers, Colombo, 1953, p.v.

[57] B. J. Perera 'Some political trends in the late Anuradhapura and Polonnaruwa period', in *Sri Lanka Historical Journal*, Vol. X, 1960, p. 60.

[58] *Culavamsa*, 44. 130. English transl., Pt. I, p. 86.

[59] *Culavamsa*, 44. 133.

[60] Perera, 1960.

[61] Perera, 1960, p. 63.

[62] Malalasekere, 1928, p. 175.
[63] *Culavamsa*, LXXIII. 2–8.
[64] See Nicholas and Paranavitana, 1961, p. 215.
[65] *Culavamsa*, LXXIX. 86.
[66] For details of Parakkama Bahu's irrigation works see Nicholas and Paranavitana, 1961, pp. 256–9, and for those of earlier kings, pp. 159–62.
[67] Nicholas and Paranavitana, 1961, p. 170.
[68] *Mv.* XLII. 16–24.
[69] Nicholas and Paranavitana, 1961, p. 111.
[70] Nicholas and Paranavitana, p. 111.
[71] Nicholas and Paranavitana, p. 169.
[72] Nicholas and Paranavitana, p. 111.
[73] B. M. Morrison, 1970, p. 73.
[74] R. Pieris, 1956, p. 73.

Notes on Chapter 11

[1] Ghoshal, in *HCIP*, Vol. III, 1970 (3rd edition), p. 343.
[2] Ghoshal, 1970, p. 343.
[3] Rowland, *The Art and Architecture of India*, 3rd edn., 1967, p. 281.
[4] Rowland, 1967, p. 78.
[5] See Dutt, *Buddhist Monks and Monasteries of India*, 1962, p. 169.
[6] Dutt, 1962, p. 174.
[7] Hsuan Tsang, Vol. I, p. 240.
[8] Lalmani Joshi, 1967, p. xvii.
[9] For the evidence that Buddhism had reached Bengal in the Ashokan period see the author's '*Buddhism in Bengal*' in the S. G. F. Brandon Memorial Volume, 1973.
[10] Kosambi, 1965, p. 178.
[11] Sushil Kumar De, 1961, p. 26.
[12] J. C. Ghosh, 1948, p. 24.
[13] Bhakat Prasad Mazumdar, 1960, p. 170.
[14] Mazumdar, 1960, p. 171.
[15] *Dacca District Gazetteer*, 1969, p. 49.
[16] *Dacca District Gazetteer*, 1969, p. 49.

Notes on Chapter 12

[1] See, e.g., Ludowyk, 1966; Malalasekere, 1928, G. C. Pieris, 1963; P. E. Pieris, 1920.

[2] See Nicholas and Paranavitana, 1961, chapter 18.

[3] Malalasekere, 1928, p. 259. On this period see also J. E. Tennent, 1859, Vol. II, chapter 1; and P. E. Pieris, 1920, *passim*.

[4] Ludowyk, 1966, p. 9.

[5] Ludwoyk, p. 12.

[6] *Mv.* XCVIII.

[7] *Mv.* XCIX. 7–11.

[8] *Mv.* C. 73–6.

[9] Tennent, 1859, Vol. II, p. 76.

[10] de Silva, 1965, p. 64, n. 2.

[11] R. S. Hardy, 1893, pp. 12 f, p. 44.

[12] P. E. Pieris, 1950, pp. 596 ff.

[13] de Silva, 1965, p. 65.

[14] Quoted by de Silva, 1965, p. 65.

[15] On the Sinhalese view regarding the inalienable right of the Buddha over the island, see above, chapter 10.

[16] de Wijesekere, 'Theravada Buddhist Tradition Under Modern Culture' in *Proceedings of the 11th Congress of the International Association for the History of Religion*, 1968.

[17] Ludowyk, 1966, p.116.

[18] See Rahula, 1966, p. 284.

[19] Copleston, 1908.

[20] C. Eliot, 1921, Vol. III, pp. 41–4.

[21] Eliot, Vol. III, p. 42.

[22] Eliot, Vol. III, pp. 48 f.

[23] Copleston, 1908, pp. 275 f.

[24] Copleston, p. 282.

[25] Ludowyk, 1962, p. 171.

[26] N. Yalman, 1966, p. 210.

[27] L. Woolf, 1913, p. 106.

[28] B. Ryan, 1958.

[29] Ryan, p. 90.

[30] Ryan, p. 106.

[31] Ryan, p. 101.

[32] Ryan, p. 105.

[33] Obeyesekere, 1963, p. 143.

[34] Obeyesekere, 1966, p. 10.

[35] Obeyesekere, 1966, p. 16.

[36] R. L. Slater, *Paradox and Nirvāna*, Chicago, 1951.

[37] M. Ames (i), 1964, p. 78; (ii) 1964, p. 35.

[38] Ames (ii), p. 37.

[39] Ames (ii), p. 25.

[40] Ames (ii), p. 27.

[41] Ames (i), p. 80.

[42] Ames (ii), p. 40.

[43] Ames (ii), pp. 47 f.

[44] H.-D. Evers, 1965, p. 98.

[45] Ryan, 1958, p. 90.

[46] On Japanese religious movements since the Second World War, see Clark B. Offner and Henry Van Straelen, *Modern Japanese Religions*, 1963; D. C. Holtom, *Modern Japan and Shinto Nationalism: A Study of Present-Day Trends in Japanese Religions*, Revised edn., 1963; Harry Thomson, *The New Religions of Japan*, 1963; H. N. MacFarland, *The Rush Hour of the Gods*, 1967; *The Sociology of Japanese Religion*, ed. by Kiomi Morioka and William H. Newell, 1968; H. Byron Earhart, *Japanese Religion: Unity and Diversity*, 1969.

[47] Another feature of Sinhalese culture which is of importance to social anthropologists, but which has not been dealt with here, is the relationship between Buddhism in Sri Lanka and the caste system. On this, see E. R. Leach, 1960, for further references. The degree to which the Buddhist community in Sri Lanka recognizes caste distinctions appears to be a case of a feature of 'pan-Indian civilization' (Leach, 1960, p. 5) proving stronger than the resistance to it which is implied in Buddhist theory.

[48] See Leach, 1954, especially chapter 2.

[49] See Ling, 'Buddhist Factors in Population Growth and Control', *Population Studies*, Vol. XXIII, No. 1, March 1969, pp. 53–60.

Notes on Epilogue

[1] M. Anesaki, 1930, p. 51.

[2] Anesaki, p. 52.

[3] Anesaki, p. 57.

[4] Anesaki, pp. 57 f and see also Ling, *History of Religion East and West*, 1968, pp. 239 f.

[5] See Ling, p. 248.

[6] The subject of Buddhist civilization in South-East Asia is a large and important one, and deserves treatment in a separate work.

[7] Gouldner, 1970, pp. 433 f.

[8] *Udana*, VIII. 3.

[9] Mendelson, 1964, pp. 86 f.

[10] See Note 49 to chapter 12.

[11] Rahula, 1966, pp. 76 f.

[12] Review by Muriel Clark in *The Middle Way*, London, Vol. XLVII, No. 1, May 1972, p. 49.

[13] See chapter 1, p. 29.

[14] Preamble to the Constitution. See D. D. Basu, 1962, p. 25.

[15] R. N. Spann, 1963, p. 23.

[16] W. H. Morris-Jones, 1971, p. 55.

[17] D. D. Basu, 1962, p. 43.